This highly original book provides a stimulating, and at times provocative, view of the Neolithic in southern Britain. Employing ways of thinking which are new to archaeology (sometimes described as 'post-processual' archaeology), it attempts to question old interpretations of the period, and it is a radical departure from previous works about the Neolithic. It considers subsistence economy, monuments, depositional practices, pottery, burial, and their regional variability. The novelty of *Rethinking the Neolithic* lies in the attempt to relate ambitious theoretical frameworks to the data in a very detailed and well-informed way. It will therefore appeal to those interested in the period, but also to those concerned with the use and development of archaeological theory.

Rethinking the Neolithic

# NEW STUDIES IN ARCHAEOLOGY

*Series editors*

Colin Renfrew, *University of Cambridge*
Jeremy Sabloff, *University of Pittsburgh*

*Other titles in the series*

Ian Hodder and Clive Orton: *Spatial Analysis in Archaeology*
Kenneth Hudson: *World Industrial Archaeology*
Keith Muckelroy: *Maritime Archaeology*
Graham Connah: *Three Thousand Years in Africa*
Richard E. Blanton, Stephen A. Kowalewski, Gary Feinman and Jill Appel: *Ancient Mesoamerica*
Stephen Plog: *Stylistic Variation in Prehistoric Ceramics*
Peter Wells: *Culture Contact and Culture Change*
Ian Hodder: *Symbols in Action*
Patrick Vinton Kirch: *Evolution of the Polynesian Chiefdoms*
Dean Arnold: *Ceramic Theory and Cultural Process*
Geoffrey W. Conrad and Arthur A. Demarest: *Religion and Empire: The Dynamics of Aztec and Inca Expansionism*
Graeme Barker: *Prehistoric Farming in Europe*
Daniel Miller: *Artefacts as Categories*
Rosalind Hunter-Anderson: *Prehistoric Adaptation in the American Southwest*
Robin Torrence: *Production and Exchange of Stone Tools*
M. Shanks and C. Tilley: *Re-Constructing Archaeology*
Bo Gräslund: *The Birth of Prehistoric Chronology*
Ian Morris: *Burial and Ancient Society: The Rise of the Greek City State*
Joseph Tainter: *The Collapse of Complex Societies*
John Fox: *Maya Postclassic State Formation*
Alasdair Whittle: *Problems in Neolithic Archaeology*
Peter Bogucki: *Forest Farmers and Stock Herders*
Olivier de Montmollin: *The Archaeology of Political Structure: Settlement Analysis in a Classic Maya Polity*
Robert Chapman: *Emerging Complexity: The Later Prehistory of South-East Spain, Iberia and the West Mediterranean*
Steven Mithen: *Thoughtful Foragers: A Study of Prehistoric Decision Making*
Roger Cribb: *Nomads in Archaeology*
James Whitley: *Style and Society in Dark Age Greece: The Changing Face of a Pre-Literate Society 1100–700 BC*
Philip Arnold: *Domestic Ceramic Production and Spatial Organization*

# Rethinking
# the Neolithic

*JULIAN THOMAS*
*St David's University College, Lampeter*

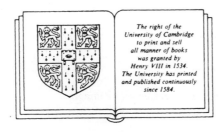

The right of the
University of Cambridge
to print and sell
all manner of books
was granted by
Henry VIII in 1534.
The University has printed
and published continuously
since 1584.

CAMBRIDGE UNIVERSITY PRESS
Cambridge
New York   Port Chester   Melbourne   Sydney

Published by the Press Syndicate of the University of Cambridge
The Pitt Building, Trumpington Street, Cambridge CB2 1RP
40 West 20th Street, New York, NY 10011-4211, USA
10 Stamford Road, Oakleigh, Melbourne 3166, Australia

First published 1991

Printed in Great Britain by Ipswich Book Co. Ltd., Ipswich, Suffolk.

*British Library cataloguing in publication data*

Thomas, Julian
Rethinking the Neolithic. – (New studies in archaeology).
1. British Neolithic civilization
I. Title II. Series
936.101

*Library of Congress cataloguing in publication data*

Thomas, Julian.
Rethinking the Neolithic / Julian Thomas.
     p.     cm. – (New studies in archaeology)
Includes bibliographical references and index.
ISBN 0 521 40377 4
1. Neolithic period – Great Britain. 2. Neolithic period – England.
3. Archaeology – Philosophy. 4. Great Britain – Antiquities.
5. England – Antiquities. I. Title. II. Series.
GN776.22.G7T48 1991
936.2 – dc20   90–24159   CIP

ISBN 0 521 40377 4 hardback

For Sue

# CONTENTS

# FIGURES

This book has taken a long time in its writing, since in the course of the past four years I have found that both my objectives and my theoretical orientation have changed. In the process, the book has shifted from a geographical to a thematic focus. What has remained is the intention to write about Neolithic Britain in such a way as to contest the accepted understanding of the period. It is perhaps this central aim which has led me to concentrate upon the 'genealogical' approach to history advocated by Foucault, which has as its *raison d'être* the undermining of conventional assumptions concerning the past (Minson 1985, 7).

This philosophical position has been put into practice in the present work by investigating different aspects of the archaeological evidence in separate chapters, and presenting an analysis which is essentially diachronic. The search for change through time is itself seen as a means of disrupting the presumed continuities which underlie conventional wisdom. This mode of practice should not be taken to imply that 'the economy', 'monument building', 'depositional practice', 'pottery' or 'mortuary practices' constituted integrated spheres of action which maintained a separate identity for themselves throughout the Neolithic. Rather, each category of evidence is like a text, in that it represents a set of phenomena which have been arbitrarily grouped together and which can be probed and dissected in the process of analysis.

It follows that since each chapter uses a different 'text' as the basis for an interpretation, each represents a kind of parallel narrative, concentrating on different aspects of Neolithic life. Written from different evidence, there is no particular reason why any of these five narratives should have a greater truth value than the other four. This being the case, it is interesting to contemplate why different aspects of the evidence lead one to different (and perhaps contradictory) conclusions. At the least, this must count as a useful source of autocritique.

The study itself concentrates on six counties in the centre and west of southern England: Avon, Dorset, Gloucestershire, Oxfordshire, Somerset and Wiltshire (see map). No hesitation has been shown in extending the discussion beyond these geographical bounds, although the reader should recognise that only in the study area are any claims made for thoroughness in data collection. The region in question was originally chosen to combine geographical variability with a bulk of available information. It might be objected that any further study of areas like Wessex and the Thames Valley only serves to bias yet more our understanding of the Neolithic in favour of these well-investigated regions. However, while it might be worthy to look beyond these and a handful of other areas (Orkney, east Yorkshire, parts of East Anglia

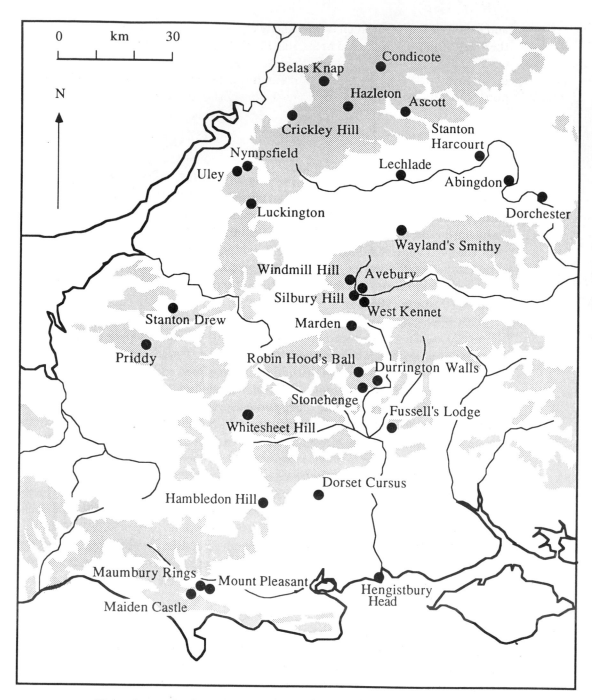

The study area, showing major sites mentioned in the text

and southern Scotland), such is the paucity of excavation and survey elsewhere that the kinds of analysis presented here could hardly be contemplated.

Chronologically, the scope of the volume extends from the first Neolithic presence in the British Isles (at around 3200 bc) until some time after the first use of Beaker pottery (*c.* 1700 bc). All dates are expressed in uncalibrated radiocarbon years bc.

# ACKNOWLEDGEMENTS

The present volume represents in some ways the outcome of a lengthy period of study, and provides me with the opportunity to thank all of those who have given their help, friendship and support over that time. First amongst these I should mention Andrew Fleming, John Barrett and Robin Torrence, who between them have provided me with the opportunity to evaluate many of my own preconceptions concerning prehistory. Research is never undertaken in a vacuum, but I have been particularly lucky over the years to be in contact with a number of scholars who have helped in innumerable ways to provide a creative atmosphere in prehistoric studies. Particular mention should go to Richard Bradley, Ros Cleal, Mark Edmonds, Roy Entwistle, Ian Kinnes, Frances Raymond, Colin Richards, Nick Thorpe and Alasdair Whittle. Much of the material in this book could not have been written without lengthy conversations with these people, and several of them have generously provided unpublished information from their own research. In Lampeter, I owe much to my colleagues, David Austin, Martin Bell, Barry Burnham and Chris Tilley, for providing a constructive working environment.

Parts of the manuscript were read, and extensive comments provided, by John Barrett, Richard Bradley, Mark Edmonds, Ian Hodder, Keith Ray, Chris Tilley, Alasdair Whittle and Norman Yoffee The remaining faults are entirely my own. Richard Bradley, Claire Halpin, Ian Hodder, Roger Mercer, Alan Saville and Geoffrey Wainwright kindly provided the photographs. The manuscript was typed by Maureen Hunwicks, and the drawings were executed by Chris Jones. The cost of the illustrations was met by a grant from the Pantyfedwen Fund of Saint David's University College, which I gratefully acknowledge. Much of the unpublished information in the volume derives from research undertaken for my Ph.D. thesis, and I repeat my thanks to the many museums and units who provided access to this material. Part of Chapter 1 was originally published as 'Same, other, analogue: writing the past' in F. Baker and J. Thomas (eds.) *Writing the Past in the Present* (Lampeter 1990), while parts of Chapter 6 are drawn from 'The social significance of Cotswold–Severn burial rights', published in *Man* 23, 540–59 (1988).

Finally, the greatest debt of thanks is to Sue Pitt, who has endured much in the course of the writing of this book.

# 1

# An archaeology of difference

## Introduction

It is singularly ironic that prehistoric archaeology systematically destroys that which attracts us to it in the first place. When we come across a megalithic tomb, its presence is one which can be at once intriguing and disturbing. It is an object which is foreign to our own culture, yet it exists in the same space as we do. Although it may be integrated into folklore, or a road map, or a heritage park, its material existence is one which jars with its surroundings. What such a monument offers to us is the opportunity to encounter the Other in our own immediate lifeworld. It is doubtless this experience of something which is mysterious and alien which first inspires many of us to take up archaeology as a study. Being engaged by the past, we want to know more about it. Yet it is precisely in trying to find out about the past that we destroy its unfamiliarity. We introduce techniques of classification and rationalisation which homogenise and tame the past.

While accepting it as inevitable that as soon as we write about the past we fail to capture its alterity, it is the central contention of this book that our image of the Neolithic in Britain is one which is unnecessarily tied to a series of assumptions. It may be impossible to mentally escape one's own cultural context, and to grasp a dead and alien culture in its own terms. Nevertheless, it is a reasonable goal to account for the reasons why our present understanding has been constructed in the way that it has, and therefore to present a more satisfactory interpretation. This book is thus not presented as a definitive account of the British Neolithic so much as a critical writing of the British Neolithic.

While the social sciences have long stressed the way in which our personal experience forms the frame through which we apprehend reality (Bourdieu 1977, 2), the problems faced by archaeologists in casting aside their preconceptions are singular. Inevitably we always judge the object of study in relation to ourselves and the way that we live. But as archaeologists who inhabit the same space as the past society we study we are also tempted to see that society as part of an unbroken developmental continuum which leads upward to ourselves. All of prehistory and history do no more than document the process of emergence of our present order. The consequence of this for the Neolithic has been that in addition to the imposition of a modernist economism which seeks to find a 'rational' explanation for all aspects of prehistoric society, the period has been seen as a simplified, more barbaric form of those periods which succeed it. This can take the relatively crude form of interpreting the 'Beaker folk' as a community of *foederati* brought into Britain to quell the rebellious natives

(Ashbee 1978). But equally, Neolithic pits have been interpreted as storage devices, despite their manifest unsuitability for the purpose, by analogy with Iron Age pits (Field, Matthews and Smith 1964). Causewayed enclosures have been seen as the equivalent of hillforts (Renfrew 1973; Barker and Webley 1978), and Neolithic pottery was originally categorised according to an ABC sequence following schemes devised for the Iron Age (Piggott 1931; Hawkes 1931; Warren *et al.* 1936). It can be contended that all of these interpretations are grounded in a meta-narrative of continuous and progressive development toward the present. The notion that the Neolithic might in certain respects be qualitatively and categorically different from what followed it, and that major horizons of cultural discontinuity might exist in pre-history at a more fundamental level than that of migration, invasion and diffusion is one which has been difficult to entertain under these conditions.

This book is addressed to the problem that, while any prehistory we write is a modern production, written within a given set of circumstances, the past achieves its greatest political potency when it retains its sense of difference and 'otherness'. It is therefore a book which is concerned with neither theory nor practice exclusively. It has recently been suggested that textual production in archaeology is dominated by descriptive, 'common-sense' works, and that works of theory are few and far between (Shanks and Tilley 1987a, 14–15). However, while we might agree with this argument in principle, another point needs to be added. Texts concerning abstract theory have been a constant, if minor, element of the archaeological canon over the past twenty years (e.g. Clarke 1968; Watson, Leblanc and Redman 1971; Gardin 1980; Hodder 1986; etc.). However, what have been even less common have been works which take a body of integrated theory as the basis for a sustained excursus into a given period or problem. Within the 'processualist' tradition there have been honourable attempts to use theory as a means to throw new light onto certain problems (e.g. Renfrew 1972; Randsborg 1980; Hodges 1982). Nevertheless, in these instances the method which has usually been followed is to recruit 'bits' of theory to explain particular phenomena, rather than to start with theory as first principle.

**Writing prehistory**

In recent years archaeologists have become increasingly aware of the textual nature of their enterprise. Part of this awareness has taken the form of the adoption of a textual model for the archaeological record (Patrik 1985), yet here I will concern myself more with the status of archaeological discourse as writing, and some of the implications which follow from this. History, Frederic Jameson tells us, is only available to us textually (1981, 35). This point is forcefully seconded by Shanks and Tilley (1987a, 19), when they suggest that archaeological evidence is only made comprehensible when it is placed in the context of a narrative – that is, when we tell a story. Such an admission clearly contradicts the positivist dictum that we should allow the facts to 'speak for themselves', and the notion that we could ever collect a full set of data which would reduce the past to a transparent and self-evident state.

Despite what archaeologists may claim to the contrary, our problem may not be one of a paucity of evidence, but one of defining which elements of the evidence are significant. Roth (1988, 10) has recently considered the positivist historian's dream of a 'perfect chronicle' containing every event in history written as it happened. Such a chronicle would still produce an imperfect understanding of the past, since the significance of events is perceived only in context, and often only in hindsight. The relevance of an historical event is judged in terms of its contribution to the development of an historical plot. This is why we laugh when we hear that in a particular film a character was given the line 'Forward, men of the Middle Ages: we are about to start the Hundred Years' War!' What we define as significant evidence, what we choose to look on as facts, will vary depending on the preoccupations and preconceptions under which we write history.

The starting point, then, is the position that the archaeological past is inherently written, and is written in a present which is itself 'in history'. What makes this different from writing a novel is the 'trace' of the past in the present, the evidence. As Nietzsche says, 'the past is a rock you cannot move'. However, to write the past is to tame it; to place the evidence in a comprehensible narrative is to rationalise the perspective of a particular context. What I would like to do is to suggest that there are a number of different ways in which archaeologists can and do write the past, and explain the way in which I am trying to come to terms with the problem, before broaching the vexed question of how we evaluate rival narratives. The central motif of the first part of this discussion I draw from Paul Ricoeur's essay *The Reality of the Historical Past* (1984). Here, Ricoeur distinguishes between three tropes of historical writing: History-as-Same, History-as-Other and History-as-Analogue. Each of these 'great signs' is distinguished by a particular relation between the past and the present. Or rather, each form of writing attributes a different status to the written past.

Now, I would contend that the great bulk of archaeological writing is conducted under the sign of the Same. In order to make sense of the evidence available to them, archaeologists often employ some form of universalism, whether it is called analogy, uniformitarianism or middle-range theory. Thus the palaeoeconomic school sought to explain the evidence which was available to them concerning prehistoric settlement and subsistence by recourse to presumed universal laws of behaviour based upon animal ethology (Higgs and Jarman 1975). Other forms of Past-as-Same which prevail in archaeological discourse involve attempts to isolate anthropologically defined forms of social organisation in the past. Thus, for instance, we can note Renfrew's search for chiefdoms in European prehistory (1973), or the forms of structural Marxist archaeology which seek evidence for particular kinship systems or modes of production in the past (Thomas 1987).

Ricoeur cites the example of Collingwood as his central case of History-as-Same, and it is significant that Ian Hodder draws upon Collingwood's work in developing one of the most sophisticated archaeologies written under the sign of the Same (Hodder 1986, 90). According to Ricoeur, Collingwood's aim in historical 're-enactment' is not the re-living of events, but the re-thinking of the thoughts of the actors concerned. To get inside the event in this way means that knowing *what* happened is already to know *why* it happened: understanding consists in fusing with the mental life of another. Hodder takes this line of reasoning to imply that certain universal structuring principles allow unique events to be appreciated by all people at all times.

However, even with such an advanced form of Past-as-Same there are immediately some problems which arise. These stem, I think, from the medium through which the archaeologist must attempt to enter the minds of past individuals: that is, material culture. Taking the argument that we can look on material culture as being in some ways analogous to language, something which conveys and holds meanings, it is questionable whether any communicative medium can give a total and immediate access to the thoughts of another person. To suggest this would be to accept the Husserlian model of the meaning-giving subject expressing primordial, internally generated meanings through communicative acts (Norris 1982, 46). This effectively asserts that a pure, intelligible meaning is being expressed through the imperfect, distorted artifice of discourse, be it verbal or material. However, as Foucault says, 'there is nothing absolutely primary because, when all is said and done, underneath it all everything is already interpretation' (1967, 189). Or, to put it another way, there is nothing outside the text. We cannot assume that there is some fundamental level of deep meaning, however much our post-Freudian civilisation would like it to be so. So we cannot say that material culture is 'language-like', and yet at the same time hope that it necessarily expresses some deeper level of meaning. It seems more logical to suggest that material culture, as a symbolic system, is a part of thought; it is not an expression but an interpretation of reality. People use things to think with. So if one is able to use material items as a means of approaching the mind of some long-dead person or group of persons, one may not be so much empathising with them, or entering their thoughts, as peeling away sedimented layers of interpretation within an alien system of thought.

If this is the case, if communication is always already interpretation, our problems are compounded. We are producing an interpretation of an interpretation. This introduces a parallel with Derrida's famous discussion of Nietzsche's umbrella (Derrida 1978; Norris 1982, 71; Lawson 1985, 116). There exists in one of Nietzsche's manuscripts a marginal note, which says 'I have forgotten my umbrella'. Derrida finds almost endless play in this one sentence, speculating as to whether it can be taken at face value, or whether it represents some coded comment on or key to the rest of the manuscript. Indeed, he finds it possible to argue that it is no more or less significant than any other sentence in the piece of writing. This is because its meaning is ultimately unknowable; what we take it to mean depends upon our own reading. Thus, too, with archaeological materials – a point which Hodder would doubtless concede, and to which I will return.

If there are problems with perspectives which link past and present, the immediate alternative is a past written under Ricoeur's sign of the Other. It is here that some more of the disturbing consequences of post-structuralist thought for archaeology start to emerge. In their different ways, Derrida and Foucault have done away with the 'points of presence', the fixed points of reference outside history which might act as Ariadne's thread to guide us through the labyrinth (Lentricchia 1980, 166). Now, there is only the labyrinth. 'Nothing in man', says Foucault, 'not even his body – is sufficiently stable to serve as a basis for self-recognition or for understanding other men' (1984a,

87). What, then, if there is no stable entity which we can call human nature? What if, as Nietzsche suggested, even the most seemingly stable elements of our existence, like morality and sexuality, can be seen as historical and transient? What if there are no structural universals which extend into the past? What if there were no chiefdoms in the Neolithic? How can we ever reach into the distant past if we have only concepts developed in the present with which to apprehend it?

It is with the attempt to get beyond 'the consoling play of recognitions' (Foucault 1984a, 88) that the idea of History-as-Other begins. Such a history is based not on searching for similarities between past and present, but in the recovery of temporal distance. By recovering the *difference* of the past, such a history seeks to delegitimise the present. In this way, the difference of the past becomes one of its most political characteristics. The prototype of such a history was Nietzsche's *On the Genealogy of Morals* (1969), which served as a model for Foucault's work on penal systems and sexuality. In each case the aim was to historicise the seeming universals of the human condition by contrasting past and present. All of the common-sense values dissolve before genealogical analysis – words do not keep their meanings, desires do not keep their objectives, ideas do not keep their logic.

Genealogy, a contrastive history, can be argued to provide a paradigm for effective archaeological research. It should be possible to use a similar methodology to investigate particular areas of human practice through a search for points in time in which they were subject to structural changes. Our efforts can be directed at those supposedly static and ahistorical spheres like the appropriation of landscapes, the preparation and consumption of food, the disposal of household waste, the organis-ation of domestic space and the use of the human body in mortuary practice. Each of these has been conventionally looked on by archaeologists in universal terms: hence food remains are looked on as evidence for calorific input, while mortuary practices are seen as the raw material for mathematical indices of the degree to which a society is ranked.

Such an archaeology, then, would oppose itself to the forcing of the past into modernist categories and classifications. At each stage, it attempts to maintain the strangeness of the past, its alien quality. However, it must be admitted that in the final analysis such a process will always be incomplete and unsatisfying. One can decon-struct the forms of one's analysis of the past indefinitely. Clearly, no set of concepts or ideas developed in the present will ever grasp the whole essence of the past (see Dews 1987, 177). So just as Derrida can demonstrate the absence of any fixity of meaning by moving constantly from one signifier to the next, we might search endlessly for a written past which finally breaks its ties with the present. At some point we must come to terms with this, and simply write a story. It is at this stage that we move to Ricoeur's final great sign, that of the Analogue. Here, the narrative which we write is acknowl-edged to be something which is not the real past, but something which 'stands for' the past. A history written as Analogue is a story written in the present, which weaves together the traces of the past in a web of rationalisation. If we accept the point that to write at all is to tame and homogenise the past such a writing effects a form of reconciliation between Same and Other.

If we begin from the position that what we are striving to do is to free the past from ethnocentric and presentist deformations, our writing can begin with a radical separation of past and present through the employment of genealogy and deconstruction, yet must end with an act of domestication. Writing the past, then, is an endless task, in which each act of putting pen to paper is admitted to be a failure to grasp some elusive truth. Such a truth is always already absent from written discourse.

# 2

# More than an economic system

**The image of a 'Neolithic economy'**

The present understanding of the Neolithic in Britain rests upon its identification as a primarily economic phenomenon. Contesting this central assumption is the starting point for this book. When first employed by archaeologists, the term 'Neolithic' implied a technological rather than an economic phenomenon (Lubbock 1872). However, at some point in the history of the discipline the use of ground and polished stone tools, pottery and agriculture came to be seen as inextricably linked (e.g. Cole 1965). While contemporary archaeology has eroded the division between hunting and gathering and agriculture (Higgs and Jarman 1975), and has come to allow the existence of foragers with ceramics (Rowley-Conwy 1983), the opening of the Neolithic is still seen as necessarily the occasion of the adoption of a reliance upon agriculture (Williams 1989). The term 'Neolithic', I would argue, is seen as synonymous with 'mixed farming economy'. This point of view has been maintained by a coming together of two quite different schools of archaeological thought, one based on a traditional, culture-historical approach, and one geared to the 'palaeoeconomic' perspective which developed in Cambridge in the 1960s and 1970s. These two paradigms have found common ground in two basic suppositions: firstly, that a separate sphere of human action designated 'subsistence economy' can be discerned in prehistoric societies in general, and secondly that this practice is somehow more fundamental than all others, forming the precondition for all aspects of human life. Thus Atkinson suggests that 'It was the practice of agriculture and stock-raising, that is, the deliberate *production* as opposed to the mere gathering of food, that allowed the population of Britain for the first time to gain mastery of its environment, and so to rise from brute savagery to the higher levels of barbarism' (1956, 148; emphasis in original). Similarly, Higgs and Jarman indicate that 'The primary human adaptation to the environment is the economy, man's management of his household . . . Palaeoeconomic studies lay their main stress on a basic aspect of human behaviour which can be shown to conform to predictable laws over a long period of time' (1975, 4).

What these two points of view share, then, is a particularly crude form of the base/superstructure duality, in which the institutions of the latter are ultimately always reducible to the former. Thus Legge (1989, 224) is able to suggest that 'the modest achievements of Mesolithic peoples in Britain are a reflection of an economy based upon hunting and gathering. The major achievements of the Neolithic peoples of Britain were not . . . Only agriculture could provide the essential fuel for that degree of social elaboration'. It has been this degree of agreement which has allowed the two approaches to be welded together over the years to produce a picture of a mixed farming economy driven through successive episodes of intensification and collapse by the fragile relationship which obtained between population and resources. This is not to say, however, that all commentators within this emergent tradition draw entirely the same conclusions from this body of accepted wisdom. Given the striking lack of evidence for settlement patterns, dwellings, agricultural practices and stock management in Neolithic Britain, the contradictory statements which issue from the background of certain common-sensical notions concerning these phenomena can perhaps deliver the *aporia* which undermines the entire structure.

The conventional narrative of economic change through the period can be briefly sketched. To begin with, the British Neolithic farming system was seen as being 'mature and non-experimental' (Case 1969a, 177), whether it was introduced by colonisation as Case would have it, or by acculturation as more recent formulations suggest (Zvelebil and Rowley-Conwy 1986). Its impact on the British landscape is described as 'impressive . . . in all but a few upland areas inroads into the woodland and forest were made' (Darvill 1987, 53). The ultimate consequence of this 'most significant social transition . . . ever to have taken place' (*ibid.*, 48) was the foundation of 'networks of subsistence territories' within which was practised a 'complex agricultural system' which 'can of course be integrated with Renfrew's model of emergent chiefdoms' (Barker 1985, 200). Nevertheless,

> One must *assume* an initial period after the settlement of the British Isles in which all efforts were concentrated on the production of food and the increase in numbers both of herds and crops, where there would be little time available to devote to sites or even, perhaps, substantial settlements. One may therefore *reasonably assume* that the earliest Neolithic monuments for which there are radiocarbon dates do not in fact reflect the structures erected by the first, second, or even the third generation of agriculturalists to settle in this country. (Megaw and Simpson 1979, 79; emphasis mine)

This series of acknowledged assumptions allows the rather interesting proposition of a totally archaeologically invisible first Neolithic in Britain to be posited, a line of argument which Zvelebil and Rowley-Conwy (1986, 74) seem equally to accept. Both schools of thought have implicitly conceived of the Neolithic as essentially being composed of a set of agricultural innovations, any 'cultural' elements being secondary. The eventual emergence of Renfrew's monumental landscapes is thus entirely conditional upon this agricultural achievement.

A similar set of arguments has been constructed to explain away the comparative absence of domestic architecture in Neolithic Britain. On the one hand we have Megaw and Simpson, arguing that 'Archaeologists have been searching in the wrong places – on the tops of the downs where in general both the barrows and causewayed enclosures lie, rather than in the valley bottoms where now more and more evidence suggests, and *common sense would indicate*, that settlements would occur adjacent to water' (1979, 86; emphasis mine). This is surely what Bradley (1985) calls 'the archaeology of Mr. Micawber', the faith that in time 'something will turn up'. And this in the face of a continental European sequence in which the substantial timber buildings of the Bandkeramik and associated cultures disappear at precisely the same time as the inception of the British Neolithic (e.g. Kruk 1980; Whittle 1988a, Chapter 3). Darvill (1987, 56–7), by contrast, proceeds to discuss the very few house structures excavated in Britain as 'farmstead settlements', rather evading the problematic nature of their 'domestic' status (Kinnes 1985, 26; Herne 1988, 25). A third strategy is followed by Burl (1987, 83), who chooses to interpret the large pits with attendant stakeholes at Winterbourne Dauntsey as 'three claustrophobic round huts'. 'Their filth discouraged any idea of a prehistoric golden age. Although they were situated on a low hill, the ground appeared to have been continually sodden, bare of anything but patches of grass and scatters of decaying food thrown out from the cramped, squalid shacks' (*ibid.*).

All of these accounts take it as read that Neolithic people should live in permanent buildings, and on this basis struggle to convince us that such structures existed in the period concerned. Again, this can be argued to be the consequence of certain unexamined assumptions of archaeological thought: Neolithic people practise mixed agriculture, therefore they are sedentary, therefore they have houses. The same turn of mind obviously lies behind Fowler's astonishing suggestion that

> It will not be too surprising when we turn up our Middle Neolithic and earlier field systems. They will turn up, perhaps not on the present land surface and probably not in the 'classic' field areas, but buried beneath the erosion deposits in a lowland English valley, or just out of sight below the rim of a bog or marsh. (1981, 39)

In all particulars, then, the agricultural lifestyle of the Neolithic is assumed to have been much the same as that which obtained in Britain until the arrival of the Romans and beyond. People lived in houses, kept sheep, pigs and cattle and grew cereals. This amounts to 'mixed agriculture' (e.g. Burgess 1980, 29). On this basis, Mercer suggests that 'farming practice in British prehistory had the *potential* to support massive populations' (1981a, 236; my emphasis). Here lies another assumption, the Malthusian dictum that population will always rise to the highest level which can be supported by resources and technology, implicit in palaeoeconomy. Population pressure has come to be seen as a driving motor in many accounts of the British Neolithic. 'With more people to feed, more crops and more cattle were needed, areas of good soil were over-exploited, poorer regions were brought under cultivation, more forest was cut back and competition for land increased. In such a period of tension there came the emergence of territories, leaders and conflict' (Burl 1987, 32).

If the middle of the Neolithic is seen as a period of change in the relationship between population and resources (Whittle 1978, 34), then the later third millennium is a 'period of recovery' (Whittle 1980a, 331). In this epoch is often imagined the rise of 'a largely pastoral economy' and 'a nomadic society' (Megaw and Simpson 1979, 168). The users of Grooved Ware, in particular, are seen as practising 'pastoralism and strandlooping, with no certain evidence for the cultivation of cereals' (Wainwright and Longworth 1971, 266). This is an interesting prospect, since it seems to be suggested that the major meat animal was the pig (*ibid.*, 264), whose suitability to a nomadic lifestyle might be questioned (Grigson 1982b).

The prevailing picture of Neolithic Britain, then, is one of a society firmly grounded in a lifestyle of sedentary mixed farming, in many ways comparable with those which succeeded it until the Industrial Revolution, yet one dogged by its explosive population expansion and the fragility of the ecosystem it inhabited. The contemporary circumstances which lie behind the writing of this account are easy enough to identify: a combination of a hankering after the idyll of an 'eternal' British countryside, in which a particular way of life has remained unaltered for millennia, and a 'green' concern over the present-day environment. Within this, of course, lies a contradiction between change and changelessness. Many prehistorians seem happy to assert that agriculture was the sphere of human practice in which reasons for the development of prehistoric societies must be located, yet are unable to see that agriculture itself is changing in any fundamental way. At most, agriculture is said to 'intensify' – to increase in scale, rather than to undergo fundamental transformation. Where transformation is posited, it is generally in the form of that stock explanation of culture-historical archaeology, 'a shift to pastoralism'. A way of life which is outside our own immediate experience seems to be difficult to conceptualise within such a framework.

## The archaeology of production

One of the main reasons why this set of common-sensical and modernist ideas has come to dominate our thinking on the economic practices of the Neolithic period has been the existence of a general resistance to theory in economic and environmental archaeology. We will never understand the significance of material production in prehistory if our accounts begin and end with how many cattle would have been kept, how many tonnes of grain harvested per hectare. The provision of food, and equally of other goods, is always a social process which takes place in the context of a set of relations of production. While it can be argued that people always have to eat, this is very much a minimum consideration with respect to the form of their economic life. To attempt to explain an agricultural system, or a set of exchange transactions, in abstraction from the particular social rationale which defined the objectives of production and circulation is thus likely to be a fruitless task. Production involves the transformation of a set of natural materials by human labour, and this in itself is a process of classification and categorisation. Hence the product is socially defined, and cannot be measured purely in terms of matter and energy (Ingold 1981, 120).

The form of words 'social relations of production' can imply an economistic and deterministic view of history. In some forms of Marxism, for instance, the relations of production are seen as depending directly upon the development of the productive forces, and in particular technology (Cohen 1978). While one might wish to affirm a connectedness between the forces and relations of production, it is not necessary to see this as a one-way process of the unfurling of technological change driving social and economic development. When Marx and Engels say that 'By producing their means of subsistence men are indirectly producing their actual material life' (1970, 42), they can be taken to be stressing the materiality of human existence, rather than locating the source of social development in the subsistence economy. It is perhaps unnecessary to need to claim any lineage for one's work in the ideas of Marx, yet it could be argued that the most positive way in which the legacy of historical materialism can be interpreted does not lie in stressing the primacy of the productive forces. Instead, one could see the most important aspects of materialism as being the notion that being in the world precedes consciousness of the world, and the stress on relations of production as real rather than metaphysical. These relations are situated in the real world, existing between extant subjects and objects, and are emphatically historical in nature. At the same time, one might object to the impression that 'relations of production' need be more than a function of the production of material things than the production of human subjects, and the reproduction of society and of knowledge. What this amounts to saying is that material production is to be located in a nexus of relations of power and knowledge which are historically situated, and are thus constituted and reproduced in radically different ways in different societies.

From this it follows that the social organisation of labour undertaken by people within a given epoch is fundamental to the understanding of their historical circumstances. Yet this may be less in the sense of the quantities of food produced and consumed than in that of how labour contributed to their formation as subjects, and hence to the process of social reproduction. Any labour – hunting and gathering, pastoralism, agriculture, industrial production – implies a set of spatio-temporal rhythms, a discipline of mind and body which contributes to the constitution of subjectivity. The same set of natural materials can be transformed into a materially identical product in a multiplicity of different ways. What is important is not what is produced, so much as how it is produced.

For archaeology, what is significant is the recognition that this nexus of relations of production can be constituted in different ways in different epochs. Only under capitalism is a separate sphere of practice recognisable as an 'economy' to be distinguished (Giddens 1981). In many contemporary tribal societies, economic activities are carried out within the framework of kinship relations (Godelier 1977). The wisdom of separating off distinct areas of study as 'economic archaeology' or 'environmental archaeology' is thus to be severely doubted, since the understanding of why people adopted the agricultural strategies which they did is unlikely to reside in the bones, seeds, snails and pollen alone. An archaeology of production must be sensitive to the need to understand the internal dynamics of a society if one is to recognise why labour was organised as it was.

## Defining the Neolithic

Discourse is at once made possible and constrained by the language that we use. Very often it is the structure of that language itself which determines the course which intellectual history will take. Words which can never quite express the concepts to which they are linked in our minds fall into certain places, and a discourse emerges which gains a momentum of its own. So it is that when we come to discuss the term 'Neolithic', we may be referring to a chronological horizon, a stage in an evolutionary scheme, a form of economy or a cultural phenomenon. Thus it is that many of the debates concerning the introduction of the Neolithic to Britain or to Europe have been characterised by exchanges which take place at cross purposes, in which the antagonists are actually referring to phenomena of a quite different order. The problem is at its most acute in the work of those archaeologists (Dennell 1983; Zvelebil and Rowley-Conwy 1984; 1986) who equate the word 'Neolithic' with 'agriculture', and proceed to discuss the developments of the period concerned as if all of the cultural and social innovations were subsidiary to the inception of farming. This is not to deny the importance of the origins and spread of agriculture. What it does suggest is that *in some cases* its adoption may have taken place in the context of other changes which may have been of equal or greater significance to the communities concerned.

These problems are very evident in Zvelebil's (1989) recent comments on the spread of the Neolithic. Zvelebil expresses the desire for a clear definition of what constitutes a Neolithic society, and agreement on how this is to be recognised in the archaeological record and on those traits which might discriminate between indigenous development and incoming populations (*ibid.*, 382). The rigour of such a project is commendable, but Zvelebil appears to want the Neolithic to be something stable, which can be held constant across time and space. These aspirations are more appropriate to the physicist's laboratory than to the messy business of human cultural development. The Neolithic was a *historical* phenomenon, comparable with other such phenomena like Christianity, capitalism and communism, more a process than an object to be grasped and reduced to a series of traits. It should not be expected to comprise the same elements at different times and places, even if it maintains an identity by constituting a linked sequence of events and transformations. The Neolithic was a historical effect of the playing out of human social relations. At one point in space and time it might indeed have been primarily an economic phenomenon, at another it might have constituted an ideology.

These rather abstract points can be substantiated by a brief consideration of the development of the Neolithic way of life across Eurasia. In the Near East, a lifestyle involving a dependence upon domesticated plants and animals seems to have developed in quite different ways in two different areas, the Levant and the Zagros (Redman 1977, 534). In the Zagros foothills, a heavy reliance upon herded animals seems to have developed, together with relatively small and architecturally simple settlements like Ali Kosh and Jarmo (*ibid.*, 536). In the Levant, however, the first instances of house building, cultivated barley and legumes and symbolic paraphernalia involving the use of human skulls all preceded the domestication of animals (Clark 1977, 54). In this area one can well argue that it was the development of a settled lifestyle and a richer ceremonial and cultural life which fostered the domestication of plants and animals rather than vice versa. This particular chicken and egg have been discussed often enough in the past (Childe 1951; Binford 1968; Bender 1975). What needs to be pointed out at this stage is that from its inception, the Neolithic was an extremely heterogeneous phenomenon, at least in economic terms. One might argue that, if the post-Pleistocene transformations of the Middle East possessed any unity, it existed at the level of relations of production, rather than the extremely variable forces of production involved. A readiness to appropriate and transform nature was emerging, and this would have required a substantial shift in social orientation. Indeed, it could even be frictions internal to society which might have dealt the 'first kick' towards domestication so notoriously absent from demographic and ecological explanations of agricultural origins (Bender 1975, 34). The alteration of the relationship between humanity and nature is broader far than herding and harvesting. As Hodder suggests, 'The building of more stable houses, the aggregation and even delimitation of settlement, the more elaborate and cultural treatment of the dead, all separate more securely the domestic from the wild' (Hodder 1987, 53). Such a process of separation is as much about the definition of in-groups and out-groups, of culture and nature, as it is about survival, just as the cooking of food is in part concerned with the definition of the human domain (Lévi-Strauss 1970).

If these elements of the Neolithic way of life developed in a piecemeal way in the Near East, their introduction to Europe may have been in a more integrated form. At Franchthi Cave, for instance, cattle and pigs, polished stone tools, pottery and a blade industry all appeared together (Barker 1985, 65). As against this, sheep, goats and domesticated plants had arrived earlier at that site (Payne 1975; Hansen 1980), and there is plausible evidence for an indigenous domestication of cattle and pigs in Greece. It is at this point that we must distinguish between two quite different processes. Throughout the period in which Neolithic culture spread across Europe, there are documented instances of the domestication of animals, or of plants, or the use of pottery or polished stone tools, or of complex forms of burial being practised by local populations who may or may not have been in contact with Neolithic groups. These sporadic instances do not constitute a precocious 'Neolithisation'. It is not the adoption of the odd Neolithic trait or innovation into a Mesolithic lifestyle which represents the onset of the Neolithic: it is a wholesale transformation of social relations which results from adopting an integrated cultural system. Such a system has as its purpose not merely the provision of sustenance, the biological reproduction of the community, but its social reproduction, including the maintenance of power relations, knowledge and institutions. Owning a cow, or an axe, living in a house, or burying one of one's kin in a particular way does not make a person Neolithic. It is the recognition of the symbolic potential of these elements to express a fundamental division of the universe into the wild and the tame which creates the Neolithic world.

The expansion of the Neolithic into temperate Europe with the Linearbandkeramik in the fifth millennium bc extended the pattern set up by the Balkan Neolithic. The integrated system of farming and residence in large timber houses seems to have spread by colonisation (Starling 1985a, 41), and to have been limited to a restricted set of environmental locations (Bakels 1982, 31). Only later, with the further expansion into the North European Plain, Scandinavia and the British Isles did a fundamental change in the nature of the Neolithic lifestyle take place (Thomas 1988a). From this time on, many of the characteristic type-fossils are either absent, rare, or restricted to a very specialised set of contexts. Cereals may not have played a very large part in the subsistence practices of Neolithic Britain (Robinson and Wilson 1987), while pottery may have been used only for a restricted set of practices (Herne

1988). Large, timber-framed houses are rare in north-west Europe from the Rössen period onwards, and in Britain those few which exist are of uniformly early date. Aggregated settlements are still rarer. So, while we might concede that the Neolithic of the LBK was one which manifested itself in a highly 'economic' guise, by the time Britain entered the Neolithic community, it was a Neolithic which existed largely in the realm of ideas. Nevertheless, as I have argued elsewhere, it was this transformation which allowed it to be transmitted by acculturation rather than by colonisation (Thomas 1988a, 64).

## The evidence of lithics

At the same time as an orthodox view of Neolithic agricultural and residential patterns has been developing, evidence has been gathering which might challenge it. This evidence is in the form of tools and waste material of flint, chert and other stones, which occur as scatters distributed across the landscape. While these lithics have been recovered from ploughed fields for generations by amateur collectors (e.g. Laidler and Young 1938), the notion that their systematic collection (Richards 1982; 1984) and analysis (Gardiner 1984; Holgate 1984; 1988a; 1988b; Brown and Edmonds 1987) have much to tell the archaeologist is a comparatively recent one. The perceived benefit of the study of lithics is that, while the structural traces of prehistoric settlement might be minimal and fragile, stone tools are relatively indestructible, and remain locked in the topsoil, moving relatively little from their point of discard (e.g. Bradley, Cleal, Gardiner, Legge *et al.* 1984).

To a degree, stone tools and waste can provide a chronologically sensitive indicator of the inhabitation or use of particular areas. While the temporal resolution is extremely coarse, typochronology does allow a separation to be made between 'earlier' and 'later' Neolithic assemblages, in terms of both tool types and the characteristics of waste flakes and blades. Underlying this separation is a gradual chronological decline in the standard of flintworking, resulting in a slow change from the fine blade technology of the Mesolithic to the crude, squat flakes of the Bronze Age (Pitts and Jacobi 1979). Hence the metrical analysis of waste flakes may serve as an indicator of relative chronology, a proposition which has been followed to some degree of sophistication in an analysis (Ford 1987). At the same time, particular forms of arrowheads, flint axes, cores and other tools are also held to be chronologically diagnostic (Gardiner 1984; Bradley and Holgate 1984; Holgate 1988a).

These insights have been applied in Britain both to museum collections of lithics amassed by amateurs (Gardiner 1987a) and to material systematically collected by fieldwalking survey (Richards 1985). The results of this work can best be interpreted by placing them in the context of the European sequence alluded to in the last section. The primary Neolithic settlement of central and western Europe, the Linearband-keramik, presents a major contrast both with subsequent continental developments and with Neolithic activity in Britain. Typically, these small settlements of timber longhouses were located on the edges of minor valleys in the loess country (Lüning 1982, 26). The plateau top immediately above the settlement would have served as the location for fixed-plot horticulture fertilised by domestic waste (rather than the swiddening once proposed for this phase) (Sherratt 1980; Rowley-Conwy 1981; Howell 1983a, 132). On the valley floor cattle would have been grazed.

However, as has already been mentioned, from the late fourth millennium onwards, the horizon at which the Neolithic was established in Britain, large timber houses are rather rare in western Europe (e.g. Bakker 1982, 90; Howell 1983b, 64). This absence of substantial domestic architecture is a pattern which is maintained until well into the Bronze Age. Where structures are preserved by exceptional circumstances, as at Mosegården in Denmark, they may be flimsy in the extreme and the density of occupation material indicates a relatively short duration of use (Madsen and Jensen 1982, 66). Equally, in some areas it has been suggested that the later fourth millennium was a time when a greater dependence was placed upon domestic livestock, and cattle in particular (Howell 1982, 116). However, while this development coincided with the expansion of the Neolithic into Britain and the North European Plain, a further phase of *internal* colonisation was to take place in the middle of the third millennium (Kruk 1980; Starling 1983, 7; etc.). This involved a change of emphasis in landuse away from the water courses and towards the drier and less fertile soils, and has been connected by Sherratt (1981, 293) with the introduction of plough agriculture. This seems plausible, although these developments might constitute an essentially social and economic change played out through the medium of the introduction of new technology (Starling 1985b; Thomas 1987).

The southern British evidence has some affinity with this sequence. Those scatters of material which can be attributed to the earlier part of the Neolithic (*c.* 3200–2500 bc) tend to be small in spatial extent and to be located on light upland soils (Gardiner 1984; Richards 1984; Holgate 1988a). In contrast, later Neolithic scatters (*c.* 2500–1800 bc) are more extensive spatially and are located on a wider range of soils. This does not indicate a shift of settlement from one set of locations to another, so much as an expansion from an initially fairly restricted area, as Holgate indicates (1988a, 135).

This process can clearly be seen in Figures 2.1 and 2.2, showing the distributions of earlier and later Neolithic scatters within the study area, drawn from the author's museum data with additions from some of the works mentioned above. In a major work concerned with Neolithic settlement in the Thames Valley, Holgate (1988a, Chapter 5) suggests that only the sites which have produced five or more types of stone tools should be employed for analysis. The justification for this move is that a settlement site is expected to be the locus of a variety of types of activity, using a range of tools. While the procedure has been employed here, an immediate problem is that it assumes that the structure of Neolithic settlement would have been one based upon multi-purpose 'domestic sites' or home bases. If particular activities were carried out at special-purpose sites, using a more restricted tool kit, they might not register. Given the uneven quality of the collection of museum material, however, it might be impossible to distinguish between a genuine special-purpose site and an intensive sampling of the ubiquitous 'background' scatter of lithic material by a particularly enthusiastic collector. Given these strictures, the results generated by the analysis must be taken at a very general level.

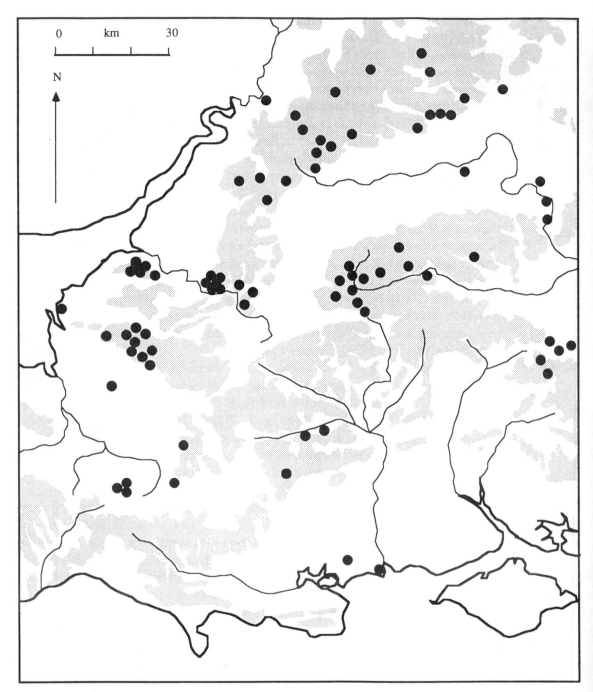

Figure 2.1 Earlier Neolithic settlement in the study area (author's data with additions from Gardiner 1987b and Holgate 1988a)

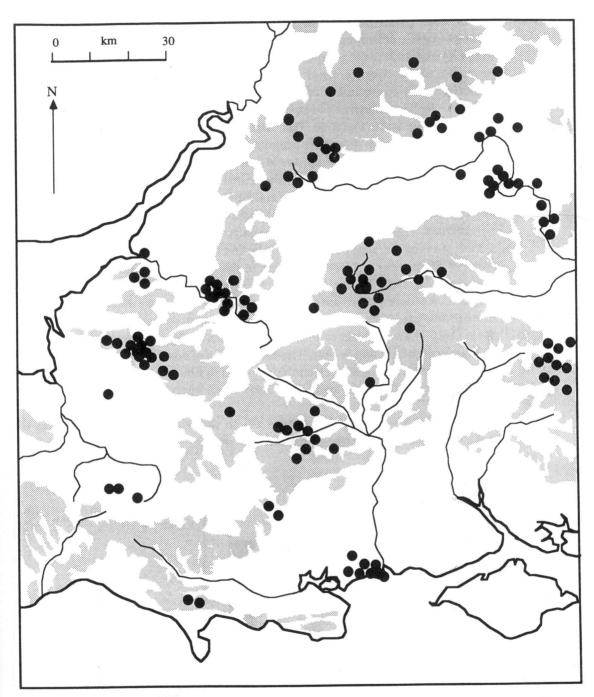

Figure 2.2    Later Neolithic settlement in the study area (author's data with additions from Gardiner 1987b and Holgate 1988a)

With these points firmly borne in mind, and acknowledging the need for more detailed analyses of landscapes as wholes rather than as isolated 'sites', the results in the study area confirm the general pattern indicated above. As far as the chronological resolution of the evidence can demonstrate, it seems that the middle of the third millennium saw an expansion of settlement onto the clays, gravels and greensand, together with a maintenance of activity on the limestones and an intensification of it on the chalk uplands (Fig. 2.3). This latter phenomenon is in part linked with the greater use of the clay-with-flints capping some areas of chalk as a location which would have afforded plentiful supplies of lithic raw material (Gardiner 1984).

As Bradley (1987a, 182) suggests, this expansion can be linked to a number of other changes in the character of surface flint assemblages. As well as the increasing size and density of scatters, and a larger number of findspots, certain technological changes can be discerned. These include the shift from narrow to broad flakes already mentioned, the use of a broader range of tools, and a decline in the use of retouched and serrated flakes. Evidently this represents a change in the way in which the raw material was regarded and used. Earlier Neolithic assemblages are characterised by careful preparation of cores, which are often rejuvenated so as to make maximum use of the stone (Edmonds 1987). Blades have been carefully removed, and often retouched for use as tools. The assemblage as a whole is one which can be put to a variety of uses: the tools are non-specific and flexible. The combination of a narrow range of tools and the careful use of cores indicates a technology suited to a mobile way of life (*ibid.*). Thus the character of the tools themselves adds to an appreciation of settlement and mobility.

By the later Neolithic an assemblage was in use which had a broader range of tool types, each more specific to particular activities. This might be seen as a 'less

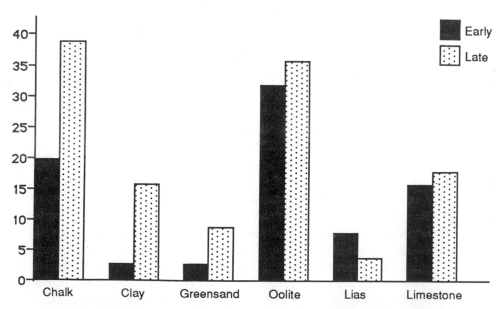

Figure 2.3   Landscape use in the earlier and later Neolithic (vertical axis represents number of sites)

economic' use of raw material than in the earlier assemblage. However, this runs the risk of imposing a modern Western concern with efficiency on the past, and an alternative reading would be that this was a set of tools suited to a changed style of life, in which portability was not at a premium. If, as Edmonds (1987, 169) suggests, the earlier Neolithic assemblage can be connected with regular, large-scale, planned movements of population, perhaps on a seasonal basis, then the later Neolithic pattern might represent the breakdown of this system, with a reduction of overall mobility. The broad spreads of tools and debitage across the landscape might indicate 'that residential locations of a fairly insubstantial nature were repeatedly moved within a well defined area' (*ibid.*, 174).

Placed in the context of the European evidence, these observations can be expanded upon somewhat. The small, nucleated distributions of lithics of the earlier Neolithic could easily relate to a pattern of fixed-plot horticulture, although one dominated by the dictates of seasonal or shorter-term movements within a way of life based upon cattle herding. By the later Neolithic this was replaced by a pattern in which the residential focus was even less fixed. Individual households might shift from one location to another over a number of years, being less closely tied to particular plots and perhaps abandoning them when weed infestation set in. That is to say, the introduction of the plough might have made the preparation of new plots less costly in terms of labour than the ridding of established plots of weeds. At a higher level of organisation, however, the later Neolithic might have seen rather less in the way of planned, large-scale seasonal movements. This might relate to purely economic factors, such as a greater dependence upon grown crops as opposed to livestock, but might equally represent the decline of some element of the social organisation of the earlier Neolithic. These claims might seem excessive on the basis of lithic analysis alone, but can perhaps be substantiated by placing them alongside the biological evidence.

## Faunal and botanical evidence

What can be said about the crops which were grown in Neolithic Britain has tended to be rather limited, in consequence of the very few seed impressions and samples of carbonised seed remains which have been recovered (Hillman 1981a). The very paucity of this evidence has contributed to its being interpreted in a particular way. Thus Legge (1989, 220) suggests that 'Most judgements of the importance of agriculture to prehistoric communities therefore rest, to a significant degree, on data other than that of the charred seeds, such as the size and complexity of settlements or the scale of monumental construction.'

However, it is far from clear that complex monuments, or for that matter involved ritual practices or social stratification, need to be based upon a system of sedentary agriculture with fixed fields and a dependence on staple crops. The massive monumental complex at Cahokia, on the Mississippi, constructed in the first millennium AD, for instance, was the product of a society which practised maize and squash horticulture in small raised gardens supplemented with many wild species (Dincauze and Hasenstab 1989, 73). Societies like the north-west coast Amerindians had complex ceremonial cycles, yet the only crops which they cultivated were those which were used as sacraments in ritual. Hunters and gatherers and those practising horticulture and other simple forms of cultivation often have many hours of spare time not engaged in productive labour (Sahlins 1974). There is thus no reason at all why monument-building or complex ritual should be dependent upon a large agricultural surplus. On the contrary, one might argue that it would be more likely that agricultural intensification to support urban populations in more recent epochs could be held responsible for the impoverishment of the ceremonial lives of traditional societies.

Given this evidence, it is no longer the case that any explanation for monument-building can be found in the development of an economic base, in the form of a transition from hunting and gathering to farming. A growth of territorialism resulting from the adoption of agriculture has often been cited as a reason for the first construction of monuments (Renfrew 1976; Chapman 1981). However, if there is no evidence for such agriculture, this becomes a circular argument (monuments are the consequence of agriculture, which must exist because of the presence of monuments).

If we remove the imperative to interpret seed remains as evidence for a complex system of fixed-field crop rotation, the quality of the record is more explicable. For some time it has been recognised that 'most of the early agricultural communities continued to be substantially dependent on a wide range of wild food resources' (Hillman 1981a, 189). Substantial biases doubtless colour the representation of various species in carbonised assemblages (Dennell 1972). Nevertheless, the domination of almost all known assemblages by wild species is suggestive (Robinson and Wilson 1987; Moffett, Robinson and Straker 1989), as is the total absence of weed faunas characteristic of plough agriculture (*ibid.*). Cereal crops certainly were grown: emmer and einkorn wheat, possibly bread wheat, and hulled and six-row barley (Hillman 1981b, 124). There is also evidence that particular crops were grown preferentially on different soils (Dennell 1976). As spelt had yet to be introduced, there would be no winter wheat, and hence a single yearly sowing. Jarman, Bailey and Jarman (1982, 142) insist that as legumes are found in rotation with cereals in the Neolithic of Europe and the Near East they were probably also present in Britain. Such a rotation fixes and replaces nitrogen in the soil, and hence is highly suitable for fixed-plot horticulture. However, the evidence for legumes is scant, and in the British climate they might prove prone to weevil and aphid attack (Green 1981). Indeed, even the relatively high productivity and sedentariness of continental Bandkeramik garden horticulture may be inapplicable to the British situation, as Moffett, Robinson and Straker indicate (1989, 254).

The earliest record of the use of the plough in Britain is provided by the marks beneath the South Street long barrow, dated to 2810±130 bc (BM-356). However, it is open to debate whether this genuinely reflects the use of an ard in routine cultivation (Reynolds 1981). The artefactual evidence for cultivation is restricted to a single digging stick recovered from the Baker Platform on the Somerset Levels (Rees 1979). Nevertheless, the evidence from the continent suggests that even in the more intensive Bandkeramik horticulture no more advanced technology than hoes, digging-sticks and spades was employed (Kruk 1980; Sherratt 1981; Rowley-Conwy 1981; Jarman,

Bailey and Jarman 1982). As Entwistle and Grant have suggested, the most likely picture in Neolithic Britain is one of 'transient, hoe-based horticulture' (1989, 208) representing only a part of a broader spectrum of plant foods. Hazelnuts, crab apples, raspberry, blackberry, sloe and hawthorn pips have all been recovered from carbonised assemblages, while edible roots, rhizomes and tubers are known from waterlogged contexts (Moffett, Robinson and Straker 1989, 246). Whether cereals and other domestic crops represented a dominant or minor element in the diet might have varied from place to place and time to time. Indeed, it is interesting to speculate whether the significance of domesticated species might have been less dietary than symbolic, a pattern which seems quite common ethnographically (Farrington and Urry 1985). This might explain the relatively major concentrations of cereals located at 'special' sites like causewayed enclosures (Legge 1989, 218).

In the past, accounts of early agriculturalists in Britain have portrayed them as tied to their fields, jealously protecting crops of cereal vital to their survival from predators and elements (Case 1969a). This perhaps underestimates the hardy character of primitive crops (Reynolds 1979; 1981). Equally, it is unlikely that such a degree of dependence upon a single food source was risked. Modern communities who combine cultivation with gathering often exhibit scant concern for their crops. Both the Ownes Valley Paiute and the Siriano of eastern Bolivia plant crops annually (in the latter case in small cleared plots, in the former involving considerable effort in irrigation), returning to harvest them as part of a seasonal cycle of hunting, gathering and collecting (Farrington n.d.). Cultivation can thus be seen as a means of extending the range of crops available within a broad-spectrum regime, either as an insurance against the failure of particular species or as a way of providing exotic plants, often for ritual purposes.

If we dispense with the prejudice that only a fully agricultural society could have produced the monuments and complex artefacts of Neolithic Britain, the evidence for domesticated plants can best be seen as representing rather small-scale, garden horticulture. On the loess soils which then existed over much of southern England (Catt 1978), it seems likely that these plots could have been used for many years without soil decline or fall in yields (Reynolds 1979, 58–64; Jarman, Bailey and Jarman 1982, 141). The degree to which these plots would have been either weeded or supervised is a difficult question, and the relationship of horticulture to the broader pattern of mobility and settlement is better addressed in relation to other forms of evidence.

Superficially speaking, we have a far better knowledge of the livestock component of Neolithic agriculture in Britain. The main domestic animals were cattle and pig, with sheep rather less frequently represented. Wild species are consistently found as a minor element in faunal assemblages. However, aside from red deer, the contribution of these species was more likely to have been as fur-bearers than as a meat source (Grigson in Smith *et al.* 1981). Conventional wisdom has it that a sequence exists in which cattle dominate the economy of the earlier Neolithic, being replaced by pigs in the face of woodland regeneration in the later Neolithic; renewed clearance of the downland allowed sheep to become of greater importance in the Early Bronze Age (representing 38 per cent of the sample at Snail Down barrow cemetery: Tinsley and

Grigson 1981, 225). However, what one finds in a faunal assemblage depends upon where one gets it from (Meadow 1975), and almost all of the animal remains which the author has personally studied from southern Britain come from ceremonial or mortuary contexts. I have previously suggested that the predominance of pigs on Grooved Ware sites is to be connected with their use as a feasting animal rather than with environmental conditions (Richards and Thomas 1984, 206). At other sites of late Neolithic date, such as the later silts at Maiden Castle, the Peterborough Ware layers in the Dorset Cursus, or the Maiden Castle long mound, cattle continue to dominate the assemblage (Fig. 2.4). If we are to postulate a return to woodland conditions in the later Neolithic, we would expect to find not only a high representation of pig, but also of wild species (Smith 1984). Figure 2.5 shows the ratio of sheep to pigs against the percentage representation of wild species in all of the assemblages from the study area. Wild species account for less than 5 per cent in all of the henge sites, and usually less than 2 per cent. Those with higher percentages of wild animals (Thickthorn Down, Wor Barrow, Maiden Castle, the Dorset Cursus) are often earlier in date.

What is particularly noteworthy about the relative representation of species is the marked emphasis on cattle in the earlier Neolithic. Later Neolithic sites show varied proportions of cattle and pig, but earlier Neolithic assemblages always have more than

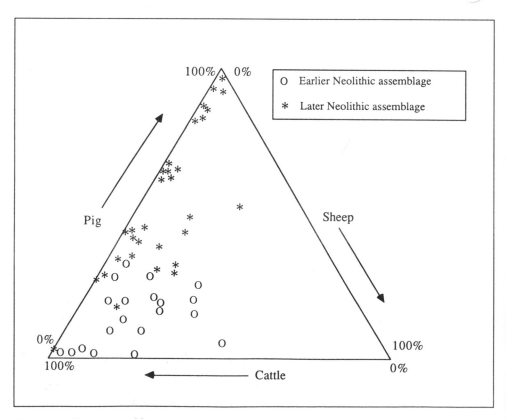

Figure 2.4   Faunal assemblages: ratio of pigs:cattle:sheep (author's data)

50 per cent cattle. Perhaps we should be less concerned with explaining the shift to pigs than with the earlier pattern of cattle dominating the assemblage.

It is evident that the consumption of large quantities of meat took place at various kinds of monuments during the Neolithic. At none of these is there much evidence for complex bone processing, marrow-splitting and butchery marks. This might be expected if the nutritional value of the carcasses were being exploited to the full. More-over, both Legge (1981) and Smith (1966) point to the presence of articulated limbs of cattle in the ditch silts of causewayed enclosures. In a later Neolithic context, it was found that at the henge monument of Durrington Walls the different parts of the bodies of cattle and pigs had been differentially distributed between the various parts of the site, indicating not merely feasting but a very deliberate way of disposing of the debris (Richards and Thomas 1984). At all the henge monuments, and also at various other sites like the Thickthorn Down long barrow and Hambledon Hill causewayed enclosure (Sieveking's 1951 excavations, Jackson archive), relatively high ratios of bones from the meat-rich parts of pig and cattle as against waste parts (as defined by Maltby 1979, 7) were recorded. These sites all seem to have been concerned with the consumption and sometimes deliberate wasting or offering of the choicer parts of the

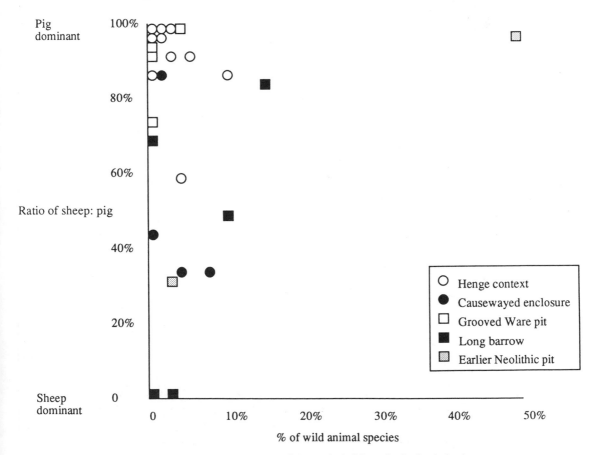

Figure 2.5   Faunal assemblages: ratio of sheep:pigs/wild species (author's data)

animals. These observations, of course, are general in the extreme, and further work might address the issue of the value placed upon different anatomical parts. We should not be surprised if these were not those judged most tender by the modern palate.

Grigson (in Ashbee 1966) has noted that at certain long barrows (Fussell's Lodge, Bowl's Barrow, Amesbury 42, Knook 2, Corton, Sherrington 1 and Tilshead Lodge) the remains of bovid foot bones (metapodia, cuboids, phalanges) have been recovered in such circumstances as to suggest the burial of ox hides, often in association with bovid skulls. This is clearly connected with the purposeful deposition of cattle skulls at the causewayed enclosures of Whitesheet Hill (Piggott 1952), Maiden Castle (Grigson in Smith *et al.* 1981, 199) and Hambledon Hill. 'Head and hooves' burials continue into the Beaker period, as at Hemp Knoll (Robertson-Mackay 1980) and at Beckhampton (Young 1950). However, the circulation and deposition of cattle hides as artefacts of some symbolic significance may be an even more widespread phenomenon. Cuboids, metapodia and phalanges are often present as a large percentage of the cattle bones recorded from causewayed enclosures and henge monuments. It seems that, at many of these sites, the cattle bones can be accounted for entirely as meat debris, skulls and hides: a high degree of selectivity.

Why this particular emphasis is made on the symbolic qualities of cattle as opposed to other species in mortuary and ritual contexts is a question which has to be addressed. A primary aspect of the social role of cattle is represented by the evidence for feasting. Legge (1981, 179) states that 'the majority of cattle killed at the causewayed camps are female, and . . . these animals represent the surplus available from economies based at lowland (and undiscovered) Neolithic sites'. As Grigson (1982a) points out, equal numbers of males and females must have been born, yet the young males culled soon after birth in the system presented by Legge are absent from the enclosures. This leads to two conclusions: the causewayed enclosures must have been tied in to a broader (regional?) economy, and this economy involved the movement of cattle from one place to another. Cattle were not at the enclosures at the time of year when young males were being culled. Any interpretation of the enclosures as economically independent defended settlements has therefore to be considered critically.

Sherratt (1981) suggests that the development of dairying economies before the middle of the third millennium is unlikely, since any major human dependence upon milk consumption can only take place once a biological tolerance for lactose has been achieved (see also Entwistle and Grant 1989). However, yoghourt, cheese, butter or ghee are largely free of lactose (Grigson pers. comm.). This being the case, dairy products could provide protein for a prehistoric diet. However, nutritional factors alone cannot provide an adequate explanation of the importance of cattle in Neolithic Britain. Arguments have in the past been made to the effect that 'wealth' in pre-industrial societies is constrained by the fact that the surplus product exists only as agricultural produce (Gamble 1981). This leads on to the expectation that such surpluses will be used to maintain craftsmen, producing prestige items. Hence the existence of craft specialisation is seen as one of the key attributes of the early state, the consequence of the ability of a managerial élite to centralise and redistribute surpluses (Renfrew 1972). As a result, craft specialisation has come to be one of the indicators of social change sought for in the Neolithic (Renfrew 1973). Yet, as has already been noted, this notion of a material surplus may not be relevant to such a society. Monument building and the production of prestige goods hardly require a separate population of specialists. Labour may be recruited as corvée. Equally, food may fuel a prestige system by other means than by supporting specialists. Notably, it may be consumed in feasts (Friedman 1975). The assembled evidence indicates that cattle were killed and eaten in large numbers at special sites like causewayed enclosures. Their remains, particularly their heads, hooves and hides, seem to have been treated with some care, sometimes buried as part of human funerary deposits. All of this might indicate that the eating of cattle flesh was not an everyday activity, so much as something to be indulged in at particular times and in particular places. These occasions would appear to have been communal feasts. If wild plants, cultivated plants, the flesh of lesser animals, and perhaps dairy products provided the staples of the Neolithic diet, then cattle meat might have been a more highly ranked food, circulating under different conditions.

Earlier in this chapter it was suggested that lithic analysis indicates a high degree of mobility in the Neolithic way of life. The botanical remains can be read as suggesting no more than a partial dependence upon cultivated cereals and pulses, with considerable gathering of wild plants. The analysis of faunal remains again points to populations who were substantially mobile, or at the least who carried out different activities in different places at different times of year. It is not necessary to evoke the existence of an independent nomadic pastoralist system in Neolithic Britain (as suggested, for instance, by Barker and Webley 1978; Jarman, Bailey and Jarman 1982). Nomadic pastoralism is usually a form of economy which arises as the consequence of the growth of state societies nearby (Gilbert 1975), and the pastoralists usually exist as an element within a more complex regional economy. Only the Masai manage to remain entirely independent of horticulturalist neighbours, and this at the cost of drinking the blood of their animals (Goldsmitt 1979). Rather, the suggestions that cattle were actually circulating within the landscape, and that their slaughter took place in monuments remote from the settlement areas, emphasise a complex inter-community division of labour, and one which was intimately concerned with movement in space and synchronisation in time.

## Standstill or reorganisation?

It is now necessary to turn to the arguments which have been put forward for economic change in the Neolithic. On the basis of pollen analytical evidence for woodland and scrub regeneration, Whittle and Bradley both proposed that 'a population grown too large on the initial riches' (Whittle 1978, 39) of clearance and cultivation fell upon a period of agricultural recession in the middle years of the third millennium. An imbalance between population and resources led to soil decline, loss of soil stability, regeneration of clearances. It would not be until the end of the millennium, with the building of the large henges and the rise of new social hierarchies associated with Beaker pottery and prestigious funerary practices that a full recovery would be effected (Whittle 1980a, 334; 1980b). Extending the model backwards in time, Mercer

(1981a) suggests that the building of causewayed enclosures in Wessex could be connected with a growth of territoriality and a pressure on land in the years between 2800 and 2500 bc.

However, it is possible that this is a model which has slipped into orthodoxy on very shaky foundations. Population dynamics models are very much a part of the baggage of the ecological archaeology of the 1970s. Where it is denied that 'cold', pre-capitalist societies are as riddled with class antagonisms and internal contradictions as are modern capitalist ones, and their adaptations are considered as homologous to those of biological organisms, only the reaction to external stimuli will be considered. The idea of an agricultural 'standstill' is the consequence of not considering internal change. Just as Whittle (1978, 34) rightly criticised Renfrew (1973) for assuming that the increasing investment of effort in monuments throughout the Neolithic was a consequence of a steady and unbroken growth in population, it is necessary to criticise Whittle for assuming that all populations will inevitably rise to carrying capacity, and for the Malthusian supposition that all social and technological innovations owed their genesis to the balancing of relations between population and resources.

There are other flaws in the model. Firstly, while valley alluviation doubtless extends back into the Neolithic (Bell 1982), there is little evidence for large-scale periods of synchronised runoff until much later (Shotton 1978). Indeed, many of the soil changes which have been blamed upon Neolithic cultivation, like the inception of lessivage, may have a much earlier origin in postglacial canopy conditions (Fisher 1982). A further complicating factor lies in exactly what is considered to have been regenerating in the third millennium. There is still considerable confusion concerning clearance in Neolithic Europe, and particularly the nature of the 'elm decline'. Rowley-Conwy (1982) argues that the scale of the elm decline was such that it could hardly have been entirely anthropogenic. Only woodland clearance on a massive scale could have had such an effect. Ten Hove (1968) shows that the elm decline also took place in areas which have no evidence of human occupation at the time, as in the case of northern Norway. If we are not clear how much of the vegetational disturbance of the late fourth and early third millennia can be attributed to human agency, it is difficult to argue that this activity decreased over time.

This last point introduces something of an imponderable into the argument, and emphasises the lack of clarity in inferring human activity from the pollen record. As Edwards suggests, it is 'rather dangerous to talk of a general third millennium regeneration . . . unless all the sites bore a relative constant and known relationship with the human community causing the inferred impact' (1979, 263). We might have to consider the possibility that the apparent change in human influence on the pollen record reflects not a decrease in the degree of influence so much as a change in the structure of that influence. For instance, under some conditions, small localised clearances may not be detected at all (Edwards 1982). At Flanders Moss in the Firth Valley, Turner argued that clearances had been too small to detect (Smith *et al.* 1981, 173). The pollen of cereals and arable weeds is produced in less abundance and travels less far than that of grasses and plantain (Edwards 1979). So in a grassland environment like that of later Neolithic Wessex (Evans 1971), cultivation might go unnoticed in the very few pollen spectra available for the chalklands (Waton 1982). Finally, one aspect of the vegetational record which contradicts any idea of an agrarian crisis is the evidence of very large tracts of woodland which had never been cleared (Smith *et al.* 1981, 206). The proposed selective pressure of scarce resources and limited land simply did not apply. Waton's (1982) pollen diagrams for Lewis and Snelsmore (Berkshire), for instance, show little evidence for clearance until the Middle Bronze Age and the Iron Age respectively.

It is an unfortunate effect of the coarse grain of the archaeological record that we have very little resolution on the artefactual chronology of the British Neolithic beyond a distinction between an earlier and a later part. Within each of these two divisions, we are aware that quite different sets of material equipment and economic practice were in use. Hence it is all too easy to emphasise the discontinuity between the two, and impose some cataclysm to account for it. It is more difficult, but more rewarding, to consider the mechanisms involved in a transition. Whittle's evidence for the cessation of cultivation on the chalk reaches its peak in the years between 2900 and 2500 bc. How can this be reconciled with the fact that it was in this same period that sufficient labour was available for the construction of the two most gigantic edifices of British prehistory, the Dorset Cursus and the Hambledon Hill complex? One could hardly suggest that agricultural decline and depopulation have not taken place in the past. Nevertheless, it is to be suspected that this is an idea which has been projected back upon prehistory from more recent European experience. Agricultural depopulations did take place in England in the fourteenth and fifteenth centuries AD, but their causes had nothing to do with an imbalance between population and resources. Still less were they a consequence of the Black Death, or any other natural calamity. The late medieval period saw the birth of both agricultural capitalism and the western European mercantile world-system (Wallerstein 1974). The crisis was the result of the imbalance between the prices of cereals and wool, and the consequent shift to sheep grazing (Slichter van Bath 1963, 164–5). All of the factors involved – market forces, capitalist reproduction, enclosure – would have been absent in prehistory.

The evidence of the lithic distributions, we should recall, is that the nucleated scatters of the earlier Neolithic gave way to more extensive and diffuse spreads (and may be interpreted as representing a changed system of landuse), while the pollen record could be read to suggest a more mobile form of agriculture. If this were connected with the use of the plough, the previous emphasis on long-lived clearances for garden plots would no longer be necessary. It is impossible to consider this phase of activity in isolation from events on the other side of the Channel, and equally impossible not to note its synchroneity with the change of residence and settlement patterns which could be linked to a restructuring of the social relations of production. This suggests that the changes evident in Wessex in the second quarter of the third millennium and subsequently are an aspect of a much broader pattern.

## Conclusion

A proper understanding of agricultural and residential practices in Neolithic Britain is far from complete. This chapter has attempted no more than the merest sketch of how these activities were organised: at the present the most pressing task is the rejection of the traditional view of Neolithic settlement and economy. The population of Neolithic Britain did not live in major timber-framed buildings, quite probably did not reside in the same place year-round, did not go out to labour in great walled fields of waving corn, were not smitten by over-population or soil decline, and much of their day-to-day food may have been provided by wild crops.

It seems highly unlikely that the significance of economic practices in the Neolithic can be appreciated solely by the level at which crops and animals were exploited. The shifting patterns of resource use which have been hinted at by various studies may only prove comprehensible in terms of the social context of production. Hence the transformation which overtook Britain in the later fourth millennium was one of the social relations of production, and the degree to which a fully agricultural society was established is open to debate. Furthermore, it seems extremely unlikely that anything approaching a market economy existed in the period, and we might expect economic relations and transactions to be congruent with and embedded in other social relationships. The evidence derived from both lithic and faunal assemblages for regular, large-scale movements of people and cattle in the earlier Neolithic is best interpreted in this light. The exchange of goods and marriage partners, the slaughter of animals and seasonal grazing might all be integrated into a yearly round, in which particular places might be occupied at particular times of year, allowing regular meetings and gatherings to take place. Thus the way of life imagined during the earlier Neolithic is a mobile one, with at least part of the population following herds of cattle seasonally between upland and lowland. The whole community might have been transient, gathering roots and berries as they went, or part (most?) of each group might have stayed in one place year-round, tending garden crops of cereals and pulses. Indeed, these two extremes might mark the poles between which actual variability existed.

If a seasonal cycle of movement lay at the heart of both social and agricultural arrangements in the earlier Neolithic, with cultivated plants contributing rather little to diet, the pattern seems to have broken down in the later third millennium. The evidence of pollen spectra and lithics together indicates a less regular pattern of clearance and mobility. Yet traces of domestic architecture are no more common in the later Neolithic. One possible explanation for this state of affairs is that the social trend towards greater personal individuation evidenced in the burial record (see Chapter 6) had some correlate in economic practice. If land and stock came to be organised at the level of the household rather than that of a larger community of kin, synchronised cycles of stock movement might indeed break down. Thus the diet, livestock, crops and domestic structures of the later Neolithic might differ little from those of the earlier, the chief distinction being found in social organisation. New areas of the landscape might be exploited, and a degree of new technology employed, but a real change in the fabric of the farming lifestyle would not take place until the mid to late second millennium. Only at that point did field systems and permanent domestic structures become the norm in the British Isles.

# 3

# Reading monuments

## Monuments in space

The most substantial trace of Neolithic activity which remains in the modern landscape of Britain consists of a large number of earth and stone monuments of a variety
of forms. From Aubrey and Stukeley down to Daniel and Piggott, these constructions
have attracted the interest of the archaeologists. However, a concern with 'monumentality' as such can perhaps be dated to Colin Renfrew's essay, 'Monuments,
mobilisation and social organisation in Neolithic Wessex' (Renfrew 1973). Renfrew's
thesis was that monuments constituted 'the natural counterparts of other features of
society' (*ibid.*, 556). As such, their scale and complexity could be taken as an index of
that of the society which created them.

More recently, Richard Bradley has provided a series of contributions which
together represent a concerted critique of Renfrew's position (Bradley 1984a; 1984b;
1985). Bradley draws upon Cherry's (1978) observation that large monumental constructions may be undertaken by dominant groups either at their time of establishment
or under conditions of stress and instability. Applying this perspective to the British
sequence, Bradley points to the discontinuous nature of monument building. Thus a
massive structure like the Dorset Cursus may be constructed as the initial act in the
settlement of a new area, while the large Wessex henges can be seen as a reaction to
social change and conflict. For Bradley, the most important feature of monuments is
their permanence. 'They dominate the landscape of later generations so completely
that they impose themselves on their consciousness' (Bradley 1985, 9).

Drawing as they do on the explicitly generalising approach proposed by Cherry,
these arguments still beg one major question. The domination of the landscape by
monuments in the Neolithic and Early Bronze Age seems to have given way to a
pattern of field systems and permanent, often enclosed settlements. This transformation of the social landscape must clearly be conceived as an historical conjuncture: a
qualitative difference exists 'before' and 'after'. It follows that the monuments of
the Neolithic are something specific, something which defines a particular social
formation. When Humphrey Case (1969a) considered the role of monuments in the
inception of the British Neolithic, he saw them as part of a phase of 'stable adjustment',
subsequent to the initial episode of colonisation. Only when a farming economy had
been in place for some generations, and a sufficient surplus had been generated, could
monuments become a feature of the landscape. This view casts monuments as a kind
of 'optional extra', to be indulged in when conditions allow. Where monuments are
seen as either a display of surplus wealth or as a medium of prestige competition

(Bradley 1984a, 20–33; Sheridan 1986), such a conception of 'optionality' can still be maintained. One of the central arguments of this chapter is that it is more consistent with the evidence to view monuments as something fundamental to the Neolithic way of life.

The starting point for such an argument is in considering monuments (and architecture in general) less as objects in themselves than as transformations of space *through* objects (Hillier and Hanson 1981, 1). In particular, changes in the configuration of space affect the way in which it will be experienced by the individual. Thus it may be that the 'objective' fact that a monument has required a certain number of worker-hours for its construction is less significant than its 'subjective' experience, an encounter perceived through the physical presence of the lived human body (Tuan 1974, 215). It follows that a major part of the importance of a monument is the way in which it affects the way in which a space is experienced and interpreted. Thus it may be useful to draw a qualitative distinction between formless space and 'place', a location which has been named and 'tamed' (Tuan 1978, 10; Relph 1976, 17). Placing space into a conceptual order, classifying it into 'centres of meaning' (Tuan 1974, 239) may be a purely cognitive process. Consider, for example, the Australian aboriginal 'songlines' which create a system of meaning within a landscape according to the mythic antediluvian wanderings of ancestral spirits. However, a more concrete means of converting space into place is through a physical transformation. Once a monument has been built in a particular space, that space can never again be interpreted in the same way as before.

This kind of perspective begins to offer a means of explaining why it is that such an emphasis on the building of monuments is characteristic of a particular phase of British prehistory. As Relph suggests: 'Existential space is culturally defined and hence it is difficult to experience the space of another culture' (1976, 15). Where we become concerned less with generalised, universal explanations of monuments, and more with cultural codes which define ways in which space is to be experienced, the opportunity for understanding the historically specific is opened up. However, at the same time, once one begins to consider the 'cultural' element in a hermeneutics of space, the phenomenological element of 'humanistic' geography must necessarily be jettisoned. The experience of space is neither innocent nor primal, but inescapably social and cultural.

The cultural and historical specificity of spatial interpretation can be understood in a number of ways. In materialist terms, we might link the experience of space with the spatio-temporal rhythms built up through the habitual movements of day-to-day life (Pred 1977, 218). If the consciousness of the subject develops through practice, the habitual use of space and time implicated in any way of life will form an element of what Foucault (1988) would term a 'technology of the self' – that is to say, a set of historically and culturally contingent social practices through which persons come to recognise themselves as subjects of a particular sort. The practice of the subject is constrained by his or her movements in space and time, the performance of tasks which are repetitive or unique, habitual or strategic, and whose timing is ordered by the cycles of day and night or of the seasons. Hence it follows that the way in which hunter-gatherers become aware of themselves as beings within a world, moving seasonally through a forest between a series of temporary camps, will be quite different from the experience of agriculturalists, continuously investing their labour in plots of land. Hence, in a way, Giddens' suggestion that social control can be based on the control of the movement of individuals in time and space (1984, 145). Cycles and patterns of movement, of encounter between body and environment, generate people's understanding both of themselves and of their surroundings. Acting as 'stations' in this network of movements, features which have been constructed by people will have a constraining effect on the interpretative process. Thus a society like that of the British Neolithic, engaged in structuring a landscape through the building of monuments, is actually involved in the 'making' of subjects and their consciousness.

Alternatively, a more direct relationship between the forms of spatial knowledge and power within a given society might be postulated. Thus it might be less the realities of the productive regime which determine the way in which space will be manipulated, than cosmology, a particular understanding of the world. It is in these terms that Hirst (1985, 178) interprets the centrally planned churches of the Renaissance as 'a manifest presence and physical existence of cosmic order'. The geometry of the church was conceived as a representation of cosmic relationships, on the understanding that church architecture had a privileged position in the spiritual transformation of the human subject. Similarly, Kus (1983, 292) describes the way that Ambohimanga, the Merina capital of Madagascar, was constructed about the cardinal points in accordance with an astronomical understanding of the cosmos.

These views can perhaps be reconciled in seeing a relationship between the 'lived' and the conceptualised world. Thus discussions concerning space are themselves tied to essentially material relations of power. Hence Foucault (1984b, 243) talks about a shift in the locus of power in space through the eighteenth and nineteenth centuries, as concerns with architecture and town planning gave way to railways and electrification. Spatial control ceased to be invested in the organisation of urban space and shifted into the spheres of transportation and communications. Similarly, Cosgrove's interesting study of the relationship between economics and aesthetics (1984) suggests a connectedness between the material order and the conceptualisation of space. Cosgrove's argument is that the symbolic appropriation of space in landscape painting is a consequence of the physical alienation of land within a capitalist economy. Only where land becomes a commodity to be freely disposed of by its owner, rather than handed down from generation to generation, can it be portrayed with a dispassionate gaze severed from the location itself. This is the view of the outsider, interpreting nature as a bounded thing behaving according to causal relationships (*ibid.*, 64). It follows from both of these examples that the cultural rules governing the interpretation of space are generated in a historical context. The question which must be asked in this particular study concerns the historical context of Neolithic monuments.

## The inscribed landscape

The suggestion that monuments represent landscape features which are to be interpreted or 'read' inevitably leads to the comparison of space with text (Ricoeur

1981; Moore 1986). Again, this analogy can be understood in a number of different ways. Constructed objects can be seen as components of a discursive formation, generated by a determinate structure of rules and patterns (Hirst 1985, 175). Perhaps more radically, the landscape as a whole can be considered as a text, characterised by a 'ceaseless play of infinitely unstable meanings' (Duncan and Duncan 1988, 118). The writing of such a text is never finished, but continually altered, continually read and interpreted. Each act which leaves a mark on the landscape is the equivalent of an act of writing, each mark the equivalent of the black character on the page. This formulation places a curious inflexion on the way that Neolithic monuments have been looked at by archaeologists. Renfrew (1976) and Chapman (1981) both saw megalithic tombs as symbols of a corporate group's claim to land and resources. Hodder (1984) saw the same structures as symbolic transformations of houses of the living into houses of the dead. Morris (1974) considered megaliths as a whole to be representations of group cosmology. All of these interpretations seem reasonable enough in themselves. What they have in common is a realisation that the monuments had some symbolic content. That is, they *stood for* something other than themselves. It follows that the status of the monument is less that of signified than that of signifier.

Monuments as parts of a landscape can be seen as the equivalents of written discourse; they 'inscribe' space as parts of a chain of signification. No monument can be looked on as a system of meaning closed in upon itself. Indeed, monuments are demonstrably 'intertextual', laden with nuances of mutual reference. The cursus monuments refer in their architecture to the long mound and long mortuary enclosure traditions, and may actually incorporate long mounds within their fabric (Bradley 1983). Silbury Hill, with its stepped chalk cylinders, may have been redolent of the Boyne passage graves (Thomas 1984). The very fact that monuments seem to form 'traditions' which share constructional features indicates that the meaning of a given structure is in some way conditional upon other sites.

In a pioneering study concerned with the textual nature of space, Moore (1986) places emphasis on the way in which the same space may be experienced or interpreted differently by different people. Men and women, for instance, may think about a given space in different ways, while some members of society may be granted a privileged position with regard to legitimate interpretation (*ibid.*, 73, 86). This can perhaps be linked to the concept of 'textual communities', social groups which cluster around alternative readings of a given text (Duncan and Duncan 1988, 117). So although meaning is invoked by the physical encounter with a monument, this act of 'reading' the monument may still be open to interpretation. If we can assume that these structures had some part to play within the power relations of Neolithic communities, then it might be that the nuances of their interpretation would be a focus of struggle between individuals and interest groups.

## Causewayed enclosures

The arguments which have been put forward so far suggest that the monuments of Neolithic Britain structured the social landscape largely through the influence which they exerted upon the interpretation of space by the human subject. If such a spatial text were read 'inattentively' (Duncan and Duncan 1988, 123), this influence upon interpretation might have an active role to play in the process of social reproduction. The objective of this chapter is to present a picture of the *changing* relationship between society and monuments through time. However, at this point the argument has progressed far enough to enable us to consider one class of monuments of the earlier Neolithic, in the light of ideas concerning the control of movement in space and interpretation of space.

Causewayed enclosures are among the more enigmatic monuments of the British Neolithic. Decades of debate (Curwen 1930; Piggott 1954; Smith 1965a; 1966; 1971; Renfrew 1973; Wilson 1975; Drewett 1977; Mercer 1980; Burgess *et al.* 1988) have resulted in a variety of explanations for the function of the sites, from enclosed settlements to cattle kraals to regional fairs, exchange centres, necropoli and cult centres. Mercer (1980, 65) takes the minimal view that the term 'causewayed enclosure' cannot now be taken to suggest more than 'a constructional technique with no overall functional implication'. Barker and Webley appear equally impartial when they state that the enclosures were 'central places of some kind (or several kinds)' (1978, 161). However, their landuse model for the earlier Neolithic is based upon transport cost and least effort principles: this neglects the evidence which suggests that causewayed enclosures are in no sense central, that they existed at the edges of settlement systems (Bradley 1978a, 103; Gardiner 1984, 21; Holgate 1984; 1988a).

In the wake of Smith's (1965a) publication of Keiller's excavations at Windmill Hill the interpretation which came to be accepted was that of redistribution centre. This was taken to explain the high percentages of fossil shell and oolite in pottery from the Bath/Frome area at Windmill Hill, Robin Hood's Ball, Whitesheet Hill and Knap Hill (Peacock 1969, 145) and of gabbroic wares from the Lizard in Cornwall and of Portlandian chert at Maiden Castle, Hambledon Hill, Robin Hood's Hall, Windmill Hill, Hembury and High Peak (Smith 1971, 103). Drewett (1977, 224) summed up a problem with this view: 'if causewayed enclosures were simply trade centres, surely the foreign material would be exchanged there and then removed for use elsewhere. The discovery of such material in causewayed enclosures would suggest its use there.' Moreover, whether fine products acquired through long-distance links were redistributed from causewayed enclosures would be difficult to test using fall-off curves, since, being items which would circulate in the more highly ranked spheres of exchange, they might change hands rapidly for some tens of years. It was the recovery of fine artefacts from the enclosures which led Bradley (1982; 1984a, 31) to suggest that they represented high-status settlements.

There are problems with this interpretation also. If, for instance, Hambledon Hill were to be thought of as the residence of an élite, it would be an élite apparently separated by several miles from the nearest population (on the basis of results from a campaign of fieldwalking: R. Palmer and A. Saville pers. comm.). And yet it would also have to be one which could mobilise from that population sufficient corvée labour to enclose 160 acres of hilltop with a double ditch and palisade (Mercer 1982, 1), one whose meat was brought in from herds elsewhere and whose grain arrived at the site already threshed and cleaned (Mercer pers. comm.). Smith (1966) was originally led to the conclusion that the enclosures were not settlements, by the absence of pits in their interiors, as at Offham (Drewett 1977, 211). Pits *are* present in the central enclosure at Hambledon, yet they appear to have been concerned with the deliberate deposition of items like gabbroic vessels (90 per cent in pits; 10 per cent in ditches), axes, red deer antler and quernstones (Mercer 1980, 23; 1988, 93). The flintwork recovered from these pits often showed a peculiar bias towards a particular tool type (scrapers or microdenticulates (*ibid.*)), while two of the pits contained postholes. As fragments of human bones and teeth were also found in these pits, it might be suggested that, as with the Handley Hill pit, these represent one part of a multistage burial process: pits from which the bones were removed when defleshed. This accords with Bradley's (1984b, 24) suggestion that fine artefacts were involved in some stage of mortuary ritual. However, these items might not represent grave goods in the formal sense, so much as prestations necessary for the conclusion of rites of passage. The huge quantities of skeletal remains from the main enclosure ditch at Hambledon (Mercer 1980, *passim*) and the finds of bone from Maiden Castle (Wheeler 1943), Windmill Hill (Smith 1965a), Abingdon (Leeds 1928), Staines (Robertson-Mackay 1962; 1987), Whitehawk (Curwen 1934), Offham (Drewett 1977) and Maiden Bower (Smith 1915) need not be dwelt on here. Suffice to say that the exposure or defleshing by other means was a recurrent feature of the enclosures. As Thorpe (1984) shows, the proportions of males, females and children present indicate that these groups were equally eligible.

At Maiden Castle the study of the excavated material reveals a similar pattern to that at Hambledon: flint and stone axes are concentrated in pits (7.2 and 2.7 per cent of the assemblages respectively) as opposed to ditches (3.6 and 0.3 per cent). One pit, T8, had a concentration of microdenticulates (Wheeler 1943, 86). However, all of this neglects the fact that at Stepleton, the lesser enclosure on Hambledon Hill, a two-acre site existed with a variety of internal features of 'domestic' nature. Domestic activity is also clearly present at Crickley Hill, Gloucestershire (Dixon 1988). Nevertheless, at the latter site the house platforms can be tied to the very latest phase of a complex sequence of backfillings and recuttings of the ditches before the replacement of the causewayed camp by an enclosure bounded by a massive continuous ditch (Dixon pers. comm.). At Crickley, then, settlement appears not to have been the primary purpose for the construction of the site.

Another recurrent feature of causewayed enclosures is their coincidence with lithic sources. At Hambledon, excavations on the Hanford spur revealed a complex of shallow mines and grubbing pits which may have provided the mediocre quality flint found in the Stepleton enclosure (Mercer 1982, 2). At Offham, far more primary core reduction waste was found than could have been needed to produce the sparse implements found on site, indicating that cores were made from the poor quality flint found on site and taken away (Drewett 1977, 217). Similar poor quality flint sources are found at Robin Hood's Ball and Maiden Castle, and at the latter site the many unpolished roughout axes and waste pieces indicate that the processing of raw materials from elsewhere took place there (Care 1982). All of this is taken by Care as evidence for social control of lithic resources. With this I concur, but not in the sense that she intended: a review of some further aspects of the problem will provide an alternative framework.

Firstly, there is an obvious contradiction between the investment of effort in the building of the enclosures and their deliberate backfilling and recutting. At Robin Hood's Ball (Thomas 1964, 11) and Hambledon (Mercer 1980, 35) the richest deposits of artefactual and faunal material actually overlay the collapse of the banks, so it is clear that at least a part of the function of the sites did not depend upon the integrity of their defences. Perhaps the mere delineation of a separate space with an interrupted ring of pits/ditches was of greater import. The nature of deposition is, throughout, most interesting. The material in the ditches can be of considerably greater quantity than one would expect in an Iron Age hillfort (Thomas 1964, 11) while the pottery is often unweathered (Smith 1966) and animal bones may be articulated (Legge 1981, 173). The ceramic assemblages found on causewayed enclosure sites in Wessex are not those which one would associate with a settlement. The lack of carinations or beaded rims to allow coverings which might have permitted their use for storage, and the predominance of cups and open bowls, can perhaps be taken to suggest consumption. A similar assemblage of vessel forms came from the 'ritual' pit of earlier Neolithic date outside the Coneybury Hill henge (Cleal pers. comm.). All the above factors seem to indicate feasting activities.

Legge (1981) has suggested that the faunal remains from causewayed enclosures represent only a part of a more complex pastoral economy, involving other sites elsewhere in the landscape. Piggott (1954, 28) long ago pointed to the presence of hazelnuts and crab apples as evidence for the autumnal use of the sites, while the 'clean' grain from Hambledon could indicate occupation at a time after the harvest. The enclosure at Etton would probably have been flooded for part of the year (Pryor *et al.* 1985). Firm evidence of seasonal occupation could only really come from a detailed analysis of a large and well-excavated faunal sample, however. To this we can add Barker and Webley's observation (1978, 173) that the soils which surrounded the enclosures were best suited to pastoral activities. Furthermore, all the enclosures in Sussex appear to have been built in areas freshly cleared of woodland (Thomas 1982). In Wessex, the only two sites among the large number of molluscan assemblages studied by Evans (1971, 64) which did not show evidence for having been built in large clearances were causewayed enclosures, Knap Hill and Windmill Hill.

Causewayed enclosures in Wessex were clearly in some way connected to channels of long-distance exchange, without necessarily being redistribution centres in the full sense. A possible rationale for their peripheral siting lies in the nature of exchange in non-capitalist societies. Where the significance of an item is vested in something other than its monetary value, some control may be necessary over long-distance exchange. The circulation of material items *within* a community may have formed an important system of meaning, with implications for the generation of social position, the formation of alliances and so on. The transfer of goods between exchange systems requires an alienation of items from their source: a dangerous and potentially polluting activity for the agents representing either system. Such exchanges will often therefore be carried out at the peripheries of social territories, within bounded areas, surrounded by multiple prohibitions and prescriptions (Servet 1982, 23). A kind of rite of passage of items between communities is achieved in the liminal state of such enclosed areas, and such transaction is frequently associated with feasting and a temporary inversion of social relations emphasising the temporary nature of the arrangement (Turner 1967). This logic extends as far as the gateway communities of Mesoamerica and early historic Europe (Hirth 1978; Hodges 1982). In the present context it seems to be borne out by the presence of groups of monuments surrounding sources of lithic artefacts in prehistoric Britain, like the stone circles and other enclosures located in passes leading out from the Stone Age factories in Great Langdale, Cumbria (Burl 1976, 69; Clare 1987). The suggestion that causewayed enclosures were originally socially neutral areas wherein exchanges could be concluded in isolation from their normal social meaning can be extended to other aspects of their use. It is significant that the mortuary practices associated with these sites are predominantly those of exposure and defleshing: the liminal state between the living person and the ancestor. Likewise, ethnographic studies have shown that the extraction and processing of lithic materials is often carried out in a condition surrounded by prohibitions (Burton 1984). Finally, were cattle being moved seasonally down into the low clay vales from the chalk uplands, it would be at the enclosures of Hambledon Hill and Whitesheet Hill that the agglomeration of herds would take place, with a consequent temporary adjustment of the conditions of ownership from the minimal to the maximal group. It is not necessary to the argument that all these activities took place on all of these sites; what is important is that they worked as a bounded space at the edge of an occupied zone, which marginalised and contained influences which could be perceived as harmful or polluting to the social fabric.

Now, it is clear that some of the enclosures were more complex than others. In these cases it can often be demonstrated that the elaboration of the defensive aspect of the site, or its use for settlement, is secondary to a more modest initial construction. At Abingdon, there is evidence that the outer ditch postdates the inner (Case and Whittle 1982), while at Hambledon the complex systems of outworks and cross-dykes are additions to the original enclosure (Mercer 1988, 101) (see Fig. 3.1). Perhaps significantly, the extremely complex sites of Hambledon and Whitesheet Hill are those sites on the ecotone between chalk upland and clay vale. Those enclosures which were most embellished and elaborated produce the richest material assemblages (Hambledon, Trundle, Whitehawk), while the less complex sites (Robin Hood's Ball, Offham) are relatively poor. The eventual emergence of some of the sites as fortified settlements, presumably connected with élite activities, is a consequence of the purposeful appropriation of the powerful associations of these places. The liminal state is dangerous, yet powerful (Turner 1967), while control of the enclosure would ensure preferential access to the ancestors and the ability to control the production of value within the society.

That these activities are secondary in nature is demonstrated by the siting of barrows of mid-third-millennium date on or near to causewayed enclosures, usually with single burials. Oval barrows exist at Hambledon (Mercer 1980, 43), Abingdon (Bradley, Chambers and Halpin 1984), Maiden Castle and Robin Hood's Ball (J. Richards pers.

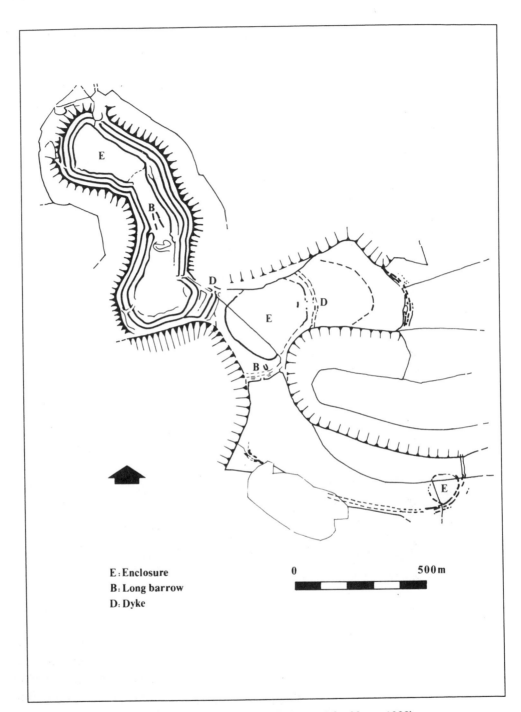

Figure 3.1    The enclosure complex on Hambledon Hill, Dorset (after Mercer 1988)

comm.), while at Whitesheet Hill a round barrow with causewayed ditch and single inhumation was set on the bank (Piggott 1952, 406). In all these cases we can suggest that a secondary monument was used to distort the original meaning of the site. At Hambledon, the ditch sequence of the barrow appeared to mirror that of the enclosure, integrating the meanings of the two monuments (Mercer 1988, 98). The later use of the enclosures also involved the deposition of Peterborough and Beaker ceramics in the ditches of the more complex enclosures in particular (Hambledon, Maiden Castle). This practice recalls that at the long barrows: in both cases the significance of old monuments was continuing to be invoked, in contradistinction to the contemporary practices associated with Grooved Ware.

## Shifting meanings

Having considered a class of monuments whose meaning seems to have changed through time, it is necessary to return to the question of how meaning is attached to space. This is best achieved by looking in more detail at how space is 'read' by the individual. Bourdieu, in his study of the Kabyle house (1973), showed the way in which cultural rules and norms were inculcated into the subject through the inhabitation of a space onto which a system of meanings had been mapped. The space of the house may be classified according to a generative scheme of oppositions, and these were internalised by living within its confines. The continually repeated experience of moving about within the house again and again invoked the meanings which had been given to particular loci. Yet, as Moore (1986, 84) points out, the meanings concerned are not inherent in the space of the house, they are attributed, and knowing the meaning of a particular space is conditional upon a particular lived, social experience of that space. 'All discourse . . . is realised as event but understood as meaning' (Ricoeur 1981, 167).

It follows that meaning is a function of social practice. Moore (1986, 81) suggests that it is not the actuality of past actions which is inscribed in space so much as their meaning. This forces a realisation that a relationship of mimesis between social space and social relations is a practical impossibility. Nothing can represent any phenomenon 'as it really is' (Norris 1987, 38). Hence the desire to 'read off' a society from its spatial arrangements must be a delusion. This argument is clearly related to the conundrum which Marx presents of how it is that ancient Greek art is the product of a particular set of historical conditions, and yet affords aesthetic pleasure in the present (Easthope 1983, 25). The answer is that the pleasure which we obtain from a Greek vase is not a pleasure *written* in it, but the pleasure of *reading*.

Obtaining the 'correct' message from any statement paradoxically depends upon knowing to some extent what the protagonist wants to say before it is said. That is to say, one must know the context of the statement. Convention holds that the signified is a place at which the movement of signification comes to rest (Harland 1987, 135). However, no discourse can ever refer unproblematically to an object which is somehow located outside language, outside time and outside context (Lentricchia 1980, 189). The chance that we, existing outside the Neolithic social and cultural context, could ever present exactly the same reading of a megalithic tomb as would an inhabitant of Neolithic Britain is hence extremely slim. However, these remarks are not intended in a negative way, merely to encourage pessimism concerning the interpretation of past architectural texts. Rather, it is important to note that these same problems of the lack of fixity of meaning are ones which would have applied as much in the past as they do in the present. 'The interpretation of any signifying chain is necessarily only another chain of signs' (Lentricchia 1980, 189). I have argued already that Neolithic monuments are inherently symbolic, and refer to things other than themselves. Even in domestic space, the process through which meaning is inscribed is generally metaphorical (Moore 1986). Furthermore, symbols of all kinds always change their meanings according to context (Macdonnall 1986, 45). Where an explicitly symbolic order is in operation, it seems likely that words and things will be polyvalent (Turner 1969), and that particular nuances of meaning will have been invoked and taken on a cardinal significance at different times. So it is extremely likely that prehistoric monuments had no one single meaning, but were a means of making material a whole system of meanings. Monuments provided a technology by which people could be reminded of different rules and codes of procedure according to the context in which they were experienced. However, it would seem that it was this condition of 'dissemination' which proved to be their most problematical element.

A landscape structured through monuments could provide a degree of control both over the movement of individuals, and over the way in which they interpreted their surroundings. The probability that a number of planes of signification intersected at the monument would mean that it had a part to play in economic, ritual, juridical and spiritual issues. Yet at this point one should remember the arguments already put forward to the effect that there will be those within a society whose interpretations are privileged. Interpretation of space may be a focus for a struggle over the definition of reality, and monuments might be expected to be axial to this kind of struggle. In the final analysis, a monument is only a heap of stones and dirt or an arrangement of holes; its significance is defined according to a set of rules; that is, it is conventional.

A number of authors have already pointed to the significance of 'secondary' activities on established monuments (Bradley 1984a; Thorpe and Richards 1984). Dealing explicitly with this kind of phenomenon, Lane (1986, 189) described a number of Bronze Age sites in South Wales, where burial mounds had been erected over the remains of earlier structures. Lane argued that this represented the reintroduction of the past into the present in a specific guise. In broader terms, it is evident that monuments of many kinds were altered radically or subtly in order to influence the way in which they were interpreted. These acts could take a number of forms. The most straightforward example might be the structural transformation of a site, as with the addition of 'tails' to a variety of heel-shaped and circular cairns of earlier Neolithic date (Corcoran 1972, 32), both to enhance their monumentality and also, perhaps, to bring them into line with a more standardised long mound tradition. Similarly, we could point to the translation of a number of later Neolithic timber circles into stone: Loanhead of Daviot, Croft Moraig (Piggott and Simpson 1971), the Sanctuary (Cunnington 1931), Stonehenge (Atkinson 1956; Burl 1987) and Mount Pleasant (Wainwright 1979a). Such structural shifts might indicate merely a more monumental form of the same 'idea', a change of function, or an appeal to the extant stone circle tradition as a means of 'rewriting' a space in the context of an already established meaning.

A second instance of subsequent activities which seem to aim at an alteration of the way in which a site is to be interpreted can be found in the deposition of secondary burials. Numerous barrows and other monuments in Britain have had inhumations or cremations inserted into them at some time after the initial use. These acts of burial, however, are not distributed evenly through prehistory. Rather, they can be argued to be a practice which results from a particular historical way of thinking about the significance of monuments. Secondary burials are very rare until the end of the Neolithic. None seems to date from the earlier Neolithic, and to the later Neolithic inhumation tradition can be attributed only a few examples like the two male individuals with lozenge arrowhead from the ditch at Wor Barrow, Dorset (Pitt Rivers 1898), the male individual with flint axe and jet belt slider dug into the long mound at Whitegrounds, Burythorpe, Yorkshire (Brewster 1984) and several of the burials at Duggleby Howe (Mortimer 1905). By contrast, the cremation burials of the 'Dorchester series' (Piggott 1954, 351), dating to the terminal Neolithic (Kinnes 1979), seem to have been preferentially deposited in secondary contexts. This would include the cremation cemeteries at Duggleby Howe (Kinnes *et al.* 1983), Stonehenge (Atkinson 1956) and the various Dorchester on Thames sites (Atkinson, Piggott and Sandars 1951). In the subsequent Beaker horizon, secondary burials continue to be placed in earlier burial mounds like Sale's Lot, Gloucestershire (O'Neil 1966), and Thickthorn Down, Dorset (Drew and Piggott 1936). These can possibly be seen as the mobilisation of a site hitherto connected with a generalised category of ancestors in support of the claims to power of an individual or dynasty. By this logic, the sequential Beaker burials at a site like Shrewton 5K (Green and Rollo-Smith 1984) might be seen as the outcome of a struggle for leadership played out over the generations, each claim legitimated by the interment of a family ancestor in a significant barrow. At the same time, the deposition of individuals with Beakers at sites like the Sanctuary (Cunnington 1931), in the ditch at Stonehenge (Evans 1983) and in the bank of Durrington Walls (Hoare 1812, 170) indicate an actual shift in the kind of discourse to which the site was appropriate. So while the same kind of claim to legitimacy sanctioned by the influence of the past as is noted with secondary burials in barrows may be equally important in these occurrences, a further feature is the removal of the site from the sphere of the living into that of the dead.

It seems likely that certain aspects of the deposition of material items in monumental contexts are related to this practice of 'translation'. Axes of stone and bronze are commonly found in contexts which relate to very specific depositional practices: in rivers and in hoards (Bradley 1987b; Needham 1988). Yet very often these items are encountered deposited in significant locations in monuments, frequently in connection with the termination of activity at the site. A stone axe was found blade down in the bank of Henge A at Llandegai (Houlder 1968, 218) and another in the forecourt blocking at Ty Isaf (Grimes 1939). Bronze axes have been found deliberately buried in the extension of the ditch terminal at the Mount Pleasant henge

(Wainwright 1979a) and in the forecourt blocking at Newgrange (O'Kelly and Shell 1979). Given the arguments which have been advanced to the effect that the axe represented a singularly potent symbol throughout the Neolithic and Early Bronze Age (Hodder and Lane 1982; Kristiansen 1984), yet one which was engaged in practices essentially separate from monuments and burials (Barrett 1985), these would seem to be very significant acts. They again represent an attempt to move a monument out of one sphere of discourse and into another. 'Discourse' in this case can be taken to mean practice which both comments upon and interprets an object.

The way in which a group of monuments was re-presented and reinterpreted by their continuous structural alteration can be strikingly illustrated by reference to the Dorchester on Thames complex in Oxfordshire (Atkinson 1948; Atkinson, Piggott and Sandars 1951). Here, a complex sequence of building and rebuilding can be demonstrated (Bradley and Chambers 1988). The complex began as a grouping of a long mortuary enclosure (Site VIII) and one or more oval mounds containing burials (Site XI and perhaps Site I). Sites VIII and XI share a common axis with the round mound Site II (Fig. 3.2). Only later was the alignment of the whole complex changed by the construction of the cursus across Site VIII but abutting Site XI. The incorporation of these sites into the overarching spatial configuration of the cursus is paralleled by the construction of a square-ditched enclosure surrounding Site I. The cursus and the square enclosure between them place the earlier structures into a context of rectilinear space. Finally, a series of pit- and post-circles were built on the site, including structures at Sites I and XI. This sequence of changes seems to suggest that over a period of some hundreds of years a number of different spatial orders were imposed on a given space, each one transforming the way in which previous configurations could be 'read'. The exact significance of the sequence is open to question. Possibly, a single community refurbished its monuments periodically in order to come to terms with changing social reality. Alternatively, this pattern of monuments may fossilise a process of struggle over the interpretation of space played out over the centuries by competing factions, each new hegemonic group imposing its own reading of the landscape through physical alteration of the traces of the past.

## The body in space

The problematic nature of the use of monuments as a means of ordering people's existence is a consequence of the way in which they can be interpreted in a fashion other than that intended by their builders. However, despite the argument concerning the lack of fixity of meaning, there is one sense in which the reading of space differs from the reading of a book. This is that the actual physical presence of the human body is required for 'reading' to take place (Moore 1986, 85). The encounter is a physical one, in which the kind of power relations involved are not merely discursive, but are relations of force. Architecture can be considered in terms of the mark it makes on the landscape, but at a microspatial level it can actually constrain the body's movement through space. The way in which the physical body progresses through a space may limit the way in which that space is experienced, and hence constrain interpretation. It can be argued that the development of Neolithic monumental architecture is the

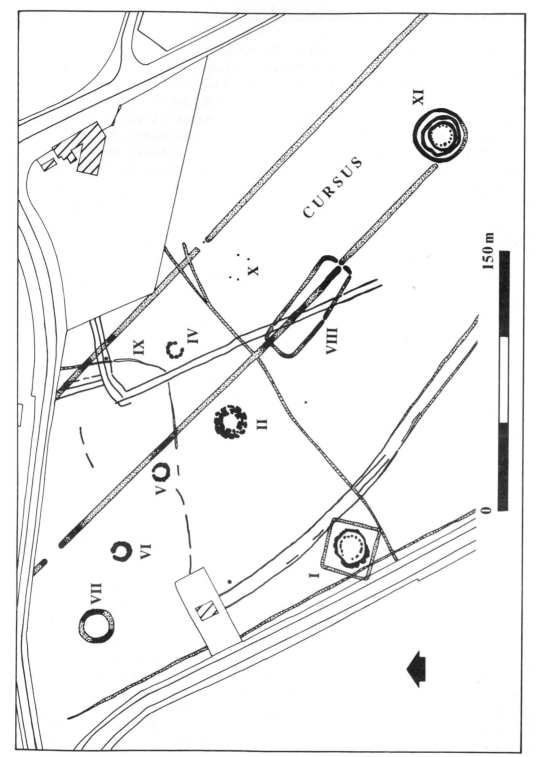

Figure 3.2   The Dorchester on Thames complex, Oxfordshire (after Atkinson, Piggott and Sandars 1951)

consequence of cumulative efforts to control the ways in which particular spaces were interpreted.

The first stage in this process is evident in the tombs and barrows of the earlier Neolithic. Burl (1987, 28) has recently suggested that the eastern orientation of long mounds may often indicate a general and imprecise alignment on the rising moon. Only later were barrows aligned to the south, in an arc which Burl suggests corresponds with the part of the sky occupied by the moon at its zenith (*ibid.*, 29). While Burl's observations apply to the long barrows of the Salisbury Plain region, the same change in orientation appears to have taken place within the Cotswold–Severn tradition (on the basis of alignments quoted in Powell *et al.* 1969). The separation of 'earlier' and 'later' chambered cairns here depends upon the chronological sequence of laterally chambered followed by terminally chambered tombs (Darvill 1982, 57; Thomas 1988b). This spatial layout is significant in itself. The earlier tombs may have up to four chambers, each approached by passages entered separately through the sides of the cairn. By contrast, in later monuments, the chamber space is reached through a single entrance in the end of the mound. Thus in the case of the transepted chambered tombs three (Wayland's Smithy), five (West Kennet, Uley) or more (Stoney Littleton) chambers can only be entered through a single entrance and antechamber. This entrance itself is set in the façade of the monument, and entering it entails crossing the forecourt area. Kinnes (1981, 84) has drawn attention to the focal role of façades within Neolithic architecture, while the forecourts of Cotswold–Severn tombs often contained hearths, pits and deposits of animal bones which may relate to ritual activities carried out in the focal area (Thomas 1988b, 550). To enter the chamber thus involved movement through a symbolically charged area containing media (pits, burnt material) which may have been redolent of boundaries and transition. These features would serve to constrain the conditions under which the space of the chamber could be experienced: it could be reached only from a certain direction, and only by the process of traversing the forecourt space. The alignment of some of these mounds on the moon at its height would place another condition on the entry to the chamber, in this case a temporal one. In this way, a degree of control over the interpretation of space could be achieved. The movement of the body in the internal space of the monument could be prescribed in terms of direction and timing.

This desire to control the movement of the body through space can be seen in the development of a more 'linear' aspect of monuments in the first half of the third millennium bc. This process is evident, for example, in the changing architecture of megalithic tombs and the emergence of the passage grave tradition. These tombs involve an enhancement of the linear approach to the chamber. In Ireland, Sheridan (1986) attributes the lengthening of the passage to her Stage 3, dated 2700–2500 bc. Stage 3 also saw the development of 'roof slots' of possible astronomic significance. Several passage graves seem to have passages aligned upon celestial phenomena: the 'roof box' at Newgrange which admits the light of the midwinter sunrise, or the way that the midwinter sunset shines down the passage at Maes Howe (Moir 1981, 223). At Bryn Celli Ddu on Anglesey, five postholes were found in an area 14 feet outside the entrance kerbstones (O'Kelly 1969, 45). These were interpreted by the excavator as evidence of 'squatting' habitation on the site after the main period of activity within the tomb (Hemp 1930). The southernmost of these posts is in direct line with the southern wall of the passage, and with a further, larger posthole located behind the chamber (O'Kelly 1969, 27). The external posts are reminiscent of the 'A' holes at Stonehenge, which Burl (1987, 66–9) holds to have been a device for recording the risings of the midwinter moon and which thereby determine the axis of the monument. The last post erected represents the extreme rising position before the moon began to retrace its own path. It thus seems highly likely that the postholes at Bryn Celli Ddu record a series of observations upon the rising of some heavenly body in order to ascertain its standstill position(Fig. 3.3). This alignment was then formalised by its incorporation into the layout of the passage and chamber (Fig. 3.4). Significantly, the southern wall of the passage is straighter than the north, as if the latter had been laid out according to a series of offsets from the former. Moreover, the southern wall of the chamber appears to continue the same straight line as the passage. Intriguingly, a standing stone in the next field to the west from the monument appears to lie on

Figure 3.3    Bryn Celli Ddu, Anglesey: the entrance (photo: author)

almost the same alignment as the passage, to within 4° (field observation summer 1990).

As with the Cotswold–Severn tombs, then, the passage grave tradition integrates temporal control into the control of access to the chamber. Here, though, there is more of an emphasis on the linear progression to the chamber space. Richards (1988) has noted the difference in relative height of the passages and chambers of the Maes Howe-type passage graves of Orkney. The architecture of the Maes Howe tombs again seeks to influence the individual's perception of space, and hence the way in which it is interpreted.

These developments seem to be largely contemporary with the emergence of another group of structures whose architecture is overwhelmingly linear, namely the cursus monuments. While Stukeley's interpretation of the Stonehenge Great Cursus as a chariot track (1740, 4) may be unlikely, it shares a conception of linear movement in space with Atkinson, who suggests that 'whatever ceremonies took place within it must have been of a processional kind' (1956, 151). Bradley (1983) has indicated a

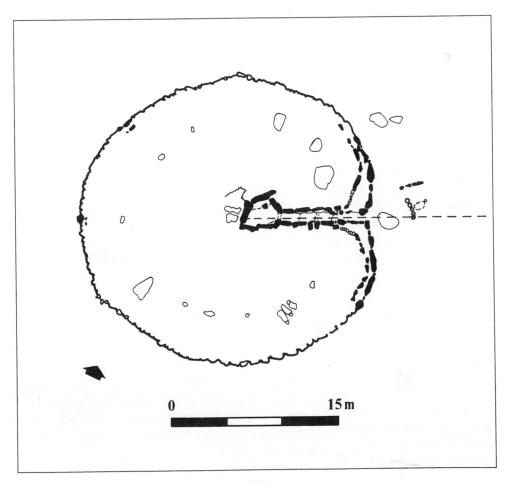

0                  15 m

Figure 3.4    Bryn Celli Ddu: plan (after O'Kelly 1969)

derivation of the cursus monuments from the long mounds and long mortuary enclosures. In this connection it is interesting that both the Dorchester on Thames and Springfield cursuses have timber circles contained within their eastern ends (Hedges and Buckley 1981, 5; Bradley and Chambers 1988). This is particularly the case in view of Clare's recent suggestion (1987, 462) that an affinity exists between the timber mortuary structures found beneath earthen long barrows and the timber circles found within henge monuments in the later Neolithic. Both have as their role the provision of a focus for the monument. In the case of the circles within cursus monuments, these structures are likely to have been the locations of ritual or ceremonial activities, yet could only have been approached by a progress through linear space.

The construction of monuments in earlier Neolithic Britain consisted in the separation of an area of space from the outside world. This applies to the provision of a chamber area in various types of tombs (Kinnes 1975) and to the causewayed enclosures, which bounded off an area by the digging of a circuit of pits. In the first half of the third millennium bc, this means of inscribing space was elaborated by architecture which limited the movement of the human body to a procession in a straight line. Thus it is very revealing that several causewayed enclosures had linear monuments erected over them. At Maiden Castle (Fig. 3.5) and Crickley Hill these are represented by bank barrows (Wheeler 1943; Dixon 1988) (for discussion of the relationship between long mounds and bank barrows see below, pp. 113–14); at Fornham All Saints and Etton, cursus monuments were built through the enclosures (Hedges and Buckley 1981, 8; Pryor 1988). Earlier in this chapter it was suggested that several changes in the earlier third millennium bc resulted in a 'reinterpretation' of the space of some causewayed enclosures. In their original form, these enclosures were open to being 'read' in a number of different ways. By drawing a linear monument across an enclosure, an attempt was being made to restrict or otherwise transform the way in which its space was experienced, and hence interpreted. In the same way, linear monuments also restricted access to and evaluation of the ritual space of the timber circles and tomb chambers. They represent an attempt to enforce some fixity of meaning upon these sites. Related phenomena may include the avenues of posts which were aligned upon the chambers or façades of some of the later long mounds, like Kilham (Manby 1976), Streethouse Farm (Vyner 1984) and Wayland's Smithy (Atkinson 1965). These in part represent an extension of the 'focussing' aspect of sepulchral architecture, but again would have involved a restriction on the way in which these spaces would have been physically encountered.

The simultaneous emergence of 'linear' monuments and an enhanced interest in celestial phenomena is worthy of note. The 'roof slots' and aligned passages of the passage graves have already been mentioned, but one could add the possible astronomical significance of certain cursus monuments. While Penny and Wood's (1973) claims that the Dorset Cursus represented a complex observatory are probably overstated, the monument does incorporate an alignment on the midsummer sunset (*ibid.*, 55). However, although these alignments on the sun and moon are not to be ignored, monuments are just as often oriented upon other monuments or upon natural features of the landscape. For instance, the henge monument at Old Yeavering is so oriented as to provide a view through its entrance of a notch in the hills around Kirknewton (Harding 1981, 129). This might easily be either a place of some spiritual or mythic significance, or a pass providing contact with an important group of strangers. What these orientations indicate is that astronomical phenomena were not privileged over ancestral monuments or landscape features. We are not witnessing evidence for scientific observations of the heavens, so much as a perceived unity of sky and land, past and present, all being manipulated to bring more and more emphasis onto particular spaces and places. This would tend to heighten the significance of whatever transactions and performances took place there. At the same time, it would also limit access to these spaces in terms of both direction and timing, and would contribute to the way in which the space was experienced by promoting the impression that it stood at an axial point of an integrated cosmos.

## Concentric spaces

By the latter part of the third millennium bc, a new monumental tradition prevailed in much of Britain, the henges. Attempts to seek a lineage for henge monuments in any one earlier class of sites (Wainwright 1969; Clare 1987) have proved rather inconclusive, and it may be more realistic to see their development as the coalescence of a variety of traits drawn from a common cultural pool in accordance with social needs. In terms of their organisation of space, henges seem to involve a greater complexity of classification. The causewayed enclosures which preceded them sometimes consisted of multiple concentric rings, yet their central space was relatively undifferentiated. At Etton, the central area of such an enclosure was bisected by a ditch, but this kind of arrangement seems rare. Earlier Neolithic monuments, then, are largely connected with the separation of a space from the outside world, be it an enclosure interior or a

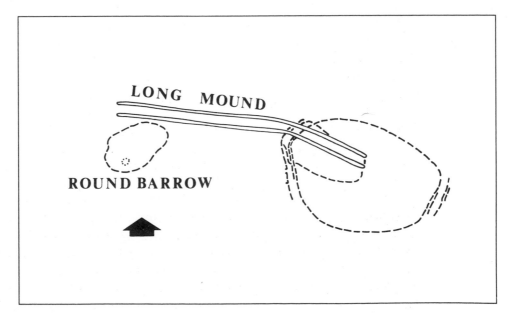

Figure 3.5    Maiden Castle, Dorset: causewayed enclosure and long mound (after Wheeler 1943)

tomb chamber. With the henges, one sees a more complex arrangement of concentric spaces divided by a variety of boundaries: banks, ditches, pits like the Aubrey Holes at Stonehenge (Atkinson 1956), shafts like those at Maumbury Rings or Wyke Down (Bradley 1975; Barrett, Bradley and Green forthcoming), and circles of posts. These are often combined to provide a series of spaces about a common centre, as with the henge at Milfield North, where a circle of pits was dug outside and concentric to the bank and ditch (Harding 1981, 101).

As with the architecture of earlier Neolithic monuments, it is reasonable to suggest that these features have as part of their role to draw attention to a particular point, the central space. At the same time, they divide up the space passed through on the approach to that point. Interestingly, at several of these sites unenclosed structures may be the primary feature, the ditch and bank being a later addition. In this connection, Clare (1987, 459) cites Cairnpapple and Balfarg Riding School. The banks of henges, while generally unsuitable for defence by virtue of being outside the ditch (Atkinson 1951; Burl 1969), would often have restricted the visibility of actions taking place in the interior. This is especially the case with the large henges like Durrington Walls, Mount Pleasant and Avebury, although Burl suggests that a stockade may have originally surmounted the bank of Stonehenge I (1987, 51). If the interior of the henge could only be seen by those approaching along the axis of the monument, a further limitation was being placed upon the experience of that space. Patterns of visibility and hiddenness may have played an important part in the use of many other monuments. For instance, activities in the Stone Cove at Stanton Drew would have been invisible from the interior of the nearby stone circle (Burl 1976, 105). Both this and the henge architecture suggest a social division between those who were and were not eligible to witness certain acts.

One strand of continuity which can be detected between the timber mortuary structures of the earlier Neolithic and the henges is in the provision of façades for timber circles, as in the case of the Northern and Southern Circles at Durrington Walls (Fig. 3.6) (Wainwright and Longworth 1971) and perhaps the original central circle at Stonehenge (Burl 1987). It could again be argued that these were focussing devices, a possibility which is borne out by a closer investigation of the Durrington Southern Circle (Figs. 3.7 and 3.8). The façade actually belongs to the first of two phases of construction of the circle (Wainwright and Longworth 1971, 27). The depths of the postholes indicate that the posts would have risen in height towards the middle, the tallest ones flanking an entrance. As with the façades in many funerary sites, then, this structure served to draw attention to the place of entry into the monument. The disappearance of the façade in the second phase of the circle is comprehensible if one considers that this later structure is contemporary with the construction of the bank and ditch of the henge (Richards and Thomas 1984, 195). With the circle no longer 'floating' in carrier space, the direction from which it would be approached was determined by the position of the southern entrance to the enclosure (Fig. 3.6). The view through the entrance from outside, restricted by the presence of the banks, would have been dominated by the circle of upright timbers, and centred by the members set in the particularly large postholes 22 and 23, flanking the entrance. In order to pass between these pillars, one would have to cross the rammed chalk and gravel platform. Just as with the forecourts of Cotswold–Severn tombs, this important transitional area seems to have held a hearth, and to have been a focus for the deposition of pottery and animal bones (Wainwright and Longworth 1971, 32). A further hearth was found in the centre of the concentric circles of timbers.

Crossing the platform, the individual would have been funnelled between posts 66 and 67, only to meet head-on post 84 (Fig. 3.7). At this point the progress towards the

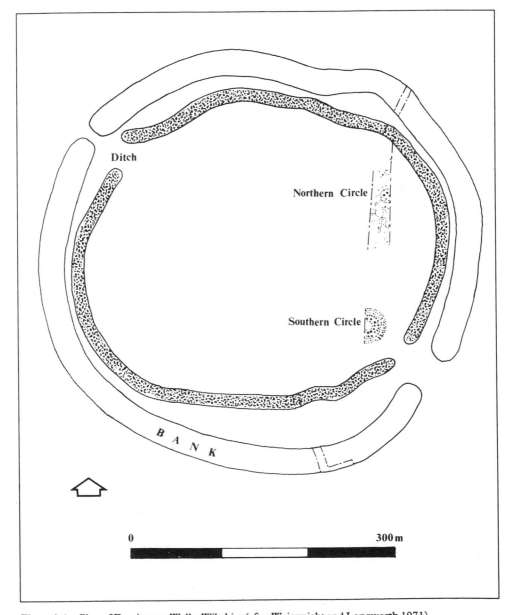

Figure 3.6    Plan of Durrington Walls, Wiltshire (after Wainwright and Longworth 1971)

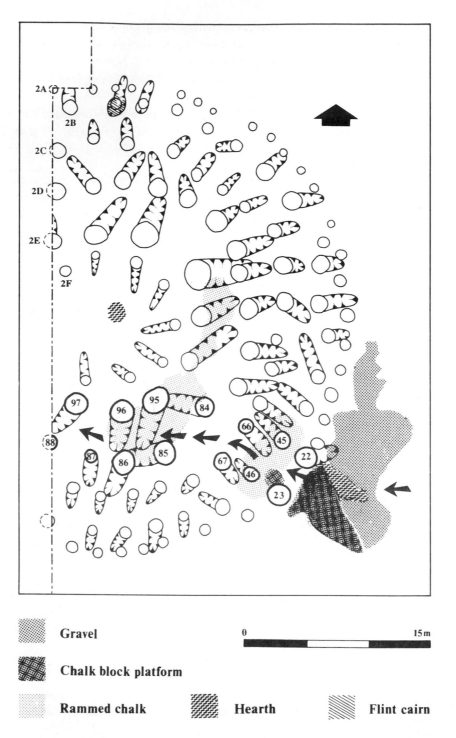

Figure 3.7    Durrington Walls: plan of the Southern Circle (after Wainwright and Longworth 1971)

centre of the circle would have been halted, and it would have been necessary to turn aside. The spacing of the posts seems to suggest that the intended direction was left, through the setting of four large posts 85–86–95–96. This brings one between the two circles 2E and 2D. These concentric circles are those between which there is the largest gap in the whole structure, and are also separated by an area of rammed chalk which could have functioned as a 'walkway'. The inescapable conclusion to be drawn from this is that the architecture of the Southern Circle was so designed as to encourage the individual to progress through the outer four circles, and then to turn aside and process around the inner two circles.

Just as a social division may have existed between those taking part in activities inside the henge and those observing from outside, some distinction may have been drawn between those in the centre of the circle and those being encouraged to process around them. The fact that a hearth existed in the centre of the circle indicates that the central space was sometimes occupied by *someone*. A similar pattern of movement seems to be indicated by the nearby monument of Woodhenge (Cunnington 1929).

Figure 3.8   Durrington Walls: the Southern Circle (photo: G. Wainwright)

There, the bank and ditch constrain entry to a single axis, which takes the individual through an entrance between the two outer circles of posts (Fig. 3.9). This entrance gap does not exist in the inner circles of uprights, suggesting that a circular movement was now intended, again within the most widely spaced concentric circles of posts.

The 'linear' and 'circular' patterns of constrained movement are actually combined in a single recently excavated monument. At Crickley Hill in Gloucestershire, a stone platform and circle built within the causewayed enclosure were reached by a linear walkway which later provided the site of the long mound (Dixon 1988 and pers. comm.) (Fig. 3.10). Advancing up this walkway towards the circle, persons would eventually meet an orthostat which would turn them aside from the centre of the circle (and the central hearth), and force them to move clockwise around inside the circle. This pattern of movement seems to have been recorded by wear patterns in the surface of the platform. Hence it is significant that at Balfarg, the recognition of the five lesser concentric post-circles within the henge depended upon the patterning of stones on the surface (Mercer 1981b, 110). Circular movement within the monuments of the later Neolithic may thus have been a rule rather than an exception. Even more than the linear monuments of the mid-third millennium, the henges seem to have been concerned with the use of architecture to control the movement of human bodies in space. Equally, the concentric division of space within henges indicates that a more complex classification was in operation than a simple inside–outside dichotomy. With the henges the physical control of the way in which space was 'read' reached its highest level of sophistication.

## Conclusions

The monumental landscapes of the Neolithic were qualitatively different from the spatial orders which preceded and which then succeeded them. By constructing artificial landmarks which placed the bones of ancestors or other symbolic media in space, an attempt was being made to condition the reading of that space. However, as with any symbolic system, the essentially arbitrary nature of this way of attributing meaning to place meant that an endless series of alternative readings was always possible. An example of this lack of fixity of meanings is provided by the causewayed enclosures. In the changing social circumstances of the earlier third millennium bc, it was possible for particular elements of the meaning of the enclosures to be brought to the fore, dismissed or subverted, with a resulting reinterpretation of the monuments.

In the latter part of the third millennium, the development of monumental architecture can be seen as a response to this problem. These newer monuments acted directly upon the human body, controlling the spacing and timing of the encounter with particular places. This process culminated in the sophisticated architecture of the large Wessex henges at the end of the third millennium. However, while it seems that in the subsequent era large monuments were no longer built (with the exception of the later phases of Stonehenge and Mount Pleasant), the same spatial order seems to have prevailed. Space was still symbolically integrated, through smaller rather than large structures. Round barrows contributed to an inscribed landscape by a process of accretion, each one adding to a complex pattern, aligned on earlier structures and subtly shifting the overall configuration. Thus the Early Bronze Age sees not a new spatial discourse, but an attempt to achieve the same effects on the landscape using labour organised on a much smaller scale. Possibly this reflects the emergence of a more devolved society, composed of many mutually competitive communities.

A real change in the way in which the landscape was organised only came with the later second millennium, and the imposition of field systems onto the land. The significance of fields, and their contemporaneity with the lapse of monument-building,

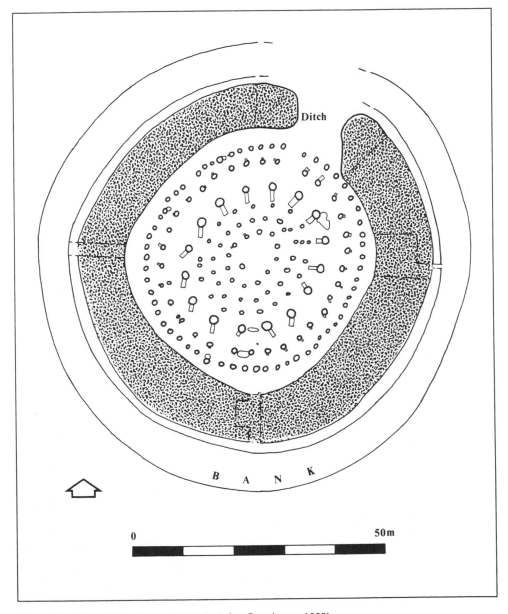

Figure 3.9   Plan of Woodhenge, Wiltshire (after Cunnington 1929)

Figure 3.10 Crickley Hill, Gloucestershire: the long mound (after Dixon 1988)

is that they too restrict and constrain the bodily movements of people, but that they do so in the context of day-to-day life and of productive tasks. Monuments may have provided 'stations' in space keyed into the movement of people and animals, but field systems actually represented the locales in which labour was invested. It would be misleading to suggest that there were no monuments and no ritual in the later Bronze Age and the Iron Age. Rather, in the Neolithic, ritual and monumentality had provided the context for day-to-day productive tasks, while a landscape laid out according to the rhythms of production provided the context for ritual and monuments in the later Bronze and Iron Ages. This can be seen both in hillforts located on 'ranch boundaries' and in burials deposited in grain storage pits (Bradley 1971; Whimster 1981).

# 4

## Pits, pots and dirt: a genealogy of depositional practices

### Laws of behaviour, cultural rules

It is a commonplace that archaeology is concerned with the rubbish of past generations. Archaeologists study materials which have been discarded, abandoned or purposefully deposited by human agents at some time in the past. However, actual processes of deposition have rarely been central to the writing of prehistory. This has latterly been the consequence of attempts to problematise 'the formation of the archaeological record', which have generally involved the isolation of universal factors affecting or transforming archaeological materials. There has been a general failure to treat deposition as a social and cultural practice *in itself*. Schiffer (1972; 1976), for instance, distinguished between natural and cultural agencies which affect archaeological deposits, yet failed to see these 'n-' and 'c-transformations' as fundamentally different in their ontological status. Just as lawlike statements could be generated to predict and filter out the effects of rodent burrowing, water sorting and transport, erosion, animal scavenging and trampling on deposits, structures and artefacts, so c-transforms were seen as universal laws governing the way in which human agency acted upon the archaeological record. Schiffer (1976, 15) gives as an example of one such law the prediction that, as settlement sites increase in size, so the distance between the use and discard locations of an artefact can be anticipated to increase. Clearly, the aim of formulating a catalogue of potential c-transforms is to enable them to be stripped away, leaving an undistorted record of human behaviour. The operation of what Schiffer calls a c-transform is nothing other than human social life. If it is this which the analysis is aimed at excising, one is left to wonder what remains as the object of study. Schiffer's scheme effectively places artefacts at the centre of the stage, only bringing human beings on in a subsidiary capacity to 'do' things to them.

An alternative to Schiffer's behaviourism can be found in insisting that 'cultural transforms' are precisely what this name would imply, and hence that the formation of archaeological deposits is a culturally specific process. Nothing in the way in which people have conducted their lives through the millennia is necessarily stable and unchanging. It follows that depositional practices are interesting in themselves, rather than constituting an irritant, obscuring the path to the elucidation of general laws of human behaviour. If archaeological deposits are generated in accordance with cultural rules rather than natural laws (Moore 1981), one must acknowledge that these rules are arbitrary and conventional, and are open to being manipulated and reinterpreted as time goes on (see, for instance, Bourdieu 1977). Hence, the study of the way in which particular materials were being deposited, or how deposits were formed, through time, has the potential to inform us of shifts in such cultural rules and norms. This chapter consists of an analysis of a number of related deposits which have hitherto been described as 'rubbish' or 'refuse'. Its intention will be to consider whether such a designation is appropriate, to determine whether recurrent patterns can be discerned in these deposits and their processes of formation, and to discuss whether their changing nature has anything to tell us about the preoccupations of Neolithic society in Britain.

'Rubbish' and 'dirt' are by no means categories which are common to all cultures (Moore 1982, 48). The arbitrary conceptual schemes through which people impose a system of sorts onto an inherently untidy existence may result in conceptual anomalies which may be rejected as unclean (Douglas 1966, 9; Leach 1976, 33). But equally, particular substances may be discarded, deposited or set aside without being thought of as rubbish (Moore 1986, 102). Thus Moore (*ibid.*) describes a situation in which ash, animal dung and chaff each has its own place in a conceptual scheme, each with its own set of associations and connotations which dictate that they cannot be deposited together. We ourselves may have a single category of 'dirt', but in some situations rotten material, or faeces, may not be regarded as dirty (Panoff 1970). Similarly, the sherds from broken pots may be left lying within settlements as a result of their taking on a supernatural significance (Welbourne 1984, 22). Depositional practices, then, are wholly guided by the way in which items and substances are classified. The disposal of animal bones, for instance, frequently depends upon the way in which animals are classified (Bulmer 1976). Thus different patterns of bone deposition might result according to whether animals were principally classified in terms of their habitat (Bulmer 1967), their domestic or wild status (Tambiah 1969), their conceptual distance from being 'men' (Buxton 1968), in terms of homologies with particular types of human beings (Lévi-Strauss 1969), or according to their physical characteristics (Douglas 1957). The classification of animals may even result in their being totally avoided; thus fish may not be eaten if they are considered to be the same as snakes (Kesby 1979, 46).

Of course, none of these ethnographic examples could or should be taken as direct parallels for the classificatory schemes which we might expect to find in operation in prehistoric Britain. At most, they act as a corrective against the expectation that a single undifferentiated category of refuse would necessarily have existed throughout prehistory. Each of these examples represents the outcome of a particular set of social circumstances: the classification of the material world will not be a cultural 'given', but will exist in a state of dynamic tension created by the social actions of a community. Thus, for instance, the principle of purity which Hodder observes guiding the deposition of materials within Mesakin compounds (1982a, 162) is directly related to a transient and historical set of social relations (*ibid.*, 168). It follows that the study of depositional practices is particularly suited to the 'genealogical' approach to archaeology outlined in the opening chapter of this book.

That a rather different attitude to domestic waste from our own prevailed in Neolithic Britain has long been evident. Case (1969b, 12–15) has described the burial of sherds, flints and charcoal in pits within an enclosure ditch at Goodland in County

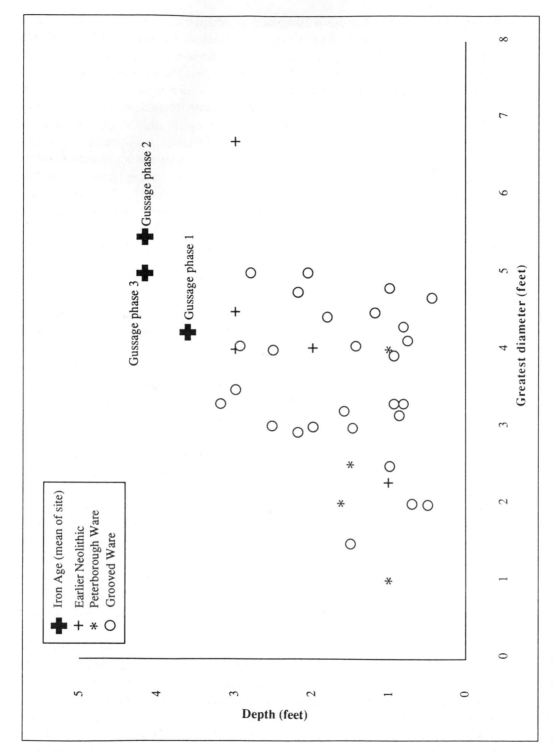

Figure 4.1   Pits: length and depth

Antrim. He suggested that this represented the scraped-up debris of settlement sites used as symbolic manure in rites of sympathetic magic designed to ensure fertility. No less striking is the use of midden material in the domestic architecture of Neolithic Orkney. The walls of the later Neolithic houses at Rinyo, Skara Brae and the Links of Notland are all surrounded by mounds of well-rotted midden, which appears to have been curated for the purpose (Clarke and Sharples 1985, 58). Similarly, at the Knap of Howar, midden had been used to fill in the wall cores (Ritchie 1983, 58). Depending upon one's interpretation of the radiocarbon dates at the latter site (*ibid.*, 57), this material could have been generations old by the time that it came to be used. While prosaic features like the thermal properties of midden material may have favoured its use for these purposes, the mere fact that the Orcadian people were happy to surround themselves with the rotted detritus of their communities is evidence enough of an attitude to 'dirt' distinct from that of the modern Occident. Beyond this, it may hint at a specific preoccupation with domestic debris, arising out of its intrinsically cultural properties and connotations.

## Pits

Evidence for domestic activities is little more substantial in the Neolithic and most of the Bronze Age in southern Britain than it is in the Mesolithic. House sites are few and scattered, and are often atypical of the general pattern of settlement in one way or another (for instance, being located inside defended enclosures: Dixon 1988, etc.). In the absence of this most basic of information, more meagre resources have been drawn upon in the development of economic models. One source of information which has been exploited has been the existence of subsoil pits, containing cultural material, and often held to be the sole surviving structural component of flimsy settlement sites. It was on the basis of the distribution of such pits that Isobel Smith suggested a basic economic division between upland and lowland Britain in the Neolithic (in Field, Matthews and Smith 1964). Such a division followed Piggott's (1958) suggestion that two separate economies could be discerned in the British Iron Age, a lowland grain-producing regime and the pastoral 'Stanwick' economy of the north and west (Bradley 1978a, 29–30). In the absence of definitive evidence, then, Smith suggested that the Neolithic economy was comparable with that of the Iron Age. As an alternative, I should prefer to emphasise the contrasts between Neolithic and Iron Age pits, which are perhaps more compelling than the similarity of their geographical distribution. On the basis of this contrast, we can go on to place the contents of the pits into the context of a number of other contemporary deposits.

Differences between Neolithic and Iron Age pits can be distinguished in a number of different aspects of their morphology. Principal amongst these is shape: Neolithic pits are almost universally shallow, bowl-shaped forms, whilst their Iron Age counterparts are flat-bottomed and either straight-sided or of 'beehive' form. Furthermore, pits of Neolithic date are considerably smaller in size, particularly in terms of depth (Fig. 4.1). Another important contrast lies in the filling of the pits. Figure 4.2 shows the numbers of layers of fill in a variety of Neolithic pits compared with Iron Age pits at Gussage All Saints and Little Woodbury (Wainwright 1979b; Bersu 1940). Such a marked difference cannot be explained purely by the lesser volumes of the Neolithic pits, and seems likely to reflect different patterns of backfilling. The Iron Age pits appear to have been used in the first instance for storage, and then to have provided a convenient repository for domestic waste, which would have built up over a period of time. The more homogeneous filling of the Neolithic pits indicates a prompt backfilling.

While shallow, bowl-shaped pits might be suitable for storage of foodstuffs in a desiccating climate (see the discussion by Clark *et al.* of such pits at Fayum in Egypt: 1960, 211), this may not be the case in Britain. Reynolds' experiments with reconstructed Iron Age pits (1974, 126–7) indicate that to store grain effectively the pit should be sealed with clay or dung to prevent respiration. Such a seal is best achieved, and least grain wasted, if an acute angle between seal and pit wall is avoided, and hence the beehive profile has been shown to be optimal. A bowl is thus the worst possible shape for sealing. Darvill's suggestion (in Darvill *et al.* 1986, 35) that some Neolithic pits may have been hearths is no more plausible than that they had a storage function, since despite the presence of much burnt material in their fillings, no pit shows evidence of burning *in situ*.

There are certain features which occur repeatedly in pits of Neolithic and Early Bronze Age date. Almost invariably they contain burnt material: ash (Stone and Young 1948, 289), burnt chalk (Frere 1943, 35) or charcoal (Thomas 1956, 167; Manby 1974, 11). This material may contain carbonised plant remains (Jones 1980), yet these are highly mixed in their composition and are generally dominated by wild species (Moffett, Robinson and Straker 1989), thus clearly not relating to the burning out of germinated grain. Another recurrent feature, often remarked upon by excavators, is that the sides of the pits are fresh, showing little evidence of subsidence or weathering (Calkin 1947, 30; Smith and Simpson 1964, 82). This is the case even on friable gravel subsoils (Case 1982, 121), and confirms the impression that they were backfilled soon after they were dug.

At a number of sites, more spectacular depositional practices alert one to the likelihood that something more complex than the routine disposal of waste material was happening. At Coneybury Hill, in Wiltshire, a large pit of earlier Neolithic date contained sherds and animal bones which had been pressed into the sides and floor of the feature (Richards 1982, 99). Similarly, at Carnaby Temple Sites 7 and 15 (Yorks.), animal bones had been pressed into the pit walls. Manby's interpretation, that these objects had been pressed back by a wickerwork lining (1974, 43), seems implausible. If the pits had been lined to store plant foods, why did they already contain animal bones? The material contained within Pit 1 at Woodlands, in Wiltshire, seems to have been covered with a flint cairn (Stone and Young 1948, 289), while Pit 4 contained a deposit which resembled the contents of a basket or bag of burnt material (Stone 1949, 122–3).

The deliberate nature of these fillings is also suggested by a range of deposited artefacts which would seem to be out of character for everyday household waste. Lithic artefacts often show a high ratio of tools to waste (Cleal 1984, 148). The tools themselves are frequently unbroken, and may include such items as finely flaked

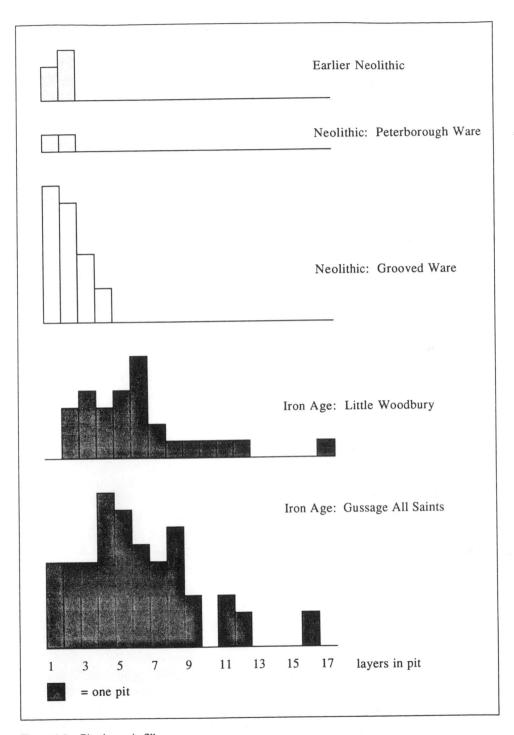

Figure 4.2    Pits: layers in fill

arrowheads (Stone 1935, 60), flint and stone axes (Leeds 1934, 264; Stone and Young 1948, 290; Stone 1949), and stone maceheads (Smith 1968). At Blewbury, a flint scraper had been snapped in two, and half placed in each of two pits (Halpin 1984). The disposal of these items was evidently not related to their no longer being usable in a functional sense, and it seems equally unlikely that they were simply overlooked in the process of 'tidying up' domestic refuse. One possibility which does remain is that these were items which were discarded on account of some form of pollution or of particular connotations attached to them which made them no longer suitable for use. The range of artefacts deposited in these pits extends to such items as bone pins (Leeds 1934), inscribed chalk plaques (Vatcher 1969; Harding 1988) and pottery vessels of rare and highly decorated types (Gell 1949; Chadburn and Gardiner 1985). Even the animal bones found in many pits defy simple explanations. Particularly in the case of those pits associated with later Neolithic Grooved Ware, like those at Larkhill (Wainwright *et al.* 1971), Stonehenge Bottom (Vatcher 1969) and Ratfyn (Stone 1935), the faunal assemblages consist almost entirely of bones from the meat-rich parts of animals (author's data). Moreover, the pits at Blewbury (Oxon.) contained bones which appeared to have been deposited as articulated joints (Halpin 1981, 1). In contrast, one pit on the King Barrow Ridge, near Stonehenge, contained an assemblage made up entirely of the foot bones of pigs (Richards 1984, 183), and one at Black Patch in the Vale of Pewsey was dominated by a large number of pig jaws (author's data). Bones of brown bear have been found at Ratfyn and Down Farm (Stone 1935; Bradley pers. comm.), while the shells of marine molluscs have been located at a number of sites.

A final feature which is worthy of note is the inclusion of human bones in pit fills. At sites like Astrop, Northants (Ashmolean Museum), or Sutton Courtenay Pit Q (Leeds 1934), these consist of no more than a few skull fragments included with an assemblage of pottery, flint tools and animal bones. At South Lodge and Handley Hill (Dorset), and in the pits within the central enclosure at Hambledon Hill, parts of human bodies were found with stone axes and pottery vessels (Pitt Rivers 1898; Mercer 1980). In two other pits at Sutton Courtenay, more extensive deposits of human remains were encountered. What this range of variability seems to demonstrate is that in practice no division existed between the enactment of 'mortuary ritual' and that of the 'routine' depositing of items in pits. This forces one to consider the difficult question of differentiating between items that constitute 'grave goods' and human remains as artefacts in themselves. Whatever the significance of deposits buried in pits, it is clear that this was not a context to which the presence of the dead was inappropriate.

The foregoing discussion of a particular set of depositional practices has established the degree to which they differ from later pits which can more reasonably be claimed to have performed a storage function, and has identified some of the principles plausibly governing their filling. To summarise, Neolithic and Early Bronze Age pits are unsuitable both in size and shape for the storage of foodstuffs. They seem to have been dug and backfilled within a relatively short span of time, with a matrix of material that shows evidence of burning, but containing artefacts which have not been burnt. In some cases the material may have been brought to the site of the pits in baskets or bags, and in one case taphonomic analysis of the bones indicates that the material had been exposed for some time before burial (Bradley, pers. comm.). Sometimes, but not always, the faunal remains indicate material which might be associated with the consumption or deliberate wasting of prime meat, while the pottery assemblage from the Coneybury pit consists of shallow, open bowls which might be argued to be best suited to the consumption of food (Cleal, pers. comm.). Whole pots are sometimes encountered, but more often parts of a number of vessels are found, perhaps implying that the material has been selected from more substantial deposits. Finally, the material culture associated with these pits includes a range of finely crafted artefacts, which tend to be rare as stray finds, often in pristine condition, and which were sometimes deliberately broken.

What is most striking about this set of practices is that they represent a phenomenon which is temporally bounded. As a histogram of the number of pits containing pottery of sequential styles within the study area demonstrates (Fig. 4.3), this is a phenomenon which became more widespread through the Neolithic, reaching its apex at the end of the third millennium bc with pits associated with Grooved Ware, yet rather less frequently connected with Beaker pottery. Collared Urn pits are extremely rare, and Food Vessel pits non-existent. Ignoring for the moment the degree of chronological overlap between these ceramic traditions, a prosaic interpretation of this sequence might be one of a shift of economic practice away from cereals and toward pastoralism. This would present an interesting inversion of the traditional model of Grooved Ware users as having 'a pastoral economy with a little hunting which was supplemented by strandlooping and fishing' (Wainwright and Longworth 1971, 264) and of Beaker-folk as 'energetic mixed farmers' (Case 1977, 71). In truth, if we remove the evidence of pits from the equation, the evidence for any kind of change in subsistence practices through this period must be slim, at least until the advent of Deverel–Rimbury settlements and field systems.

Not only does the number of pits dug seem to peak with the use of Grooved Ware, but also the amount of care expended in their filling, the degree of formality and the scarcity of the artefacts deposited. This, then, is a practice which is historically circumscribed, which was engaged in by people at one time, and which they ceased to undertake at another. When pits began again to be dug in the later second millennium bc, associated with Deverel–Rimbury settlements, they were larger, flat-bottomed and straight-sided (e.g. Drewett 1982, 332). In other words, the first digging of pits suitable for the storage of grain coincided temporally with the establishment of substantial, permanent settlements and the division of the landscape into fields. This complex of features represents the earliest sound evidence for a regime geared to intensive cereal production. By contrast, the pit-digging of the Neolithic seems to relate to a quite different set of preoccupations. In order to interpret these concerns it is necessary to consider a number of other practices which also involved the placing of objects in the earth.

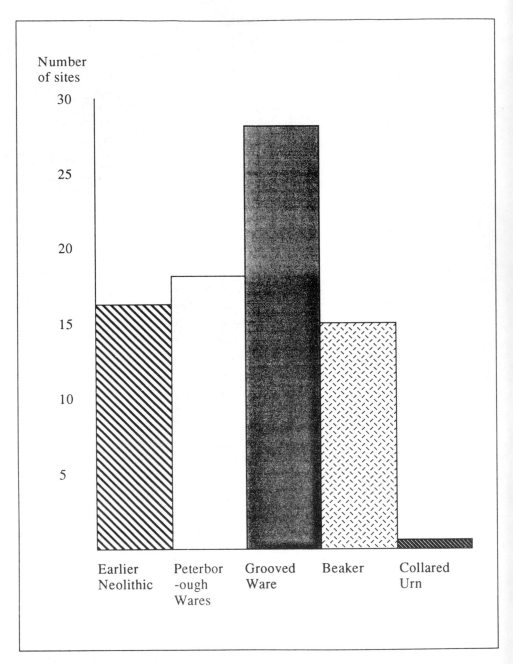

Figure 4.3   Numbers of pits containing particular styles of pottery from the study area

## Causewayed enclosure ditches

Another practice dating to the Neolithic period which involves the digging of pits of a sort (and the deposition of items therein) is the construction of the ditches of cause-wayed enclosures (Fig. 4.4). The excavation of interrupted rings of ditch segments has been interpreted in common-sense terms as an expedient means of quarrying material for a bank, given a labour force working in small gangs (Curwen 1930). However, the possibility that some enclosures may have had no bank at all (Evans 1988, 133) must place this reading of the evidence in question. The ubiquity of causewayed-ditched enclosures in north-west Europe, from Poland to Ireland, suggests that some symbolic importance was attached to the delineation of a bounded area by a discontinuous perimeter. The significance of the circuit of ditch segments itself is indicated by the number of sites at which the ditches have either been cleaned out (Mercer 1988, 100) or repeatedly recut (Smith 1971, 98; Darvill 1981, 55; Dixon 1988, 81). Parts of the enclosure at Briar Hill in Northamptonshire had been recut successively up to five times (Bamford 1985, 32), while the final 'slot' recut of the central enclosure on Hambledon Hill respected all of the original causeways (Mercer 1980, 36).

The specific significance of the ditch segments is emphasised by the way in which particular deposits have been placed in their terminals at a number of sites. At the waterlogged site of Etton these include such items as rafts of birch bark, whole pots and bundles of cattle ribs (Pryor, French and Taylor 1985, 293). That these practices were more widespread has been demonstrated by the recent excavations at Windmill Hill, where discrete (perhaps bagged) deposits of animal bones have been located within terminals of segments of the inner and middle ditches (Whittle 1988b). Still more elaborate deposits may mark the entrances through ditch circuits. At Haddenham, an entrance was flanked by ditches containing complex structural arrangements, associated with a broken stone axe butt, human skull fragments and *in situ* burning (Evans 1988, 134).

The presence of skull fragments at Haddenham prompts the observation that finds of human bone have repeatedly been made in causewayed enclosure ditches, either on ditch bottoms or in recuts. Their significance in these two kinds of contexts need not have been the same. At Hambledon Hill, the interpretation of the central enclosure as a necropolis given over to the exposure of the dead gives a plausible explanation for the mass of skeletal material located in the ditches, but there are also skulls which have been placed on ditch bottoms both here and at the lesser Stepleton enclosure (Mercer 1980, 30 and 52). It could, of course, be suggested that *all* the bones were actually placed in the ditches, rather than just the skulls. It need not follow that ditch deposits are representative of activities carried out inside an enclosure. Human skull fragments are also known from the ditches of several other sites, notably Abingdon and Staines, the latter site also boasting a sheep's skull set in one ditch terminal (Robertson-Mackay 1987, 46). Complete burials have also been recorded in ditch-butts, as at Offham (Drewett 1977, 209). As with the pit sites, the deposition of human remains, and particularly portions of the skull, seems to have been considered appropriate in the context of causewayed enclosure ditches.

While complex sequences of recutting may be specific to the enclosures, the deliberate and formal backfilling of both primary ditch cuts and recuts provides a further link with the isolated pits. Possibly the most spectacular deposit of this kind is that found on the ditch bottom of the main enclosure at Hambledon Hill. This consisted of a mass of organic material containing animal and human bones, flint flakes and potsherds. So spatially constrained and apparently deliberately placed was this deposit that the excavator expressed the opinion that it might have been placed there in a series of bags (Mercer 1980, 30). At a number of other sites, layers of organic and/or burnt material have been encountered in the ditches. At Robin Hood's Ball the richest of these postdated the collapse of the bank, underlining the point that for depositional purposes it was the ditch which was of greater significance (Thomas 1964, 11). The ditches of the inner circuit at Abingdon provided a particularly instructive set of deposits. Here, dark, silty organic lenses containing a great deal of charcoal were interbedded with relatively clean gravel (Avery 1982, 17). These layers appeared to be made up of individual heaps roughly one foot across, suggested to represent basketfuls of material (*ibid.*). Moreover, the excavator indicated that the organic material appeared to have been well rotted and composted before its deposition. At Briar Hill, lenses of material containing charcoal and fragments of ironstone, reddened by fire appeared to have been sealed almost immediately after their deposition by clean layers above them (Bamford 1985, 36). All of this seems to recall Smith's suggestions that particular deposits of material in the ditches at Windmill Hill had been promptly buried (1966; 1971). It appears, then, that certain types of matter were purposefully placed in the ditch segments and buried. Repeatedly, such deposits involve material which had been burnt – the 'ash-filled pits' recutting the ditch at Hambledon (Mercer 1988, 96), or the scorched redeposited silts at Haddenham (Evans 1988, 136). Great fires seem to have burnt in the ditches at Crickley Hill as part of the process of backfilling (Dixon 1988, 81).

Causewayed enclosure ditches and contemporary isolated pits are thus linked by a number of similarities – the presence of a burnt soil or organic matrix, the deliberate deposition of material items, ceramic and faunal assemblages which appear to relate to the consumption or deliberate wasting of food, and the presence of human bones, especially skull fragments. These similarities suggest that deposition in these two contexts was governed by a common set of ideas. Moreover, they underline the likelihood that the digging of pits and ditches, and their refilling, presumably with symbolically charged items and substances, was an important practice within Neolithic society. Further, it was a symbolic resource which could be manipulated in a number of different ways. These would include the delineation of an enclosed area in the case of the causewayed camps, but one may also note the existence of alignments of pits, often found in association with complexes of field monuments (Harding 1981; Miket 1981), and clearly involved in the process of orienting and imposing a pattern on a landscape. Throughout the Neolithic period a number of types of monument were enclosed not by a bank but by a circle of pits. These would include some of the Dorchester on Thames monuments, where the pits were filled with a mixture of burnt and organic material (Atkinson, Piggott and Sandars 1951, 119–21), or the Aubrey Holes at Stonehenge, backfilled with burnt soil and charred wood (Atkinson 1957,

Figure 4.4    Causewayed enclosure ditches at Hambledon Hill, Dorset (photo: Roger Mercer)

27). The action of fire, then, seems to be intrinsic to the significance of these prehistoric excavations.

## Long barrow ditches

A further context in which the deliberate deposition of material items has been recognised but relatively little commented upon is in the flanking ditches of the earthen long barrows of southern Britain. While a range of materials has been recovered from these features, there is a tendency for only the most spectacular deposits to be acknowledged as having been deliberately placed. Thus, at North Marden in Sussex, Drewett has speculated that a collection of carved chalk objects in a ditch section at one end of the mound, and a human skull with charcoal and potsherds at the other, were ritual paraphernalia connected with the burial rite and later buried (Drewett 1986, 32, 49). Likewise, the complete ox in the ditch of the Skendleby barrow and the skull of *Bos primigenius* in that at Thickthorn Down (Drew and Piggott 1936, 82) are commented on as having been purposefully deposited. However, where clusters of knapping debris have been found in the ditches of sites like Thickthorn (Fig. 4.5), Fussell's Lodge and Alfriston, these have been explained either as the 'testing' of nodules encountered in the digging of the ditch or as the consequence of its providing a shelter from wind and rain (*ibid.*; Ashbee 1966, 15; Drewett 1975, 126). These collections of flakes frequently refit to form complete nodules, without implements having been made and taken away (Edmonds and Thomas 1987, 196).

The way in which this material has been considered seems to depend largely upon the preconceptions of the archaeologist. That which is spectacular and baffling to economic and ergonomic logic is 'ritual', that which appears more prosaic is not, even where it is recovered from the same context. In seeking to transcend this logic it is important to consider the full contents of these contexts in terms of both composition and spatial distribution. A clear division of the evidence into the 'rational' and the 'irrational' is untenable in reference to the distribution of artefacts in the ditch of the long mound at Barrow Hills, Radley, Oxfordshire. Here, within a continuous ditch enclosing the mound, a strikingly formal pattern of deposits was located. At one end of the barrow the ditch contained groups of pottery sherds and flint scrapers, each discrete and barely overlapping. The other end contained four deposits of antler, flanked by two groups of human skull fragments (Bradley, Chambers and Halpin 1984, 5). The spatial organisation of deposition thus appears to have been guided by the principle of correspondence between, but segregation in deposition of, particular substances. Further analysis by the author of a number of other published sites confirmed this impression: the cumulative patterns which emerge are ones of segregation *within* association. Thus, certain materials occur together repeatedly but are kept separate from each other within the long barrow ditches.

In brief, these deposits are commonly concentrated at the butt-ends of ditches, and the patterns of 'segregated correspondence' emerge from items either being placed in ditches on opposite sides of the barrow or at opposite ends of the same ditch. One of the most significant of these patterns is that the bones of domestic animals are rarely found in direct association with red deer antler: at Horslip these items were found at opposite butt-ends of one ditch (Ashbee, Smith and Evans 1979, 214). Potsherds and antler, similarly, seem to be kept apart, as do antler and flint flakes, found in opposite butts of the south ditch at Kingston Deverill G1 (Harding and Gingell 1986, 11). On the basis of a rather smaller number of occurrences, it may also be possible to suggest a segregation of carved chalk and potsherds. These patterns are difficult to interpret, but what might be occurring is the representation of systematic contrasts along several different axes. One such contrast would seem to be between 'the wild' (antler) and 'the tame' (animal bones), although these might only be one element of a more complex system of overlapping classifications.

These deposits in the primary silts of barrow ditches can be contrasted with material introduced at a much later point in the silting. A very widespread pattern is evident of

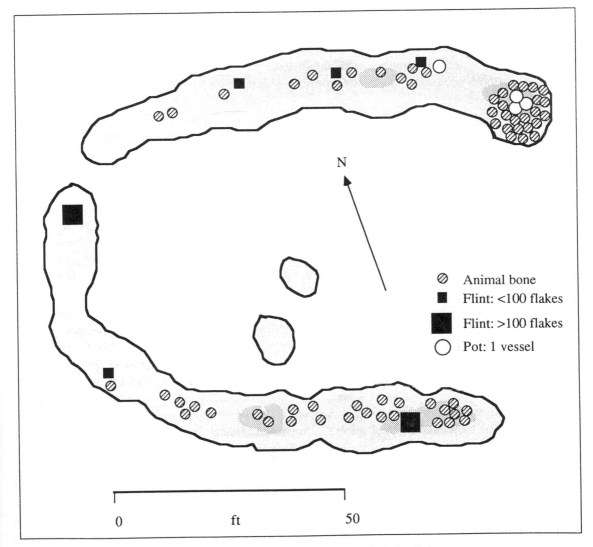

Figure 4.5    Thickthorn Down long barrow, Dorset: deposits in the ditch

burnt material, pottery, animal bones and flint tools and waste being introduced into the proximal butt-ends of barrow ditches in the later third/early second millennia bc. Almost without exception, the pottery concerned consists of both Peterborough Ware and Beaker sherds, Grooved Ware being conspicuous by its absence (in contrast, of course, with pits). These deposits seem far less structured than those of the earlier Neolithic, and might indicate no more than that feasts or other ceremonies were being held in the forecourt areas of the mounds, and material was finding its way haphazardly into the ditches, were it not for certain similarities with both deposits in pits and recuts in causewayed enclosures. Burnt material was being placed in the ditches, together with animal bones, pottery and sometimes fine material items (the jet belt slider at Skendleby, for instance: Phillips 1935, 71). Here, then, was another context for deliberate deposition, and one for which some kinds of pottery were, and others were not, appropriate. There is every indication that deposition in long mound ditches was one element of a broader tradition, and that this tradition as a whole was transformed as time went on, with the rules which guided it being changed in relation to new social realities. The significance of these changes can be considered once evidence concerning further contexts of deposition has been presented.

## Henge monuments

The likelihood that depositional practices in Neolithic Britain might be guided by sets of formal rules was first discussed in a paper concerned with the henge monuments of Wessex (Richards and Thomas 1984). That this group of sites should have provided the point of entry to the question is itself revealing, for it is in the context of henge monuments that the formality of structured deposition is most pronounced and hence most easily recognised. It will not be necessary to repeat the arguments of that paper in detail here. We can take the basic recognition of pattern and structure as read. Rather, an attempt will be made to isolate the major structuring principles which underlie the patterning recognised in the henge monuments, in order to relate them to other contexts of deposition.

The excavation of the large henge enclosures at Durrington Walls in Wiltshire and Mount Pleasant in Dorset (Wainwright and Longworth 1971; Wainwright 1979a) provided the opportunity for an assessment of how objects were treated in a number of different contexts within a given monument. The purposeful nature of the deposition of sherds, flints and animal bones on these sites was underlined by the circumstances of their recovery at the Southern Circle at Durrington Walls. Here, the concentration of artefacts at the bases of the weathering cones of the timber uprights was explained by their having been placed around the posts, 'possibly as offerings' (Wainwright and Longworth 1971, 25). It is only a short step from the recognition that some significance was attached to the disposition of certain material items within henge monuments to the proposition that formal sets of rules dictated what was to be placed where. In accordance with this hypothesis, it was discovered that the different structural elements of the Durrington monument – the Southern and Northern Circles, the enclosure ditch, the Midden and the Platform – all showed remarkably different patterns of deposition with regard to the decoration of Grooved Ware pottery, the numbers of flint tools, the parts of animal carcasses and the relative proportions of bones of different animal species recovered (Richards and Thomas 1984, 197–214).

When one considers the results of the analysis of Durrington Walls and Mount Pleasant in the context of other excavated henge monuments in southern England, it is possible to identify a broader pattern of formal deposition. In each case, one is struck less with the recurrent associations of types of material item than with the patterns of contrast and segregation. At each site, there are particular objects and types of material which seem to be kept separate, or are restricted to certain areas. It would seem, then, that the essence of the classificatory scheme which can be discerned in operation in the henges lies in a series of contrasts and oppositions expressed through deposition in spatially discrete locations. Some of these oppositions can be discerned at a number of different sites. More often, the impression gained is that a hierarchy of oppositions exists, some of which are chosen to be emphasised at each site. It is important to stress that what is manifest archaeologically is the operation of a complex conceptual system, rather than the simple mapping of a set of categories onto space. We should not be surprised that different aspects of this system are deployed at different times and in different places.

A case in point is the henge monument of Maumbury Rings in Dorchester, Dorset. The Maumbury henge is composed of an ovoid circuit of large pits or shafts, each up to 35 ft in depth (Bradley 1975). Radiocarbon dates from the site indicate that no great chronological distance separates the material deposited in the tops and bottoms of the shafts, yet these appear radically distinct in their composition (Bradley and Thomas 1984). Just as the different areas of Durrington Walls appear to have been appropriate for the deposition of different types of material, so at Maumbury it is the vertical rather than the horizontal spatial axis which is manipulated to express difference. At Durrington, bones of wild boar and of *Bos primigenius* were restricted to the outer ditch of the enclosure (Richards and Thomas 1984, 214). Precisely the same pattern can be observed at Mount Pleasant, Woodhenge and Marden. At Maumbury, a similar wild/tame opposition seems to be expressed in a different way: bones and antler of red deer represent 72 per cent of the assemblage in the top 15 ft of the eight shafts for which information from Gray's excavations exists, and 6 per cent of that from below 15 ft. The remainder is made up largely of domestic cattle and pig. Human bones are restricted entirely to the upper parts of the shafts, which also contain the greater number of struck flints. Potsherds, by contrast, are restricted to the lower parts of the shafts.

These patterns find some echoes in a number of other sites. At Durrington Walls, different ratios of cattle to pig bones were recognised in the different parts of the site, with 'special' contexts like the Platform showing a higher proportion of cattle bones (Richards and Thomas 1984, 207). At Woodhenge this pattern is all the more emphatic: not only are the bones of wild animals restricted to the outer ditch, but the ratio of pig to cattle changes between each of the six concentric rings of postholes, pig dominating the outer holes, cattle the inner (Fig. 4.6). It has long been recognised that Grooved Ware is rarely to be found associated with funerary monuments or burials in the south of Britain. The sporadic finds of human bone on henges with Grooved Ware associations are thus all the more interesting, for they correspond precisely to the locations from which the bones of undomesticated animals have been recovered. Thus at Durrington, human bones came from the ditch and the Southern Circle, at Mount Pleasant skull fragments came from the west terminal of the north entrance, at Marden a female skeleton came from the west ditch terminal, at Wyke Down human bones concentrated on the pits flanking the entrance (Bradley pers. comm.), and at Wood-henge a male skeleton came from the ditch. This emphasis on 'outside' locations (tops of shafts, outer ditches), and particularly on entrances, is shared by a number of other classes of materials. Heaps of antler picks were found in ditch terminals at Marden (Wainwright 1971, 223) and Durrington (Wainwright and Longworth 1971, 187). At Mount Pleasant, six of the seven carved chalk items in Grooved Ware contexts came from the terminals of the outer ditch. Furthermore, at Durrington and the Wyke Down henge, sherds of Grooved Ware bearing spiral motifs are concentrated around entrances and ditch terminals (Cleal pers. comm.).

In the light of these findings, it is highly significant that the classification which Colin Richards used to detect spatial patterning in the Grooved Ware at Durrington Walls was based upon two binary oppositions: bounded/unbounded and decorated/undecorated (Richards and Thomas 1984, 192–5). Each of the elements of the classification of material items which we can distinguish from the deposits in henge monuments seems to be concerned with drawing contrasts and emphasising

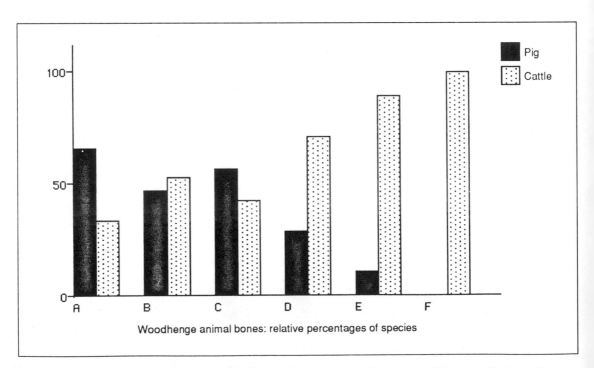

Figure 4.6    Woodhenge: ratio of bones of cattle to bones of pig in successive concentric circles of postholes (A, outer; F, inner) (author's data)

boundaries between inside and outside, tame and wild, culture and nature, and with an emphasis on entrances and transitions. The segregation of flints and potsherds detected in the individual holes of the Southern Circle at Durrington (Richards and Thomas 1984, 204), and also discernible in the holes at Woodhenge and the Maumbury shafts, fits into this scheme: flint as 'natural', pottery as 'cultural'. There are clear indications, then, of a positive conceptual scheme guiding the separation and deposition of material in the henges. The exclusion of human remains to 'outside' contexts is particularly interesting. It suggests that the dead were 'outside' and 'wild', to be kept away from the 'cultural' 'inside'. Significantly, at Durrington the single context containing the most heavily bounded and decorated pottery and high proportions of cattle bones and flint arrowheads and knives, the Platform, also appears to have held a hearth, while the nearby Midden contained a burnt, ashy deposit (Wainwright and Longworth 1971, 25, 38). Once again fire, both an agency of transformation and a supremely 'cultural' phenomenon, seems to have served as a key symbol.

## Wet places and hoards

In the preceding sections I have tried to hint at the connectedness of practices of deposition in a variety of different contexts. It follows from the argument being developed that their similarities stem from certain unities at a conceptual level: particular ideas about the connotations of specific items and substances dictated that they must be treated in distinctive ways. However, the recognition that any depositional context one cared to mention contained the same set of items treated in the same ways would of itself tell us relatively little about the ideas of the people who put them there. This introduces a major problem concerned with representation: a deliberate act of deposition may be a means of presenting relations between things as they are, should be, or could never be. In a 'ritual' context, items could come into association which would never be mixed in day-to-day life, or could be treated in thoroughly abnormal ways (Douglas 1957). The recognition that a code of rules underlies these archaeologically attested depositional practices only becomes interesting when we realise the potential for recognising further contrasts in both space and time: that is to say, when *other* sets of rules can be distinguished operating contemporary with the complex which we have identified, or when changes in these rules can be discerned through time.

Precisely such a contrasting set of rules can be recognised in another major class of depositional practices. From the start of the Neolithic onward it is clear that certain items were being deposited in wet places such as rivers and bogs. These were a far more restricted range of articles than those found in pits, enclosures, henges and barrow ditches. Initially, they consisted exclusively of pottery vessels and flint and stone axes. By contrast with dry-land deposits, the pots concerned seem to have been deposited whole, rather than as sherds, a feature which finds a parallel in earlier Neolithic bog deposits of pots containing food in Scandinavia (Bradley 1987b, 352). Finds of pottery in bogs and rivers in southern Britain are restricted to earlier Neolithic bowls and Peterborough Wares, Grooved Ware and Beaker material are entirely absent.

Moreover, the earlier Neolithic vessels are exclusively carinated or shouldered bowls. Kinnes (in Coles and Orme 1979, 52), for instance, remarks that the vessel from the Sweet Track Drove Site, while fitting into the Hembury style in terms of technology and finish, is of a form more characteristic of Grimston Ware. Similar vessels came from the Railway Site (Coles and Orme 1976, 63), where at least one pot contained a deposit of hazelnuts. This evokes Nielsen's suggestion (1986, 242) that the very widespread distribution of the carinated bowl form in fourth/third millennia bc Europe may be connected with an equally generalised set of ideas about how food should be handled and consumed (see also Herne 1988). The deposition of offerings of food in a particular type of vessel in wet places might equally be part of a widespread set of ideas. These vessels, of a sort perhaps suited to storage, contrast with the open bowls found in causewayed enclosure ditches and pits like that at Coneybury. The representation of later Neolithic pottery is equally selective, dominated as it is by (carinated) Mortlake vessels like the three from Mongewell (Smith 1924) or the one from Meare Heath (Taunton Museum).

The numerous finds of stone and flint axes from wet contexts (e.g. Adkins and Jackson 1978) have repeatedly been commented upon (Bradley 1987b, 354; Holgate 1988a, 126). Their significance as purposefully deposited items is underscored by their being larger in size than those found on land (M. Edmonds pers. comm.), and may be further emphasised by the presence of the wooden 'tomahawk' found by the Sweet Track at the Drove Site (Coles and Orme 1979, 49). Equally significant is the suggestion that continuity exists in deposition over a considerable depth of time. There is a high degree of correlation between the areas where Neolithic axes and Bronze Age spearheads have been recovered from the Thames (Ehrenburg 1980, 5–6), while one of these areas, west of London, also shows a concentration of mace-head finds (Field and Penn 1981, 15). The types of artefacts in Bronze Age river and bog finds show a similar degree of restriction to that of the Neolithic. In the Early Bronze Age, halberds were commonly deposited in bogs (Needham 1988, 230). Of the items listed in Rowlands' survey of Middle Bronze Age metalworking (1976), those found in rivers and bogs are dominated by weapons: rapiers, dirks and spearheads. This contrasts with the stray finds, which are predominantly axes, chisels and palstaves, and the hoards, which contain a variety of ornaments as well as palstaves.

If it can be postulated that throughout the period 3200–700 bc a limited range of items was deposited in wet places, dominated by weaponry, the same degree of continuity cannot be suggested for dry-land deposits. While Grooved Ware and Beaker pits undoubtedly run contemporary with the first introduction of metalwork into Britain, none of them ever contains metal items. Equally, hoards of metalwork are rarely found with other items: at most they may be contained inside a pottery vessel. They may be beneath stones (Britton 1963, 311) or buried immediately below the surface of the earth (Forde-Johnstone 1964, 99), they may sometimes be located in pits as such, but animal bones, flint tools, potsherds and burnt or organic material seem to be generally absent. Hoards may often have been deposited in places of some significance, perhaps in relation to spectacular landscape features (Gourlay and Barrett 1984). This suggests that three quite different depositional traditions can be distinguished in the Neolithic and Bronze Age of southern Britain: pits, hoards and wet places. Of these, the pit deposits seem to decline from the later Neolithic onwards. While some hoards of stone axes are known (e.g. Radley 1967), the practice of hoarding is one which seems to have escalated with the introduction of metal. The separateness of these traditions is emphasised both by their spatial discreteness and by the items judged appropriate to each. Burgess and Cowen (1972, 178), for instance, remark on the mutually exclusive concentrations of particular types of metalwork generally found in burials, hoards and river finds. Hoards of the major Early Bronze Age metalworking traditions, Migdale and Arreton, are largely absent from the 'core areas' of Wessex, the Upper Thames and East Yorkshire, where pit deposits are most numerous. The exclusion of metal items from pit deposits has already been noted, but equally striking seems to be the restriction of particular ceramic types to certain contexts of deposition. By the later Neolithic, Grooved Ware was suitable for deposition in the large henges of Wessex, while Peterborough Ware was not. Similarly, Peterborough Ware was appropriate for deposition in long barrow ditches and rivers, while Grooved Ware was not. Coming into this milieu, Beaker pottery was placed within a new and distinctive set of depositional contexts, being found in mortuary contexts and henges, but being absent from river finds.

## Commentary and interpretation

In this chapter I have chosen to highlight certain depositional contexts, and suggest a degree of connectedness between them. This is itself an act of interpretation. After all, why should these types of sites be considered, and not others? Why should these particular features be chosen to indicate similarities, and others be ignored? However, in this final section, the interpretative process is of a different order. Up to this point the argument has been constructed so as to place conventional views in question. Turning from this essentially critical process, it is now possible to put the dissected fragments of the evidence back together in such a way as to rationalise them. On the basis of the deposits located in pits, barrow ditches, enclosure ditches and henge monuments, it has been suggested that certain rules may have governed the items placed there, and their relative spatial ordering. The isolated pits, for instance, seem to have been dug specifically for the burial of particular materials, and backfilled immediately afterwards. These materials generally include a matrix which has been subject to the action of fire. While some of the items buried in these pits are finely crafted (axes, bone pins), and seem unlikely to be chance losses, many of them could be argued to be appropriate to domestic activities. Indeed, it may be that one reason why these pits have so often been taken as the remnants of settlements is because their contents are intentionally redolent of home and hearth, possibly in the context of a society which was relatively mobile, and whose attachment to places was more emotional than real and continuous. The way in which midden material was manipulated in Neolithic Orkney has already been noted, and it may be that these practices are not unrelated.

Given that fine artefacts, potentially of some significance, had been added to the pit deposits, it seems most likely that their contents had been derived for the most part either from domestic middens or from the debris of communal feasts. In either case, the activities which have produced this material are some of the most basic of human social life: eating, cooking, drinking, burning fires. Moreover, they are activities which are very explicitly social and cultural: food, and the charcoal and ash, have been transformed by fire (Lévi-Strauss 1969; Hugh-Jones 1978); food has been stored, and so on. The frequent presence of human remains in these pits is also significant: in a society in which (to judge from the effort lavished on tombs and barrows) the dead seem to have been of especial significance, the remains of the ancestral departed are overtly connected with the remains of fires and of feasting. It is logical to suggest that what is being evoked is the continuity between past and present, in terms of the continuity of the kin group, those who share hearth and food. We must remember that this was a time when the British landscape was still in the early stages of being 'tamed'. Given a relatively mobile lifestyle, the 'fixing' of the evidence of domesticity in the landscape may have been a means of domesticating the wild. The possibility that the deposition of material in a pit may have been a means of exerting an influence on a place is strongly suggested by some of their locations. Grooved Ware pits, for instance, are often found in or around earlier monuments. These include pits in the immediate vicinity of the causewayed enclosures at Etton (Pryor, French and Taylor 1985), Abingdon (Bradley, Chambers and Halpin 1984) and Maiden Castle (Wheeler 1943), and the cursus monuments at Lechlade (Jones 1976) and Sutton Courtenay/ Drayton (Leeds 1934).

If depositing certain items in pits was a way of 'fixing' a place, this would be all the more true of a place which was surrounded by pits. Here, the act of digging the pit is itself a part of the transformation of place. With the more complex arrangements of space afforded by monumental constructions, it becomes possible to draw distinctions between items deposited in different locales, and with rings of pits broken by entrances it is possible to fix more closely a location and to choreograph activity so as to emphasise the transitional. Similarly, the flanking ditches of a long barrow, incorporating the polarity between two of the cardinal points, allow certain simple distinctions to be made between types of material deposited separately. In each of these cases, the simple messages which can be inferred are much the same: they include the divisions between culture and nature, tame and wild, and the significance of burning (especially in transitional/boundary locations). The monument is bounding off an area from the wild through the manipulation of that which is domestic and ancestral, and within these boundaries further distinctions are drawn between that which is closer to and that which is further from humankind.

It is arguable that the still more formal depositional practices of the later Neolithic stress these same oppositions more forcibly. Just as the digging of pits escalates, and the deposits within the pits become more complex, so the henge monuments of Wessex consist of a more complex arrangement of space which enables still more distinctions to be made between things. However, these oppositions are variations on the same themes: inside/outside, culture/nature, domestic/wild, bounded/ unbounded, burnt/unburnt, decorated/undecorated. One significant shift seems to be that in the interim the role of the dead has changed: from being central to earlier Neolithic ritual life they have been marginalised and left on the outside. This is probably significant in a society in which divisions and boundaries were being more thoroughly enforced. The remains of the dead had either become a symbol too ambiguous to include, or one whose connotations had changed over time. If the Neolithic consisted less of an economy than of a set of social relations and the ideas which sustained them, the process of drawing boundaries was one which was central to social reproduction. The categories 'tame' and 'wild' or 'inside' and 'outside' are probably only aspects of a more inclusive and overlapping system of classification. In the earlier Neolithic this system was mobilised largely in order to exert an influence over a landscape. Nevertheless, we should note that the principle in operation was one of segregation within association: the 'wild' and 'outside' were tamed as much by being brought into a system of thought as by any physical process. At the same time, such an inclusive system provides a pattern of homology for the definition of human groups into insiders and outsiders. It may be this division of humanity by allegory which is one of the more fundamental aspects of the Neolithic.

Another aspect of the same system of contrasts and divisions would be the opposition between order and disorder. By the later Neolithic, it can be suggested that something of a shift can be recognised in the deployment of the conceptual scheme. Increasingly, the contrasts concerned were used as a means of representing divisions internal to society. The later Neolithic thus saw the rise of a particular kind of power, a particular discourse about how the world was which would have been expressed in words, actions and gestures, and one of whose elements would have been this set of depositional practices. The relatively abrupt end of this tradition in the earlier second millennium bc suggests that this strategy had ceased to be effective.

This set of practices can be distinguished from a variety of other ways in which people deposited material items. All of these, the placing of items in graves, hoarding and the deposition of objects in rivers and other wet places, increase in their intensity as the pit/ditch complex declines. Significantly, they seem to relate to a quite different set of concerns and preoccupations. If the pit and ditch deposits connote the domestic and the transformational, these other traditions seem to be more concerned with the manipulation of material wealth. Increasingly, the items found in hoards, bogs and rivers are objects which are not merely no longer elaborations of domestic artefacts, but which are never recorded from settlements. The eventual rise to dominance of these practices seems to mark a major shift of social and cultural orientation. The Neolithic society which had become established in Britain in the later fourth millennium bc was built around a set of conceptualised relationships. By maintaining a whole series of distinctions between cultural categories, this set of relations could be reproduced from one generation to the next. The construction of monuments and the deposition of materials in pits introduced these categorisations into the landscape and into the practicalities of everyday life. What can be recognised archaeologically is the development of parallel traditions of depositional practice which drew upon distinct material resources, and which were aimed at different strategic ends. The shift in favour of these arrangements with the introduction of metalwork can be seen as a significant process of social realignment.

In this chapter what has been undertaken is the archaeology of a material tradition.

A series of activities has been traced, gradually shifting through time. However, it must not be overlooked that these traditions are both maintained and transformed by the actions of people in the course of their routine activities. These depositional events are part of a broader field of human practices, doubtless elements of festivals, observances and feasts. It is the advantage (and perhaps also the burden) of the archaeologist to see these practices as dynamic phenomena, whereas to those engaged in the activities concerned they would probably have been unchanging, unquestioned and eternal. Such a conjuncture as the necessary exclusion of the remains of the human dead to the 'outside' non-cultural world is an example of the way in which history may sometimes burst in and disrupt tradition. Nevertheless, this should not allow us to lose sight of the fact that this history of depositional practice, written as discontinuity, would have been experienced as continuity.

# 5

# Portable artefacts: the case of pottery

## Portable artefacts

In a previous chapter a textual analogy for material culture was used as a means to work through the chronological changes in monumental architecture through the Neolithic. In this chapter, a similar approach will be applied to pottery. Although ceramics form one of the classes of evidence which have traditionally attracted the interest of archaeologists working in many different periods, it must be emphasised that the decision to consider pots, as opposed to stone axes, flint tools, bonework or chalk carvings, is an essentially arbitrary one. While each of these classes of artefacts would doubtless have had cycles of production, distribution and consumption peculiar to themselves, the aim of this chapter is to investigate the changing use of one particular class of portable items in contrast to stationary architecture, and in this respect pottery serves as an example.

The choice of pottery as an exemplar condemns one to consider some very specific cultural problems. The basic pattern which has to be interpreted is one of localised earlier Neolithic style zones (Abingdon, Mildenhall, Windmill Hill) (Fig. 5.1) giving way to exclusive, but spatially overlapping styles (Peterborough Ware, Grooved Ware) (Figs. 5.2 and 5.3) in the later Neolithic (Bradley 1982, 28). The issue is complicated by evidence for considerable chronological overlap between different styles and traditions of pottery, which undermines any simple chest-of-drawers model of cultural change. Bradley (1984a, 72) has recently proposed an interpretation of these phenomena based upon Miller's (1982) discussion of emulation, in which each successive ceramic tradition is adopted by the dominant group within a society, and filters down to the lower orders, only to be replaced by another style as the élite seeks to maintain its hegemony over the rare and the exotic. Such a point of view has much to recommend it, since it sees material items as being bound up with human social strategies, rather than fulfilling an exclusively functional role. However, what it shares with the latter perspective is an assumption that pottery had an essentially static and continuous role throughout the period under study, namely to express social rank (higher or lower), as opposed to simply acting as containers. The position of a given style within the hierarchy might change with time, but the use of pottery as a generic whole did not. Bradley suggests that 'virtually all of the ceramic styles of the second millennium could have played rather specialised roles' (1984a, 72). I suggest that a more radical reading of this statement is necessary than is perhaps implied: the possibility needs to be entertained that different styles of pottery were used in quite different practices, each of which might be engaged in social relations in a quite different way. The display of social standing might represent only one such option.

It is necessary to emphasise before going any further the somewhat obvious point that 'pottery' is a category of evidence recognised by twentieth-century archaeologists. That all baked clay containers were classified as elements of a single class of artefacts by Neolithic people is an unwarranted assumption, even in synchronic terms. Diachronically, the possibility that pots 'meant' the same thing to a person living at 3000 bc as they would to his or her descendant a thousand years later seems scarcely credible. Thus the word 'pottery' must be read as if written *sous rature*: it adequately describes a class of evidence existing in the present, yet is inadequate to express the potentially dispersed and unstable meaning of fired clay vessels at different times in prehistory. In this chapter I will present a study of a group of material whose unity can only be guaranteed in the present: all of the indications are that what that material was used for, and how it was considered, changed and shifted repeatedly in the period under study.

### Things as texts

The notion of material culture as being analogous to a written text is by now familiar enough in archaeology (Patrik 1985; Moore 1986; Hodder 1988; Tilley 1989), while the 'reading' of constructed space was a major theme in an earlier chapter of this book. What I should like to do in this section is to draw out some of the consequences of such a perspective for the evaluation of portable artefacts. What aspects of mobiliary items are deserving of particular note by the archaeologist? In our own society, the potential

Figure 5.1   Earlier Neolithic pottery

of inanimate things to convey messages or to introduce particular connotations into discourse is undeniable, and is one which has been thoroughly manipulated by the advertising industry (Baudrillard 1988). Nevertheless, it may be that our own social circumstances lead us to underestimate the role of material things in signification. The opposition between words and things may be a Western peculiarity (Appadurai 1985, 4), as much a legacy of Platonic systems of thought as is the priority of speech over writing. One way of explaining this is as a consequence of the development of literacy: where writing exists, other forms of material culture may be less important for the storage and preservation of ideas (Llamazares 1989, 242). But alternatively, we might choose to locate the difference in the interrelated processes of alienation, objectification and commodification (Miller 1987), the creation of the 'thingness' of things. The rupture of the social relationships surrounding material things which this precipitates curtails the ability of people to use them to 'think through' the reality which surrounds them. Hence the structure of analogue and homology which Lévi-Strauss (1966) defines as characteristic of the 'savage mind' may have been lost in gaining the ability to contemplate objects in a more 'objective' way. This indicates one more way in which capitalism stands out as entirely anomalous in world history, in the way that it constitutes objects and subjectivity (Giddens 1981).

It follows from this that we might expect artefacts to function in non-capitalist societies less as things to be thought *about*, in quantitative terms, than as things to be thought *with*, in qualitative terms. Speech, writing and material things should be

Figure 5.2    Peterborough Ware

considered not so much as alternatives than as part of a unity of discourse. Speech possesses a certain immediacy, while writing preserves discourse, making of it an archive for individual and collective memory (Ricoeur 1981, 197). Yet where neither words nor things can be separated from a social context, the division between them becomes less clear. Both belong, first and foremost, to a discourse, which *says* things about people (either face-to-face or in their absence), and which in the process creates the spaces in which their identities are formed.

One positive point which arises from the suggestion that all aspects of discourse are interlinked is the likelihood that a common set of structuring principles will underlie the material and the linguistic order of a given culture (Shanks and Tilley 1987b, 153). In thinking the world in both abstract and concrete terms, people impose a set of categories upon reality (Hawkes 1972, 84). The other side of this coin is that the interpretation of material things will be at least as difficult as that of utterances and written texts. In a language, Derrida tells us, there are no positive terms, only differences (1986, 403): 'The signified concept is never present in and of itself, in a sufficient presence that would refer only to itself. Essentially and lawfully, every concept is inscribed in a chain or in a system within which it refers to the Other, to other concepts, by means of the systematic play of differences' (1986, 404).

With material things, one might hope that it would be easier: one can touch and hold a pot or a stone axe. Yet the problem is that we generally want to know more than that the meaning of a pot is 'pot'. If, to give Hodder's (1986, 21) example, we want to make statements of the order of 'this fibula functions to symbolise women', one is necessarily taking the artefact to refer to a signified which is absent from itself. Material culture is thus, no less than spoken language, caught up in an endless process of the deferral of meaning, in which one can never encounter a signified, only more signifiers (Derrida 1986, 402). Just like words, the meanings of things are determined less by what they are than by what they are not, by a structured grid of absences (Shanks and Tilley 1987a, 103). Interpreting any one item thus becomes very like the reading of a text: it requires a hermeneutic act on the part of the reader. One must enter into the act of the construction of meaning, rather than merely abstracting a meaning which is somehow locked into the artefact itself. Meaning is thus dispersed endlessly through the web of relations between things. The native, steeped in a particular tradition of reading, routinely performs such hermeneutic acts as part of the process of day-to-day life. The act of the archaeologist, too, is one of reading and interpretation (Hodder 1988, 68), yet taking place from a different cultural context can hardly be of the same order.

If discourse forms a unity, the production and deployment of material items has to be seen as part of the process by which a society continually brings itself into being (Barrett 1988a, 7). Material things may sometimes convey overt messages, but equally often they form a 'frame', conditioning the way in which verbal and gestural exchanges may proceed (Miller 1987, 102; Tilley 1989, 189). Things create the context for discourse, but are themselves 'read' and interpreted in a setting, and may change their meaning according to context. In structuring the context of discourse, material culture thus contributes to the creation of unconsidered or habitual attitudes through 'inattentive' readings. Material culture has a continuum of significance between 'background' and 'foreground' meanings. The ways that items are deployed to build up a context, knowingly or not, may thus do much to give a natural or unquestioned character to essentially conventional arrangements (Shanks and Tilley 1987a, 112). In this way, the creation of a material context for society may contribute much to social reproduction.

Most of the foregoing applies as much to stationary objects as to portable artefacts. What distinguishes the latter is the potential for 'play' (in both senses of the word) afforded by bringing artefacts into different configurations, in which each object provides the context in which each other is to be interpreted. An apt example of this kind of practice can be found in Turner's study of the Ndembu Isoma ritual (1969, 39). By bringing certain objects into a ring of consecrated space, the Ndembu feel that they bring with them certain powers and virtues which they possess. By bringing these items together, the ritual makes the qualities which they seem to represent manipulable. So while architecture may provide the settings for action, artefacts can be orchestrated within these settings to provide more detailed and explicit contexts for social discourse. As Turner suggests, the play or bricolage of such deployment involves the evocation of particular meanings from a potentially limitless repertoire: the appreciation of a given configuration of artefacts again depends upon inculcation into a tradition of interpretation.

Just as with spoken language, material discourse is able to evoke meanings from

Figure 5.3   Grooved Ware

multiple 'planes of signification' (Turner 1969) as a consequence of its ambiguity. The instability of meaning in language which Derrida describes, while it undermines the possibility of a definitive reading, actually makes discourse *possible*. 'All forms of discourse consciously or unconsciously exploit the polysemic potential of language to transmit ambiguous, undecidable meanings' (Reugg 1979, 146).

All language is hence fundamentally metaphorical, relying upon ambiguity to provide untranslatable information (Hawkes 1972, 64; de Man 1978, 29; Ricoeur 1978, 143). The same may be true of material items, which may become associated with personal or elemental qualities through either metaphor or metonymy (Ray 1987, 67). In this way material culture can act as both euphemism and mnemonic, pointing out what can or cannot be done or said by its presence. Hence in our own society, the parliamentary mace metonymically related to the person of royalty serves as a reminder of required decorum in debate. Equally, material items may subtly alter the nature of given interactions by their presence. Thus Ray (1988, 220) gives the example of Igbo-Ukwu ware, made by women as skeuomorphs of basketry (associated with female marketing activities), thereby introducing a symbol of female economic power into male-dominated ritual contexts. Equally, Barrett (1989) discusses the role of material things in signifying the actual presence of the person of the emperor, in the Roman imperial cult.

**Decoration and tradition**

When we turn to pottery, the particular concern of this chapter, two specific issues will be of importance. These are the question of the significance of decoration on ceramic vessels, and of how it is that the form and decoration of items like pots form discrete traditions of manufacture. It would be unwise to suggest that any generalised explanation for the decoration of material items can be produced. Interpretations which can be justified by ethnographic examples include the use of decoration as a means of displaying ethnic affiliation (DeBoer 1984, 550), as a symptom of social stress (Hodder 1979), or as a conceptual marker employed to bracket off defilement and pollution (Braithwaite 1982; Donley 1982). Decorative motifs, like the artefacts which bear them, have to be seen as essentially arbitrary signifiers. One particular aspect of decoration which has attracted much interest from archaeologists is the contrast between bounded and unbounded designs (e.g. Conkey 1982; Tilley 1984). Boundedness can be seen as a means of introducing discontinuity into design structure (Conkey 1982, 117), and thereby may even be interpreted as a means of halting the dispersal of meaning (Hodder 1988, 68). However, any suggestion that the bounded/unbounded division can be mapped universally onto an inside/outside, us/them dichotomy (Shanks and Tilley 1987b, 170) implies its status as a pan-human psychological binary opposition. Such an assumption may be unwarranted. Just as the decoration of pots need not always be an analogue for the decoration of the human body (Welbourne 1984; David, Sterner and Gavua 1988), so the option between bounded and unbounded designs is a latent opposition which can be employed to different ends in accordance with specific circumstances. This would suggest that an understanding of the significance of decoration within a given society will best be achieved through a genealogical approach, concentrating on the changing contexts in which designs are adopted and discarded.

Such an approach would have to come to terms with the notion of tradition as it applies to material culture. In Neolithic Britain one of the most striking features of the ceramic sequence is the relative stability of ways of making and decorating pots over centuries or even millennia. Given the plasticity of the medium, the integrity of these traditions is most surprising, even if it is perfectly in sympathy with the findings of some ethnohistoric studies (DeBoer 1984, 557). By contrast with the other technologies of the time, like stone or antler working, pottery presents an almost limitless set of possibilities for vessel forms, decorative techniques and motifs. The identity of ceramic traditions is thus less a consequence of what is included than of what is excluded as a legitimate way of making a pot. Sets of rules seem to have existed at one level or another which guaranteed continuity in the face of dispersal. A further set of problems lies in the observations that, firstly, certain motifs may be shared by different ceramic traditions, yet their means of execution are relatively distinctive, and secondly, that the motifs found on Neolithic and Bronze Age pottery in Britain (and, for that matter, a range of associated items like passage grave art, and metalwork) are entirely non-representational.

Whatever the specific reasons for such stability, the presence of a group of relatively unchanging artefacts which functioned in a number of important spheres of human activity would have been directly involved in the continuity of social reproduction. If the shapes, sizes and decoration of pots had any specific meanings attributed to them, the constant cycle of ceramic production and use would serve to recreate those meanings and to locate them in highly repetitive social activities. Pottery is a social production rather than the strategic creation of a decontextualised intelligence, and would always be produced in relation to what had been made in the past. Without pre-conceived plans to that effect, then, pots would fix meanings in time.

The integrity of these traditions becomes more significant when we consider the evidence for their use alongside each other. Figure 5.4 summarises the radiocarbon evidence for the use of different ceramic styles in southern Britain. Plain bowl vessels of the Grimston and Hembury traditions seem to have been in use from the start of the Neolithic, and multiple dates indicate their survival until the later part of the third millennium. Regionalised decorated styles of pottery (Abingdon, Windmill Hill, Whitehawk, Mildenhall) may be almost as early in their origin, perhaps going out of use by the mid-third millennium. The currency of Peterborough Wares is equivocal: several dates exist for the mid-third millennium, and several for the period 1700–1600 bc. The gap between them can probably be attributed to accidents of deposition and retrieval. If so, the Peterborough tradition must be singularly long-lived, covering a period of more than a millennium. Grooved Ware and Beakers, by contrast, both present date spreads indicative of sudden introduction, use and decline in popularity, with the former style perhaps merging gradually into the Deverel–Rimbury tradition (Barrett 1980). What is significant to note is the degree of chronological overlap between several of these styles, and the need to explain it.

A first line of enquiry is to consider the different types of contexts from which pottery

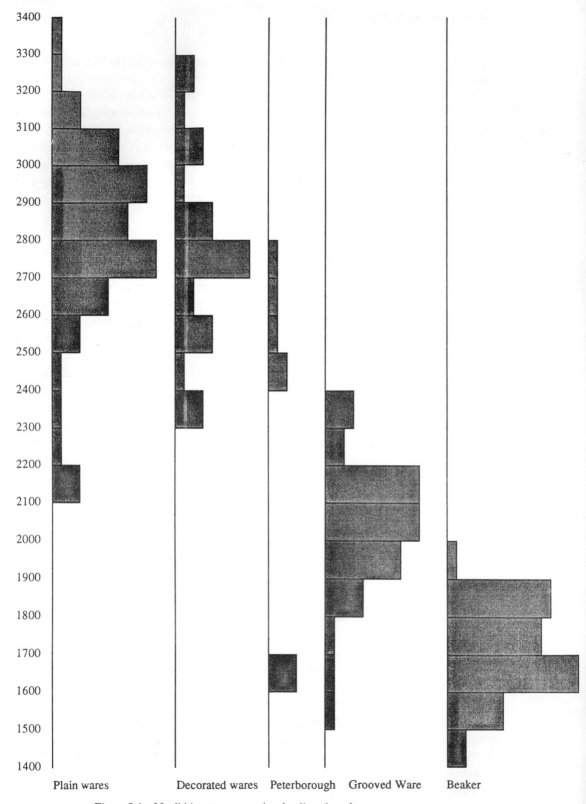

Figure 5.4    Neolithic pottery: associated radiocarbon dates

of these various styles has been recovered. These will be discussed in more detail below, but the immediate point to note is the occurrence of earlier Neolithic wares in a wide variety of contexts compared with the concentration of later Neolithic styles in a more restricted range of (sometimes mutually exclusive) depositional loci. What this might be taken to suggest is that by the later part of the Neolithic particular styles of pottery were engaged in restricted spheres of practice. That is to say, by the later Neolithic individual pot types were used for a more limited range of purposes. The full significance of this observation will be clearer in the context of a chronological discussion of the development of pottery through the Neolithic.

## Earlier Neolithic pottery

The manufacture and use of pottery vessels seems to have been a cultural innovation adopted as part of an interconnected set of ideas and practices which define the earlier Neolithic period in Britain. The earlier Neolithic pottery of Britain can be subdivided into three main groups: the plain, globular lugged vessels of the Hembury or South-Western style; the plain, carinated bowls of the Grimston or Eastern style; and a variety of regional groups with largely incised decoration, known variously as the 'south-eastern' or 'decorated' style (Smith 1974; Whittle 1977; Drewett 1980). The relative chronology of these styles is far from clear on the basis of the available radiocarbon dates. However, both the Grimston and Hembury styles find direct continental parallels in Michelsberg and Chasséen ceramics respectively, while attempts to find an origin for the decorated wares in the Rössen (Whittle 1977, 128) are both vague on stylistic grounds and chronologically untenable. Hence it seems apt to suggest that there is a degree of chronological priority attributable to the two plain ware styles, and that the decorated styles developed indigenously, even if this process took place within a generation of the first Neolithic presence in Britain. This would tend to explain why it is that the plain vessels encountered within the 'decorated' assemblages fit comfortably within the 'parent' plain styles, plain Whitehawk and Windmill Hill vessels being attributable to the Hembury style, plain Mildenhall vessels fitting into Grimston.

If we accept this chronological sequence, we have to explain why it was that the earliest pottery in this country was exclusively undecorated. This can best be done by considering the role of decoration on earlier Neolithic ceramics in continental Europe. One aspect of the trend towards regionalisation which is implicit in later Bandkeramik society is the development of regionalised traditions of band infill on pottery (Hodder 1982b; Starling 1985a). A reasonable interpretation is that pottery decoration in this and subsequent periods bore some relationship to the expression of ethnic identity, and that groups like Grossgartach, Hinkelstein and Cerny actually constituted ethnic entities by the earlier fourth millennium bc. Given such a background, the appearance of distinctive forms of undecorated pottery in western Europe, coinciding with a massive geographical expansion of the Neolithic way of life (Thomas 1988a), is intriguing. One possible explanation is that unmarked vessels, not closely identified with a particular social group, would be more able to circulate between different social contexts. Thus the exchange and replication of these vessels, bearing with them particular connotations concerning food, its preparation and consumption (Nielsen

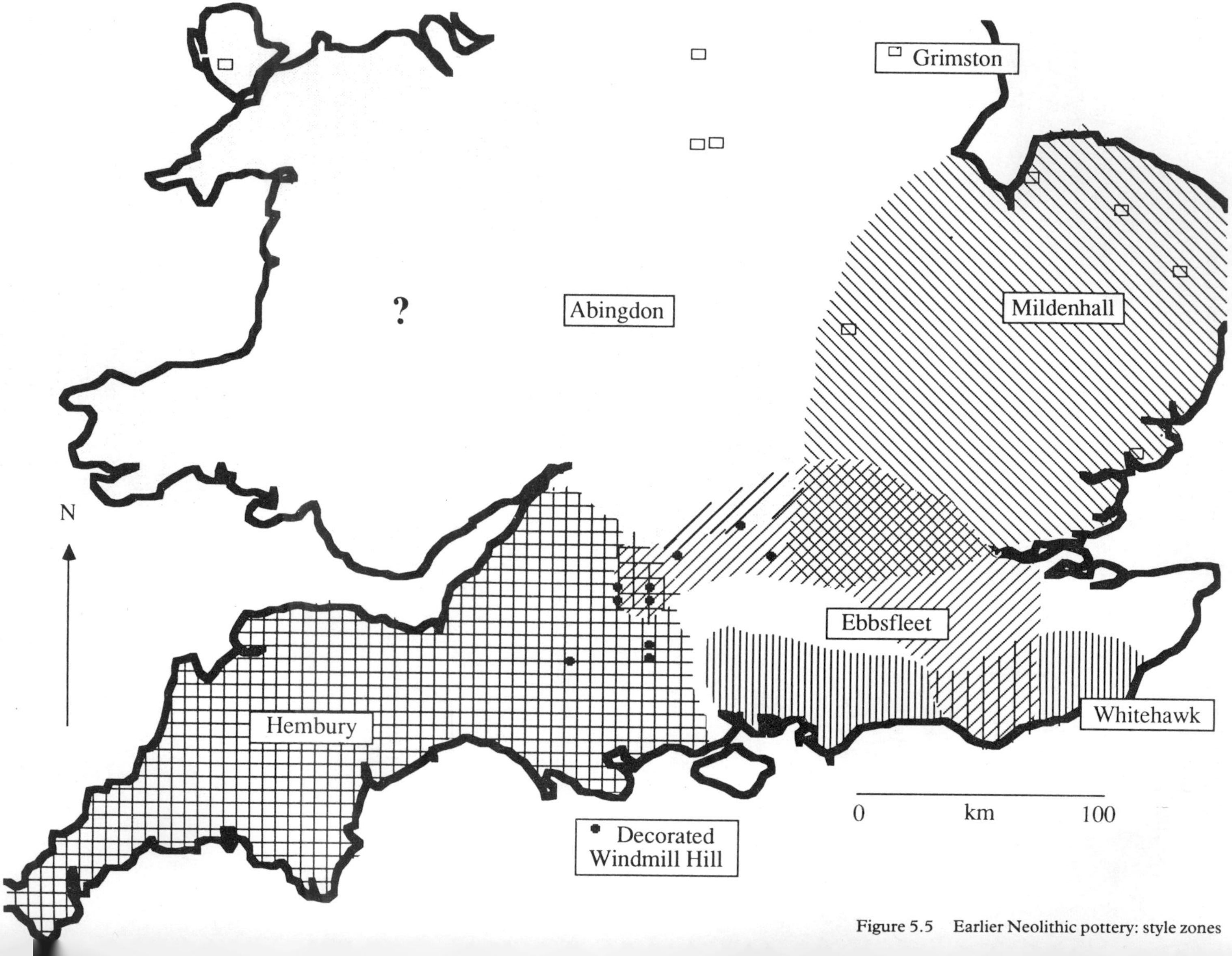

Figure 5.5  Earlier Neolithic pottery: style zones

1986; Herne 1988), would be instrumental in the spread of the Neolithic. Equally, fine plain vessels continued to be exchanged over considerable distances throughout the earlier Neolithic. It may have been their unmarked character which allowed them to be used by different social groups spatially distinct from each other.

The Grimston and Hembury traditions would hence owe their separate identities to the development of two spheres of contact between Britain and the continent at the inception of the Neolithic: one linking the south-west peninsula with north-west France, and one connecting the rest of the country with northern Europe and the Low Countries. These zones of contact may be identified in monumental as well as ceramic traditions, particularly in the morphology of causewayed enclosures. The development of decoration on pottery in the insular context seems, again, to have taken place on a regional basis. Styles like Abingdon, Mildenhall, Whitehawk and Windmill Hill each occur within geographically bounded areas (Fig. 5.5), even if these tend to merge and overlap at their peripheries (Smith 1956, 15). Decoration seems to have been applied preferentially to particular kinds of vessels: as the Windmill Hill figures suggest (Fig. 5.6), there is a distinct tendency for shouldered bowls to be decorated (a point noted by Piggott 1931, 78). Decorated pots are not always necessarily the finest vessels in a given assemblage, hence the suggestion that the regional decorated styles represent a 'fine ware' component stratified over the 'coarse wares' of the Hembury and Grimston traditions is too simplistic. On the contrary, the latter are often carefully finished vessels (Herne 1988, 25), and were often those which were exchanged over large distances (Peacock 1969). It may be necessary to cast off the impression that decoration on pottery is universally concerned with 'display' (e.g. Pierpoint 1979). As suggested earlier, decoration can be 'read' in a variety of ways. In all likelihood, the deployment of decoration on earlier Neolithic pottery related to the uses to which particular types of vessels were put.

The wide range of vessel forms is one of the more distinctive features of earlier Neolithic pottery. Modern ethnoarchaeological studies of pottery use have shown that it will often be the shapes and sizes of vessels, rather than their decoration, which form the basis for their classification (Miller 1982; Welbourne 1984). If this were the case with earlier Neolithic ceramics, it would follow that particular vessel types, used for different purposes or bearing different connotations, would be differentially represented in different kinds of contexts. A study of fifty assemblages of pottery from southern Britain as a whole indicates precisely this (Fig. 5.7). Reconstructable vessels were classified according to whether or not they were shouldered, and whether they were open, neutral or closed. Open, unshouldered bowls, which might be most well suited to the consumption of food and drink, were well represented in causewayed enclosure, long mound and isolated pit assemblages. By contrast, 'open sites' (some of which may conceivably be equated with domestic activity) contained far more of both closed and shouldered vessels. Examples would include the assemblages from several East Anglian coastal sites (Warren *et al.* 1936). This combination of vessel forms, perhaps indicating hanging-bowls and pots which could be sealed with a fabric or leather cover, would be more suitable for the storage of food. The complexities of the use of particular vessel types are doubtless far greater than such a crude analysis would indicate, but the demonstration that particular assemblages may be better suited to consumption or storage at least suggests that the various forms of pot made in the earlier Neolithic were distinguished between by those who used them.

### Peterborough Wares

Some of the foregoing observations concerning earlier Neolithic pottery are of significance to the origin of Peterborough Wares. Different vessel forms were used for different purposes, while some of these vessel forms were more likely to be decorated than others. By implication, the decoration of a vessel might be taken to be related to its context of use. The emergence of Peterborough ceramics in the early to mid-third millennium has often been seen as a development out of earlier Neolithic styles (Smith 1966), possibly with Ebbsfleet Ware (its earliest form) initially constituting a regional decorated style in the Lower Thames (Smith 1974, 112; Kinnes 1978). However, the indications are that the area in which the Ebbsfleet style developed is rather wider than this would imply, vessels conforming to Smith's criteria for 'early' Ebbsfleet being widespread in East Anglia (Cleal 1986, 122) and also present at Coombe Hill in Sussex (Smith 1956). Equally, the evident merging of earlier Neolithic and Ebbsfleet traits at Windmill Hill (Smith 1965a, Fig. 29) may indicate the involvement of the area at the headwaters of the Kennet in this process. The basic chronological sequence of Peterborough Wares, in which the emergence of the Ebbsfleet style is succeeded by that of the Mortlake and finally Fengate (Smith 1956; 1974), can probably still be adhered to. However, it is extremely unlikely that each style neatly replaces its

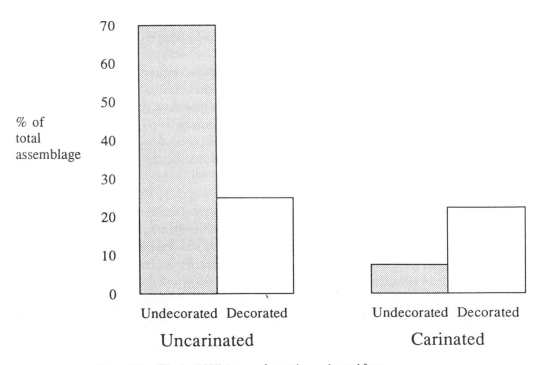

Figure 5.6   Windmill Hill pottery: decoration and vessel form

predecessor. Longworth (1961) noted that Mortlake traits were still in circulation, to be translated into the emerging Collared Urn tradition in the early second millennium bc, while several relatively late radiocarbon dates for the Ebbsfleet style and the stratification of all three styles of Peterborough Ware together in the palisade trench at Mount Pleasant (dated to 1695±43 bc), indicate their use alongside each other. The longevity of the substyles probably indicates that they were not entirely inter-changeable, and had relatively distinct meanings.

   The continuity from earlier Neolithic ceramics through to Peterborough Wares is more than circumstantial, and extends to decoration and vessel forms. An analysis of the volumes of a number of vessels of various styles (using a method similar to that described by Barrett: 1980, 316) shows very clearly that Peterborough Wares have not only the same general range of sizes as decorated earlier Neolithic pots, but that

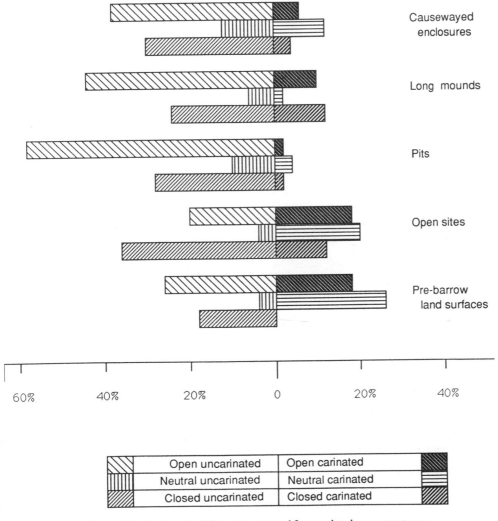

Figure 5.7   Earlier Neolithic pottery: vessel forms related to context types

similar size classes may exist in the two traditions (Fig. 5.8). The vessel form of Peterborough Wares is almost exclusively the shouldered bowl, which was the most frequently decorated form within the earlier Neolithic assemblage. Equally, the structure of decoration on Peterborough Wares is similar to that on the earlier pottery: exclusively unbounded designs concentrated on the rim and upper body of the vessel. While Peterborough Wares use a much wider variety of media (twisted and whipped cord, bird-bone impressions, etc.) and motifs (diagonals, herringbone), the decoration can be seen as a development of the same basic structure of design: the repetition of forms to fill an unbounded space, presumably starting from the top of the vessel. The chronological development of decoration through the successive styles of Peterborough Ware fundamentally consists of the filling of more of the surface of the vessel, an increase in the number of media employed on a given vessel, and a more formal arrangement of motifs on the vessel surface. This may involve the use of patterns of symmetry centred on the horizontal divisions of the vessel: the rim (or collar) or carination. The culmination of this process may be seen in Fengate assemblages like that from Astrop, Northamptonshire (Smith 1956).

In essence, then, the origin of Peterborough Ware lies in the abstraction of one element from the earlier Neolithic ceramic repertoire (the decorated shouldered bowl) and its elaboration. Such continuity with the past may have been an explicit manipulation of tradition. This much is indicated by the contexts in which Peterborough pottery was deposited (Fig. 5.9). Peterborough Ware is common in secondary contexts on established monumental sites: long mounds, causewayed enclosures, round barrows, ring ditches and cursus monuments. However, it is extremely rare as an accompaniment for burials. This would indicate a concern not with the recently deceased but with the ancestral dead, and with the veneration of places whose origin lay in the past. Of further significance is the deposition of Peterborough vessels in wet places, most notably the lower reaches of the Thames (numerous examples in Smith 1956). This again indicates a continuity of practice with the earlier Neolithic: Peterborough Wares are the only later Neolithic/Early Bronze Age ceramics frequently located in rivers and bogs, while the carinated vessels from the Sweet Track (Coles and Orme 1979, 52) indicate that this vessel form had been appropriate to that depositional practice in the earlier Neolithic. All of this contributes to an impression of continuity between earlier Neolithic ceramics and Peterborough Wares.

It is the use of a pottery vessel which constitutes its 'reading', and here meaning is actively created. If the use of Peterborough pottery was often in circumstances which evoked the past, this need not mean that decorated pottery continued to have the same meaning in the later half of the third millennium bc. The dissolution of the 'style zones' of the earlier Neolithic would indeed suggest otherwise, and the more generalised distributions of the Peterborough styles indicate that pottery decoration did not by now relate to the divisions between regional social or ethnic entities. It is obvious to suggest that, instead, pottery was being employed to signify discontinuity between individuals within groups or between distinguishable spheres of practice. This seems to accord with the more restricted set of contexts in which the pottery was deposited.

**Grooved Ware**

From some time before 2200 bc onwards, the pottery in use in southern Britain was augmented by the addition of the Grooved Ware tradition. While Peterborough Wares have been used to argue continuity from the earlier Neolithic, Grooved Ware contrasts with other contemporary and earlier ceramics in almost every way imaginable. Grooved Ware vessels are flat-bottomed, a trait absent from earlier ceramics in southern Britain. Their tub and bucket shapes are also entirely innovatory, as is the range of volumes represented. While relatively few Grooved Ware vessels have reconstructable profiles, these show no evidence of the clustering at 1500 cc or less exhibited by both earlier Neolithic and Peterborough Wares (Fig. 5.8). Furthermore, they show a continuous size range up to about 40,000 cc, almost twice the maximum volume of other styles of pottery. The extremely large vessels from Durrington Walls (Wainwright and Longworth 1971, 82) do not seem to be exceptional. This immediately suggests some major difference in the way in which the vessels were used, a proposition supported by the indication that Grooved Ware was used in communal feasting within henge monuments (Richards and Thomas 1984). Since larger vessels would be less likely to be reconstructable than small, we can argue that the admittedly small sample of vessel volumes gives an accurate impression that Grooved Ware assemblages were not dominated by vessels suitable for one person to eat out of. By implication, if Grooved Ware vessels were ever used for serving food, it would have been on a communal rather than individual basis.

The distinctiveness of Grooved Ware is also noticeable in its fabric and colour (Smith 1956, 191). Yet it is in terms of decoration that the separateness of Grooved Ware from other ceramics is most marked. Rather than adding elements into the undifferentiated space of the vessel surface, Grooved Ware decoration proceeds by dividing space into bounded units and decorating each separately. As Hardin (1984, 578) suggests, this is a fundamental choice in the way that decoration is executed. Grooved Ware design, then, is analytic, splitting up field space and manipulating it. This has consequences for the sequence of actions involved in decorating the vessel, and it may not be too extreme to suggest a complete difference in the way in which the potter conceptualised his or her task. A major break with the past is thus indicated. 'The presence of applied decoration and extensive use of cordons is basic to this problem for there is no satisfactory antecedent for these features in the known Middle Neolithic pottery of the British Isles' (Wainwright and Longworth 1971, 246).

To an extent the novelty of Grooved Ware is a consequence of its introduction to southern Britain from outside. The presently available radiocarbon evidence indicates that Grooved Ware existed in the Orkney Islands one or two centuries earlier than in southern England (Renfrew 1979, 205–8; Clarke 1983, 55). Curiously, whilst it is arguable that Grooved Ware originated in northern Scotland and/or the Orkneys, many of the motifs borne by the pots can be traced back to Irish passage grave art (Richards and Thomas 1984, 192–3). Bradley's hypothesis (1989) that these abstract symbols may in turn be derived from entoptic phenomena experienced in trance states is interesting, as is his earlier observation that 'The Grooved Ware assemblage forms a link between a series of separate regions whose monuments

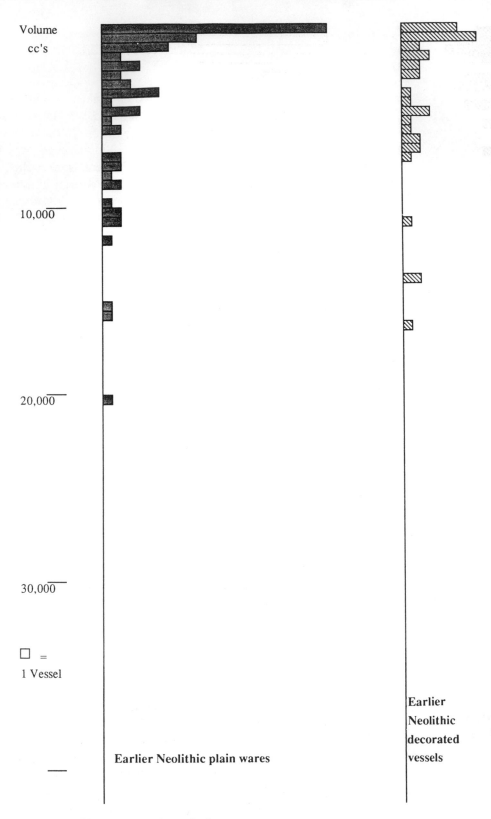

Volume
cc's

10,000

20,000

30,000

☐ =
1 Vessel

Earlier Neolithic plain wares

Earlier
Neolithic
decorated
vessels

Figure 5.8    Neolithic pottery: vessel volumes

94

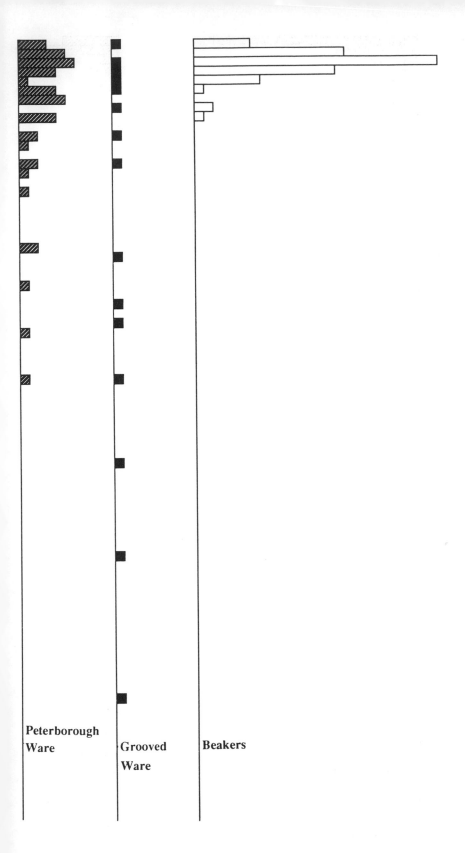

Peterborough
Ware

Grooved
Ware

Beakers

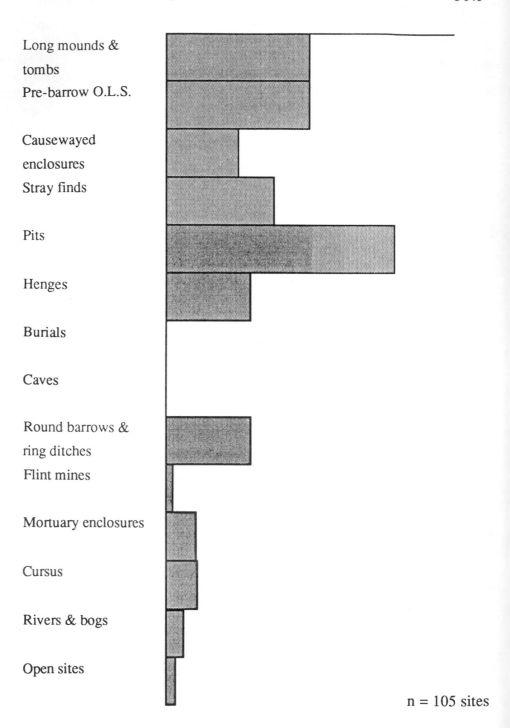

Figure 5.9    Peterborough pottery: contexts of deposition

do not show the same detailed resemblances as the artefacts found within them' (1982, 35).

Analysis of the locations of particular designs within the Irish passage graves (Fig. 5.10, based upon data from Shee Twohig 1981) suggests that those motifs which were adopted for use on Grooved Ware were not a random selection. Both lozenges and spirals are found predominantly on portal stones, defining the division between separate areas of space. The evident connections between life and death, changing states of consciousness and changing position in space are provocative indeed. The distribution of these symbols in different geographical areas, executed in entirely different media, yet consistently deployed in boundary locations (Bradley 1989, 74), suggests a sharing of meaning rather than of purely decorative traits. If the motifs in the passage graves contributed to the subjective experience of space as the individual moved through the tomb, their transfer onto mobiliary media would seem to indicate the evocation of similar meanings in non-tomb contexts. The exotic nature of Grooved Ware in southern Britain might mean that this principally took the form of making immanent distant and hence mysterious persons or beings in ritual and/or domestic transactions. More specifically, the conditions of division and transition might be recognised, the very act of interpreting the symbols contributing to the

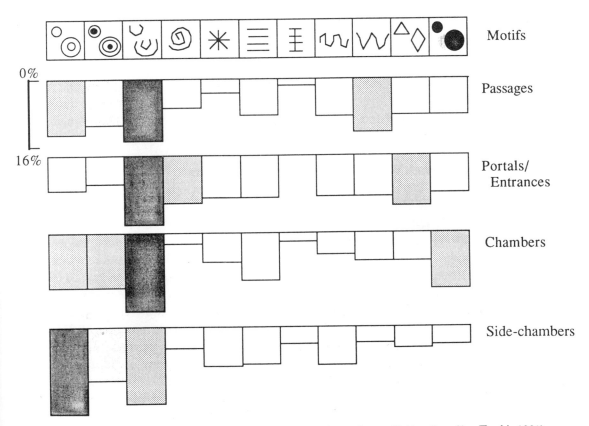

Figure 5.10   Irish passage tombs: distribution of decorative motifs (data from Shee Twohig 1981)

creation of a significance for a place or event. This much seems to be indicated at Durrington Walls, where the decoration of sherds varies according to location within the henge, principally in respect of the presence or absence of bounded designs on pots and their decoration (Richards and Thomas 1984, 197–204). Thus the use of the vessels in feasting or other activities would be actively engaged in the production of the meaning of the monument, by indicating an appropriate tenor of conduct.

More speculatively, if we were to accept the interpretation of some of the motifs as representations of phenomena encountered in trance states, a further strand can be added to the argument. The qualities being 'presenced' through the use of Grooved Ware vessels could include connotations of the otherworldly. While Lewis-Williams and Dowson (1988) claim entoptic phenomena to be universal productions of the human nervous system, their *interpretation*, like that of any other aspect of the natural world, is bound to be culturally specific. Hence it would be inappropriate to suggest that these motifs signified the realm of the ancestors, contact with a spirit world, or merely the pleasures of mind expansion, without more detailed contextual information.

A degree of confirmation for some of these suggestions comes from considering the differences between the various styles of Grooved Ware, as defined by Wainwright and Longworth (1971, 236–43). While 'boundary' motifs like lozenges, circles and spirals are present on the Durrington Walls, Clacton and Rinyo styles, they are absent from the Woodlands style. In the study area, Durrington Walls and Woodlands pottery are both common. Both are extremely restricted in their contexts of deposition (Fig. 5.11), yet in the case of Woodlands there is an almost total emphasis on isolated pits like those at Lechlade (Jones 1976) and Woodlands itself (Stone and Young 1948), in contrast with henges. While one would not wish to deny that the ladder-patterns, knots and dots of Woodlands pottery had a significance of their own, it would seem that this was not one appropriate to the monumental context.

### Peterborough Ware, Grooved Ware and Beakers

Having considered Peterborough and Grooved Wares separately, further insights may be gained by assessing the implications of their chronological overlap. The Peterborough tradition appears to have survived for the best part of a millennium, and it is not always easy to distinguish an 'early' from a 'late' vessel on typological grounds. Thus what Smith (1974) would classify as 'early' Ebbsfleet Ware was found associated with Beaker material at Clacton (Cleal 1986, 124). This seems to indicate a strongly conservative element in the manufacture and decoration of these vessels. A similar theme of continuity with the past is indicated by the use of Peterborough Wares in practices which evoke the ancestral dead and make use of old monuments. Nevertheless, Peterborough Ware does not seem to have been a predominantly funerary ceramic (*contra* Burgess 1980, 41), not being in frequent association with the emergent group of individual burials in flat graves, round barrows and ring ditches (Kinnes 1979). (The occurrence of Peterborough Ware with cave burials in various parts of the British Isles only serves to complicate the issue.)

The introduction of Grooved Ware to the south of England from further north has

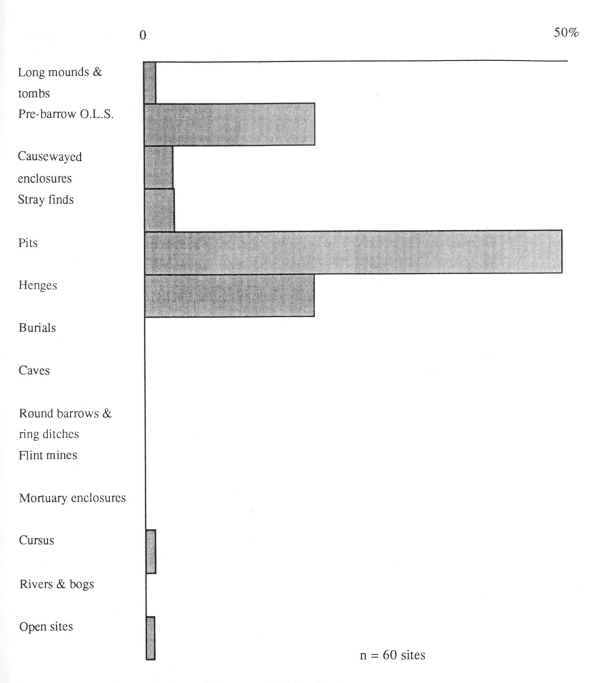

Figure 5.11    Grooved Ware: contexts of deposition

made it possible for the issue of its role to be clouded by considerations of population movement or invasion (Ashbee 1978). Similarly, it has been possible to present the users of Grooved Ware as a separate 'culture' or subculture (Wainwright and Longworth 1971), an option which contributes little towards explanation. In the British Isles as a whole it is evident that the latter half of the third millennium bc saw the establishment of parallel ceramic traditions specific less to region than to context. Thus in Ireland one has the coexistence of the Sandhills styles with Carrowkeel Ware, the latter being concentrated in tomb contexts (Case 1963; ApSimon 1986, 6). In Orkney, Grooved Ware came into use alongside the extant Unstan tradition, and it is evident that each style has distinctive domestic and funerary architectural associations (Richards 1988, 43). It is reasonable to suggest that, both in these cases and in southern England, people would have been aware of the existence and significance of different types of pottery. This being the case, one can only assume that the contrast between traditional, conservative Peterborough Ware and exotic, alien Grooved Ware was one which was fully appreciated at the time. The appearance of Grooved Ware in henges, a class of monuments which only developed in the later third millennium, and its total absence from long mound contexts indicates the same traditional/exotic opposition. What seems equally possible is that from the time that Grooved Ware was adopted in southern England onwards, the duality which it constituted with Peterborough Ware was employed as a convenient means of 'thinking through' social reality. Just as Lévi-Strauss (1969) describes totemism as a way of structuring homologies between classes of persons and things, and just as sex and age may be employed as basic divisions onto which other kinds of oppositions may be mapped (La Fontaine 1978, 2; Harris 1978, 21; MacCormack 1980, 8), so we can argue that the division between these two pottery traditions and their associated artefactual assemblages (bone, stone and chalk items) provided part of a classificatory framework. This would allow particular different activities to be separated from each other spatially, conceptually and materially. Such a framework might prove necessary in a traditional society undergoing a slow process of transformation, in which different aspects of day-to-day existence had come to contradict each other. Shennan (1982), for instance, writes of the contrast between 'individualising' and 'group-oriented' ideologies in third millennium societies. Similarly, Thorpe and Richards contrast 'ritual authority' with 'prestige goods hierarchy' (1984, 67–8). In the Wessex context Peterborough and Grooved Wares are held to represent a secular/ritual division within society, Grooved Ware users controlling ritual practice and dominating 'lower status "big men" . . . and lower ranking elite lineages' (*ibid.*, 79). This interpretation has much to recommend it, yet runs the risk of too close an identification of 'people' with 'pots'. We can agree with some elements of the prognosis concerning the sources of tension within later third millennium society (control over communal ritual versus individual aggrandisement through exchange contacts and display of personal wealth) without necessarily seeing that society as being composed of two mutually antagonistic classes locked in conflict over a period of half a millennium. Rather, we might choose to see a society in which conflicting and contradictory resources existed to be drawn upon by individuals in the pursuit of power. It might easily be the same people who engaged in corporate large-scale feasting and ritual at the great henge monuments as were honoured by individual burial in barrows like those at Handley Hill or Linch Hill Corner. What is significant is that separate material repertoires existed for use in the context of mutually incompatible activities. Hence the deposition of Peterborough Ware vessels in wet places together with stone axes becomes explicable: this ceramic, and this ceramic only, was appropriate to that particular activity.

As has already been indicated, the distinction between Grooved Ware and Peterborough ceramics runs as far as their means of manufacture. The absence of seed impressions from Grooved Ware (Jones 1980) might suggest that the pots were made at a different time of year from other ceramics, or that a deliberate attempt was made to exclude particular kinds of matter. The latter explanation fits with the use of shell as the predominant filler in Grooved Ware and the deposition of marine shells in Grooved Ware pits: an effort to include the exotic and distant in the fabric of the pottery itself. Excluding organic material (seeds, etc.) from Grooved Ware is a parallel with the culture/nature division evident within the henge monuments (see Chapter 4). The opposite is clearly the case with Peterborough Ware, in which the natural, organic world is incorporated into the pot in the form of decoration: bird-bone, leather thong, vegetable fibre and twig or reed impressions. The introduction of Grooved Ware to southern Wessex thus allowed a whole series of overlapping binary classifications to be made manifest in material culture: outside versus inside (of henges); individual versus communal (in terms of the consumption of food); unbounded versus bounded; and possibly wet versus dry (rivers and bogs as against fires and ashy pit deposits). The deployment of the two traditions allowed both a physical and a conceptual separation to be maintained between mutually contra-dictory spheres of practice: communal feasts and the destruction of personal wealth, the inauguration of new monuments and the veneration or re-presentation of old.

Between 2000 and 1600 bc considerable social change appears to have taken place in Britain, associated with the adoption of Beaker pottery. Interpretations of the Beaker presence have varied between the migration of a continental population into Britain and the introduction of a foreign assemblage of status goods. Generally, the various accounts seem to agree that this was a gradual process and that the collapse of indigenous institutions and practices was not instantaneous with the Beaker arrival (Case 1977; Whittle 1981; Thorpe and Richards 1984; Shennan 1986; Shepherd 1986; etc.). Only after some centuries were large monuments abandoned and did individual burial beneath a round mound with grave goods become the dominant archaeologically detectable treatment of the dead. The interpretation of indigenous later Neolithic ceramics which has just been outlined lends a new complexion to these events. Beaker ceramics and their material associations developed outside Britain, conceivably from Corded Ware and TRB antecedents (Lanting and Van der Waals 1976). Becoming available in Britain through long-distance exchange ties they might immediately prove desirable in consequence of their novelty, their association with distant places, or even an appearance which might be judged attractive. Yet this kind of pottery would not fit into the binary categories structured by Grooved Ware and Peterborough Ware. Beaker pottery has a decorative structure similar to that of

Grooved Ware: the vessel is divided up into bounded units (yet horizontally rather than vertically) and then infilled with motifs which are often themselves closed panels and metopes. Significantly, while the basic structure of design remained largely the same through time, the development of insular traditions of Beaker manufacture in Britain involved the insertion of motifs from indigenous ceramics into these designs. Yet the vessels are overwhelmingly diminutive in volume, suggesting a specialised purpose (Fig. 5.8). Their original designation as 'drinking cups' may not be inaccurate (e.g. Hoare 1812). Furthermore, Beaker vessels are predominantly associated with the dead. Indeed, they are the first type of pottery in Britain which is routinely (rather than occasionally) associated with individual burials. This suggests a shift in the significance of pottery to something prestigious and desirable in itself, rather than as a bearer of symbols, meanings or particular contents. For a short time elaborately decorated and finely made pottery vessels were the prime material expression of personal prestige.

In short, Beaker pottery disrupted the material order of later Neolithic Britain. Beakers were conceptual anomalies which could move between different spheres of practice, and in so doing undermined their separation and exclusiveness. The social conditions which they ushered in were ones of confusion and contradiction, in which existing social tensions began to work themselves out. Consequently, the eventual effect was that new social and ritual discourses were able to become established.

## Conclusion

Portable artefacts, as one element of discourse, do not merely reflect but are involved in the emergence of new social circumstances. On the interpretation presented here, this was the case with pottery in Neolithic Britain. Moreover, the exact role played by ceramics changed and shifted throughout the period. While the earlier Neolithic pottery was made in a variety of forms and over a range of volumes, this seems not to have been so in the later Neolithic and Early Bronze Age. Peterborough Ware, Grooved Ware and Beakers were each made in a very restricted set of shapes, and may have been used for quite restricted purposes. All of these three traditions are probably grossly overrepresented in the archaeological record, since they entered it not by chance but by intention. Grooved Ware and Peterborough Wares commonly were purposefully buried in pits, while the great majority of Beaker vessels have come from graves. The restriction of forms and purposeful deposition of pottery continued into the earlier Bronze Age, Food Vessels being rather similar in size to Beakers, while Collared Urns and Deverel–Rimbury vessels had much the same shapes and ranges of volumes as Grooved Ware. All of these are commonly found in funerary contexts. It would not be until the Late Bronze Age, with Barrett's 'post-Deverel–Rimbury' assemblage, that the variety of vessel shapes and sizes of the earlier Neolithic was regained (Barrett 1980). All of this points to the possibility that pottery was by no means used as a day-to-day medium for the preparation and consumption of food throughout the period under study. On the contrary, it seems that by the end of the third millennium it is plausible that its use was restricted to a group of more specialised transactions, culminating in the use of Beakers as vehicles for prestige expression.

# 6

# Mortuary practice

## Archaeological approaches to funerary practice

Burials of one form or another undoubtedly constitute one of the richest sources of evidence for the Neolithic in Britain. Given the amount of effort which has been expended on developing techniques of mortuary analysis in archaeology, it might be expected that these might yield much information concerning Neolithic society. However, it is clear that such methodologies are more often dictated by the preconceptions of the archaeologist than any other criteria. We thus have a dazzling battery of conceptual apparatus with which to interrogate the past, but the individual elements are grounded at a deep level in mutually antagonistic philosophies. Obviously, it is impossible to begin to operationalise these various forms of analysis without first considering one's own position in relation to these competing schemes.

Mortuary archaeology has always been carried out from within particular political and logical standpoints, and with the fulfilment of varying objectives in mind. Sir Richard Colt Hoare, in his *The Ancient History of Wiltshire*, purported to 'speak from facts not theory' (1812, 7), yet his views were obviously coloured by a romantic conception of the past. Hence particular monuments were designated by names like 'Druid Barrows'. Likewise, Thurnam (1869, 181) turned a sensibility fashioned by a classical education onto the problems of pits located beneath long barrows, and concluded that they had been the *bothroi* described by Homer as a means of communicating with the lower realms. With the close of the antiquarian phase of investigation, the emphasis in the study of burials changed from questions of religious belief to cultural affinity. Burials provided useful closed contexts for the mutual association of material traits, essential for the construction of grand culture-historic schemes (Chapman and Randsborg 1981, 3). Indeed, the theoretical orthodoxy of the time strictly denied the possibility of making inferences concerning ideational schemes on the basis of archaeological data (Hawkes 1954).

A dramatic revision of this point of view took place with the development of the 'New Archaeology' in the 1960s. The keystone of the position adopted by Binford (1964, 1965), Flannery (1968, 1972) and their contemporaries was the proposition that culture was an extrasomatic means of human adaptation. The alternative view, that common cultural traits arose as a consequence of shared values or beliefs, was rejected as 'normative'. Hence it has become a polemical exercise to demonstrate that *all* aspects of culture could be explained in terms of their adaptive significance. The task which Binford (1971) took on was to go to the very top of the Hawkesian 'ladder of inference', and show mortuary practice could be explained in adaptive terms. His researches, and those of Saxe (1970) and Tainter (1978), were intended to demonstrate that mortuary practice was a system of communication by which information about a deceased person was signalled to the living. By these means, the community might adapt to its changed circumstances. Where a society was more internally ranked, this could be 'read off' by discerning the differences in the degree of effort expended in the treatment of individual burials.

Clearly, these approaches fail to come to terms with the reality that societies rarely represent themselves in an undistorted way in death (Hodder 1982a, b; Parker-Pearson 1982; Shanks and Tilley 1982). For the purposes of this study a quite distinct means of investigating the significance of mortuary deposits is required.

## An approach to the archaeology of death

The task of reconstructing mortuary archaeology begins with the realisation that death and the dead are of different significance to different societies. We cannot simply consider the single vector of rank and hope that we have understood the social relations of a community. Societies, after all, 'do' a lot of other things beside being internally ranked. Furthermore, people do not bury themselves: mortuary activities are carried out by the living upon the bodies of the dead. It follows that the explanations for the performance of particular rites lie with the living and their attitude towards the dead. These attitudes will be highly variable, although we should agree with Binford that they are essentially social in nature. Why are the dead of little consequence to some societies, yet central to the existence of others? It is not sufficient to answer 'because of ideology'. If the dead can constitute an ideological resource, we have to ask why and under what circumstances this happens.

A partial answer is provided by Olivia Harris: 'any traditional agrarian society must be oriented towards the past. Land, the source of life, has been cleared, cultivated, improved and handed on from one generation to the next' (1982, 47). Where a state apparatus exists, with schools, police, hospitals, a legal system, a press and an army, the continuity of authority and resources from one generation to the next is assured. With hunters and gatherers, this kind of continuity is not required (Woodburn 1982). But between these two extremes are societies whose social reproduction is ensured through an orientation on the past. This requires that systems of prestige and marriage must themselves be rooted in continued relations with past generations.

Foucault (1977, 24) has emphasised 'the way in which the body itself is invested with power relations'. This point is critical. In studying the development of penal institutions through the eighteenth century, Foucault demonstrated the operation of a new 'technology of power' on the human body. 'Systems of punishment', he argued, 'are to be situated in a certain "political economy" of the body' (1977, 25). In the absolutist monarchical states, punishment had been a bloody spectacle, aimed at the destruction of the body, and designed to demonstrate the concentrated power of the ruler. By contrast, the system which replaced this aimed at the punishment of the soul through the discipline of the body. Foucault (*ibid.*, 137–43) showed how a new technology of discipline and surveillance allowed a new control over the body. Institutions like schools, hospitals, factories and asylums took the prison as their model, contributing to the control of the individual through supervision and through an organisation of architectural space which defined times and locations for particular activities (Hirst 1985). Within such 'panoptic' institutions, it was no longer possible for the individual to be aware of whether he or she was under observation at a given time: hence a complete discipline of the workforce was achieved. The body, at once an instrument of production, an agency of reproduction and a subject of domination, became 'useful' only when subjected (Foucault 1977, 25).

These conditions of total subjection (and subjectification) are clearly historically specific to the past two hundred years of the Western experience. However, the human body is always intimately bound up with the networks of power extant within a given society. Foucault's comments on punishment also apply to mortuary practice: the treatment of the body in death will also vary with the technology of power. Mortuary ritual has a crucial role to play in societies which are based upon what Bloch (1974) calls 'traditional authority', where power relations are represented as part of an unchanging natural order. A number of authors (Huntingdon and Metcalf 1979, 5; Bloch and Parry 1982, 6) have already insisted that mortuary practices do not only merely reflect the values of a society, but are instrumental in the creation and repro- duction of society. A dead body is, of course, an entirely subject body, while ritual represents a situation in which a microcosm of the world can be manipulated within a bounded analytic space (Turner 1969, 39). Where control over the movements and actions of a living body in an uncontrolled and unbounded space cannot be achieved, therefore, the technology of power may be concentrated on ritual action, and particu- larly that which concerns the dead.

Death is a threat to the continuity of society (Bloch and Parry 1982, 4). However, the aim of mortuary ritual is to replace 'biological death' (where the organs cease to function) with 'social death' (where the individual ceases to be a person). Thus the impression is given that control exists over nature, and that people cease to live when their community decrees it so. This is very often achieved through a series of rites of passage, which mark the exit of a person from society, and perhaps their reincorpor- ation as an ancestor (Van Gennep 1960; Hertz 1960). Of course, the body itself serves as a symbol in these rites. The rotting of the flesh may serve as an homology for the gradual freeing of the soul (Huntingdon and Metcalf 1979, 54), for instance. But the ways in which this symbolism is constructed tend to be specific to the social and cultural circumstances of the community. This is because the inert bodies of the dead are at the mercy of those conducting the rites.

In death, the body may be presented in an idealised manner, as an image of the 'correct' appearance for a person of a particular age, sex and status (a point suggested by the analyses in Pader 1982). Alternatively, mortuary ritual may serve as an oppor- tunity for the conspicuous destruction of wealth – irrespective of the actual status of the deceased individual (Metcalf 1981). In contradiction to the view expressed by Tainter (1978), I should like to suggest that if mortuary ritual is a communication system, it tells us more about those who conducted the ritual than those who were buried. So while analyses of the sort carried out by Saxe or Tainter might reveal a structure in data concerning body treatment, grave goods or whatever, this structure

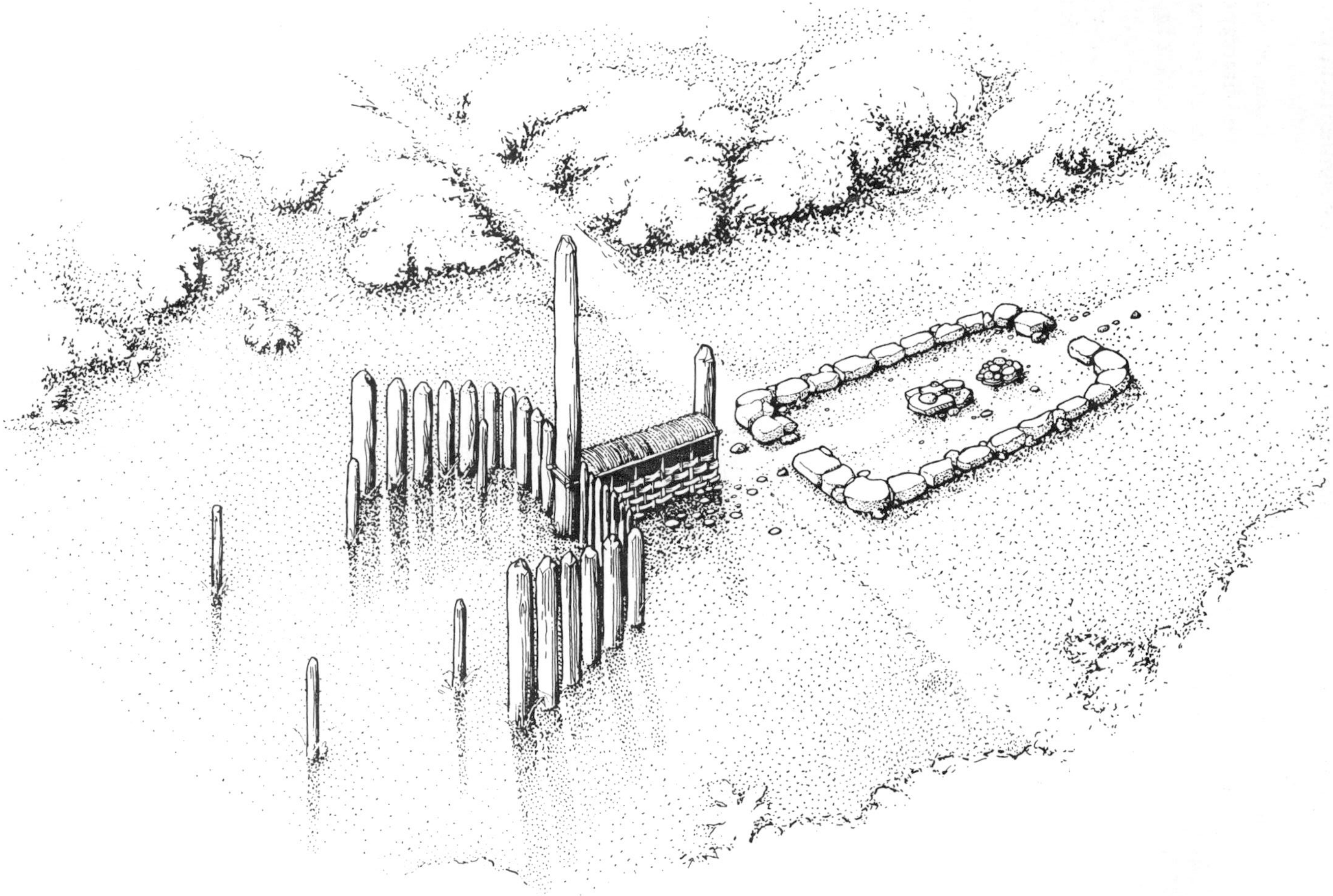

Figure 6.1    Timber mortuary structure (based on Streethouse: Vyner 1984)

need not indicate an undistorted map of the social relationships within the cemetery population.

The alternative is to take up the challenge of realising that the way in which the dead are projected in mortuary ritual is subject to what I shall call 'the strategy of representation'. They are shown to us not only through a fog of time, but also through the filter of the power strategies of their kin and contemporaries. This should not give cause for despair. Nor should it mean that the rigorous analysis of mortuary remains is worthless. Rather, we should realise exactly what it is that we are analysing. That is, we are studying a representation of society, not an objective polaroid image. It follows that one cannot hope to provide a complete reconstruction of a past society from mortuary evidence alone. What one can do is compare the way in which the dead have been treated with evidence for other activities in the hope of explaining the strategy behind the representation.

Given the central role which the dead occupy in the kind of society with which this book is concerned, it is likely that the scrutiny of the mortuary record will repay close study. Indeed, it makes it clearer why the dead have a higher archaeological profile than the living. This chapter will investigate in turn a variety of Neolithic mortuary practices. The essential aim of these analyses will be to consider the ways in which the representation of the dead varied from place to place and through time. It is important to point out before I begin that many of these practices overlapped both temporally and spatially. Consequently, it can be suggested that they represent alternative strategies for the treatment of the dead, rather than passive fossils of shared belief or cultural affinity.

## Long mounds

While the idea of a long mound designed for funerary purposes has its origin in the later phases of the Bandkeramik in Europe (Kinnes 1982; Hodder 1984; Midgeley 1985), the development of a much more specific set of rites can be observed in Britain and the North European Plain in the later fourth millennium bc (Jazdzewski 1973, 68). These involve the combination of the earthen long mound with a number of other structural elements. Chief amongst these is a simple chamber form consisting of an embanked linear zone bracketed and subdivided by wooden uprights (Kinnes 1975; 1979, 58). Such 'earth graves' are now familiar in Denmark, both as a part of the sequence of barrow construction, and equally often as independent self-supporting structures (Madsen 1979, 309).

Recent excavations like that at Streethouse Farm, Cleveland (Vyner 1984) have confirmed Kinnes' suggestion (1975, 19) that these structures were rather less complex than the ornate pitched wooden buildings envisaged by Ashbee (1970, 51). The timber and earth trough-like structure with blocked ends indicated at Streethouse (Vyner 1984, 161) would have enabled easy access to the mortuary deposit over the flanking banks, and thus would have allowed a degree of selection and manipulation of bones prior to the construction of the mound (Fig. 6.1; see Fig. 6.2 for preserved timber structure at Haddenham). There is, moreover, considerable evidence from the British barrows that these structures were open for a time before mound construction. At Kilham, the linear mortuary structure was far from being axial to the trapezoid palisade enclosure, and was thus probably built separately (Manby 1976, 123). Similarly, at Fussell's Lodge, the end pit of the mortuary structure was cut on both sides by the bedding trenches for an analogous structure, thus demonstrating its structural priority (Ashbee 1966). As with the Danish examples, we should not imagine that all of these linear chambers would inevitably be covered by a long mound. At New Wintles, Eynsham, one such linear structure was surrounded by small causewayed ditches, presumably the quarries for a low gravel mound (Kenward 1982). Likewise, several round barrows in Yorkshire contain linear crematorium structures (Kinnes 1979, 10–15).

A number of recurrent elements are found in association with the linear chamber. These are: a bedded timber façade of posts, transverse to the axis of the mound; avenues of posts aligned on the mortuary area; an enclosed area, either behind the mortuary zone or surrounding the chamber and connected with the façade. While these features might be combined in slightly different ways, the similarities between sites at great distances from each other are sufficient to suggest that what was done followed a system of rules (Fig. 6.3). In many cases the façade had been burnt *in situ*, often before the mound had been thrown up. At sites like Slewcairn, Lochill, Fussell's Lodge and Hanging Grimston, items of material culture were concentrated on the forecourt area, particularly pottery, which may have been purposefully smashed there (Madsen 1979, 307; Kinnes 1985, 36; Ashbee 1966, 20–1; Mortimer 1905, 102–5). Sometimes the uprights of the mortuary structure had themselves been burnt. Indeed,

Figure 6.2 The mortuary structure at Haddenham long barrow, Cambridgeshire (photo: Ian Hodder)

in most of the Yorkshire sites the linear zones functioned as crematoria (Manby 1970, 10). Generally, the closing off of the chamber, usually by filling with loose earth or rubble, took place as a separate act preceding the raising of the mound (Kinnes 1979, 58). In Wessex, the burial area was usually covered over with a flint cairn, often in some way associated with the skulls and hoof bones of cattle.

Long mounds both in Britain and on the continent which contain these structural elements tend to produce radiocarbon dates which fall between 3250 and 2750 bc (see Fig. 6.4). As Kinnes (1985, 32) suggests, these kinds of similarities between far-flung sites are far too often considered in terms of continental origins for British practices. The dates available for linear, post-bracketed mortuary structures in Denmark ($2960\pm90$ and $2860\pm70$ bc for Rude; $2960\pm100$ bc for Konens Hoj) are no earlier than those in Britain. We could more profitably consider that the development of a set of defined and controlled mortuary practices across this wide area was a part of a broader ideational structure whose genesis coincided chronologically with the introduction of the Neolithic to the North European Plain and Britain.

The spatial arrangements within these mortuary complexes are of considerable interest. The embanked linear chamber, usually the earliest element, is also the focus of the monument. Avenues of posts, like those at Wayland's Smithy I (Atkinson 1965), Kilham (Manby 1976, 126) or Streethouse (Vyner 1984), seem to draw the attention of the onlooker in to the mortuary zone. Likewise, the façade trenches of sites like Streethouse, Fussell's Lodge or Willerby Wold converge on one end of the linear structure, further emphasising the importance of the burial deposit. Equally, the

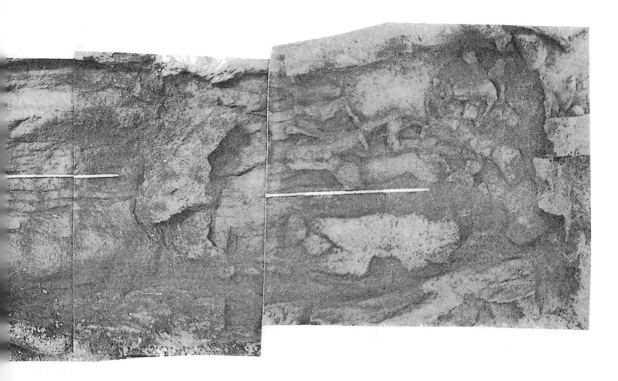

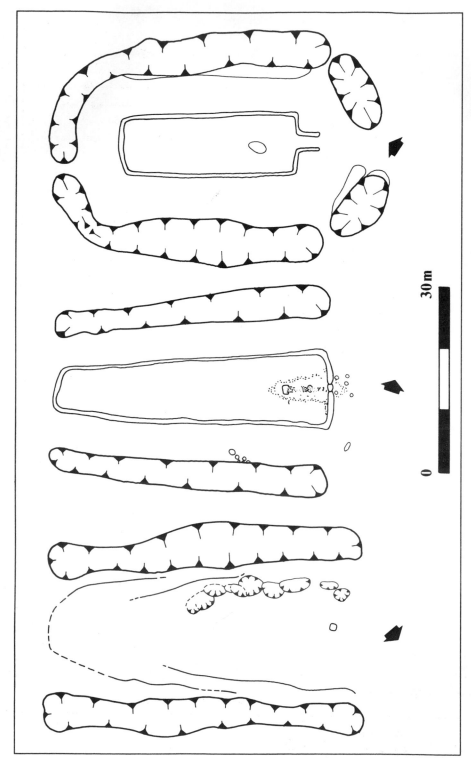

Figure 6.3    Earthen long mounds: comparative plans. From left: Wor Barrow (after Pitt Rivers 1898); Fussell's Lodge (after Ashbee 1966); Horslip (after Ashbee, Smith and Evans 1979)

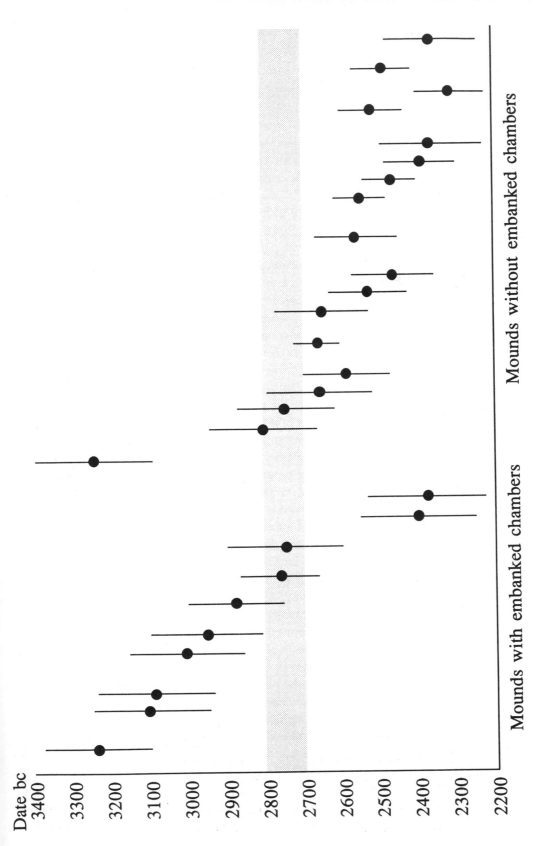

Figure 6.4    Earthen long mounds: radiocarbon dates

flanking ditches which were dug as the mound was raised clearly had the effect of limiting access to the barrow, ensuring that the monument could only be approached along its axis.

In many of these linear mortuary structures, the burials are disarticulated, a feature which has prompted the suggestion that rites of secondary burial took place. The implications of such a conclusion are considerable. Where a good deal of effort has been expended in the removal of flesh from bones, for instance to the extent of burning it off (Thorpe 1984, 47), it is clear that some major distinction is being made between the two. Such a distinction is very widespread ethnographically (Bloch 1982, 225). Often, the division is taken to imply an opposition between an enduring, male principle, associated with the bones and with order and the continuity of the community, and a mutable female principle connected with flesh, sensuality and the death of the individual (Barley 1981, 149–50). It is thus necessary to remove the decadent flesh from the bones before the individual can join the community of the ancestors. A corpse which is still fleshed represents a conceptual anomaly (Douglas 1966). Its condition is unstable, dangerous and polluting, and its transition to the defleshed state is represented as a set of rites of passage (Hertz 1960). But that such a distinction between the living and the ancestors is drawn at all is itself revealing. The need for a complex and protracted passage between the world of the living and that of the dead implies some major contradiction between the two, and hence between ideal and reality. It is thus possible that this investment of effort in the dead presents some indication of a rift between the ideals of these communities and their social experience.

Where bones are taken as the essence of order, containing the germ of future existence (Hertz 1960, 70), their separation from the flesh and constitution as the physical aspect of the ancestors imbues them with considerable symbolic power. Hence, in China, bones were placed in prominent positions as a means of gaining a symbolic control over the environment (Watson 1982, 176), while in New Guinea bones are kept in a 'head-house', and are seen as the means of access to the spirit of an ancestor (Strathern 1982, 117). Like Christian holy relics, the physical remains of the ancestors may be circulated and may be seen as the key to their blessings and power. In this connection, it is worth noting the unusual patterning of bones pointed out by Shanks and Tilley (1982) in, amongst other sites, Fussell's Lodge. They saw the arrangement of skulls and longbones and the variation in the occurrence of ribs, vertebrae and phalanges as the result of a conscious process of selection for symbolic purposes. Such an explanation may be too complicated for its own good. By contrast, Kinnes (1975, 17) suggests that the placing of bones in barrows may in some cases have been only one stage of a more complex sequence, the final deposition of remains in the barrow being by no means an inevitable conclusion. The patterning isolated by Shanks and Tilley may thus be the end product of a long sequence of additions and removals from the burial deposit while the mortuary structure was still accessible. One aspect of the patterning at Fussell's Lodge which may be of considerable relevance concerns the division of the chamber into two by the medial post, a feature which is paralleled in the orthostatic chambers of the Clyde and Carlingford cairns (Corcoran 1960). Ashbee's report calls attention to 'a relative lack of ribs, small bones of the hands and feet, patellae, clavicles and scapulae' (Ashbee 1966, 62). However, it seems that this degree of selection applies more to the larger, innermost bone groups, A and B. Bone groups C and D, on the other side of the central partition, have a more even spread (Fig. 6.5). The pattern might suggest the movement of bones from one part of the chamber to the other.

At several sites burial deposits are absent or fragmentary in the extreme. A possible explanation for this circumstance is that the remains which had been inside at one point had been removed for other purposes prior to the construction of the mound: after having been defleshed and deposited in the mortuary structure for a period they had taken on a new meaning as symbolic artefacts. Thorpe (1984, 47) notes that different anatomical parts predominate at the causewayed enclosures from those in long barrows, while Ashbee (Ashbee, Smith and Evans 1979, 83) suggests a 'reciprocal traffic' in bones between the two. Thorpe (1984, 45) suggests that many of the pits under the long barrows may be seen as the temporary resting places of burials while their flesh decayed; the interpretation of various timber structures as exposure platforms is commonplace. At Hambledon Hill, Mercer (1980) has interpreted the central enclosure as a massive centre for the exposure of the dead. At Handley Hill, Pitt Rivers (1898, 49–50) excavated the partial remains of an adult in a pit with ox bones and a large plain bowl (Piggott 1936a, 229–30). Within the pit was a hole suggestive of an upright post, which might have been a marker to enable the remains to be recovered. It is thus clear that a number of different *types* of site were involved in the circulation of human remains, both within and between sites, and that cranial fragments may have held a particular significance. If such a circulation were in operation, attempts at population estimation on the basis of the number of individuals buried in long barrows (Atkinson 1968) may be flawed.

The long mounds which were built on the chalklands of Wiltshire, Dorset, Berkshire, Hampshire and Sussex in the last quarter of the fourth millennium bc and the first quarter of the third were relatively homogeneous in form as a consequence of the sequence of ritual acts which resulted in their construction. They represented a part of a broader tradition of mound building, which it has been suggested was integrated through commonly held ritual practices. The picture of heaps of bones, burnt or unburnt, lying between two large postholes, sometimes on a chalk platform, beneath a flint cairn, is one which presents itself again and again. However, from about 2750 bc onwards this homogeneity began to be lost. This happened in a number of different ways, but each of these can best be explained by the manipulation of ritual practice by individuals or groups seeking to enhance their own prestige. The first such trajectory which can be isolated is the enhancement of monumentality. Fleming (1973, 173) pointed out that a continuum exists between those tombs which are most effective as containers of the dead, and those which are essentially monuments *per se*, whose function is to focus the attention of the individual. Bradley (1984a, 24–5) suggests that in Britain as a whole there was a shift towards the monumental end of the spectrum as time progressed, with simple mounds becoming more elaborate. This took place in two ways. Firstly, existing mounds were enlarged. At Pentridge, an existing long mound had a 'tail' added to it to more than double its length (Bradley 1983,

16–17). At Tilshead Old Ditch, it seems possible that a primary mound (Hoare 1812, 91) was enveloped in a massive long barrow, with a new burial area containing three articulated inhumations at the far end (*ibid.*; Thurnam 1869, 91–2). At Wor Barrow (Pitt Rivers 1898), Amesbury 42 and the Robin Hood's Ball barrow (Netheravon Brake) (information from J. Richards and R. Entwistle), primary ditches were recut, presumably to increase the height of the mound. Secondly, a new class of extremely long mounds, the bank barrows, were constructed. The relatively late date of these monuments is demonstrated by the running of the Maiden Castle long mound across the ditch of a causewayed enclosure (Wheeler 1943), and the date of 2722±49 bc (BM-1405) for the North Stoke example (Case 1982). Assuming the two child skeletons from a pit beneath the Maiden Castle mound to be associated with the causewayed enclosure phase (Wheeler 1943, 18–24), neither of these sites seems to have been directly connected with the disposal of the dead, but rather with monumentality for its own sake. This links the bank barrows to two contemporary phenomena: cursus monuments and the 'cenotaph' barrows (see p. 167) at Beck-hampton Road and South Street (Ashbee, Smith and Evans 1979).

The second strand which can be distinguished is a growth of regional traditions. The much-discussed oval barrows (Fig. 6.6) with individual burials (Drewett 1975; Thorpe 1984) are restricted to the south of the country, and the U-ditched examples are concentrated in, if not restricted to, Cranborne Chase (Bradley, Cleal, Gardiner, Green and Bowden 1984, 94). In the Avebury area, earthen long mounds were constructed with orthostatic sarsen chambers in their terminals, a trait possibly 'borrowed' from the Cotswolds (Thomas and Whittle 1986). Bayed 'cenotaph' barrows may also have been a particular feature of the Avebury district (Ashbee, Smith and Evans 1979). The extreme size of Winterbourne Stoke 1, Amesbury 42, Bratton, King Barrow, Old Ditch and Tilshead 7 may indicate that particularly large conventional long barrows may have been a feature of this period on Salisbury Plain, while Maiden Castle, Long Bredy and Broadmayne may indicate a preference for bank barrows in south Dorset.

The third element to mention is the shift from large numbers of disarticulated to few articulated bodies. As Thorpe (1984, 54) indicates, this is more of a general trend than a clear-cut division. It is most obvious in the case of the oval mounds containing one or two articulated individuals: Alfriston (Drewett 1975), Barrow Hills, Radley (Fig. 6.7) (Bradley, Chambers and Halpin 1984), Moody's Down SE (Grimes 1960) and perhaps Hambledon Hill (Mercer 1980), the first two of these sites having produced dates in the mid-third millennium. Given that bodies might have been placed in embanked mortuary structures fleshed as well as exposed elsewhere, there would always have been times when articulated individuals could have been found in these mortuary deposits. However, the evidence of two of the better documented barrows of later date appears conclusive. At Nutbane, two adult males and a child had been placed in a linear chamber and covered with soil or turfs, and a third male added later, after the removal of one of the timber uprights (Morgan 1959, 29–33). Clearly, here the burial deposits had not been left open. Likewise, at Wor Barrow, three male individuals and three bundles of postcranial bones, each with one skull (presumably

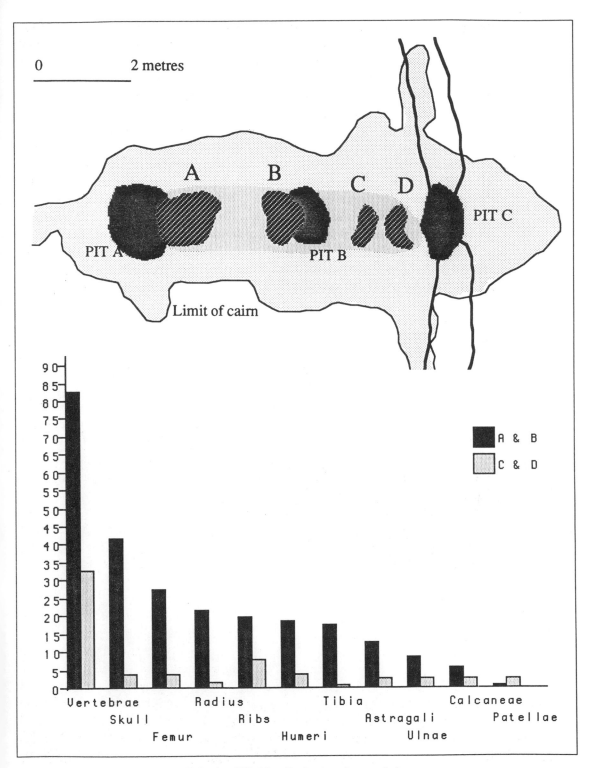

Figure 6.5   Fussell's Lodge, Wiltshire: distribution of anatomical parts

brought from elsewhere), were found within a small chamber (Pitt Rivers 1898). This might imply that a more selective procedure was in operation in the collection of the mortuary deposit. That this is coupled with a growing emphasis on the whole body as opposed to circulated 'relics' may indicate a survival of the individual ego after death. Particular named ancestors whose significance to the inheritance of prestige or property might be crucial were now replacing the generalised disarticulated bones. Additionally, given the presence of the complete but disarticulated skeletons in 'bundles' at Wor Barrow, Bloch and Parry's observation that the keeping of all of the flesh and bones within the tomb was the result of the operation of 'keeping to oneself', of endogamy (1982, 20), may apply. Since the bones no longer had to be accessible, changes were now evident in chamber form. The boxlike chamber in the irregular oval mound at Whiteleaf Hill, Buckinghamshire, containing one middle-aged male and associated with Ebbsfleet Ware (Childe and Smith 1954, 216) may not be unique.

This leads on to the final point. The use of space within the later long barrows seems to have been entirely transformed. With the oval mounds, the emphasis on a complex series of pre-mound activities was entirely lost, the mound seemingly thrown up over

Figure 6.6    Barrow Hills, Radley, Oxfordshire: long barrow (photo: Richard Bradley)

a simple grave. However, at both Radley (Bradley, Chambers and Halpin 1984) and Hambledon Hill (Mercer 1980) a complex series of ditch recuts seems to have taken place after the mound was constructed. As has already been mentioned, another characteristic of later mounds is U-shaped or surrounding ditches. These two phenomena, the raising of the mound immediately after burial and the more complete enclosure of the mound, seem to have as their objective the separation of the burial deposit from the mundane world.

This point can be further exemplified by considering the Nutbane barrow. Here, an embanked linear chamber was provided, but the bones within it were articulated and predominantly male. Rather than focussing attention on these deposits, a massive but separate forecourt area was built, and the mortuary area was enclosed within a fence (Morgan 1959, 20). Kinnes (1981, 84) and Fleming (1973) both emphasise the importance of the 'business end' of the barrow. What took place was a division between 'back' and 'front' space (Giddens 1984, 129), between private and public. Rather than being centred on the bones of the ancestors themselves, the rituals carried out in the pre-mound structure were focussed on the public space of the forecourt.

Figure 6.7   Burial with flint blade at Barrow Hills, Radley (photo: Richard Bradley)

The details and contents of the chamber were kept private, secret and mysterious. The inevitable conclusion of such an argument is that someone would have to take on the role of intercession between the community and the ancestors, and thereby control over ritual.

However, the usefulness of the dead as a resource for the living would be limited by these efforts to make access to their physical remains more restricted. Once the mound had been built there would be an inevitable distance between the dead and the living, effectively making the past unassailable. Yet were the long barrows to be left inert in the landscape their importance would have dwindled. The past is meaningless unless it is brought into the daily lives of the community (Lynch 1972, 60); places can only be kept 'alive' by involving them in practice (Relph 1976, 32). As Figure 4.5 shows, on the basis of distributions of faunal, ceramic and lithic material at Thickthorn Down (from Dorchester Museum material and J. W. Jackson's notes), there is a tendency for the cultural material deposited to cluster in the ditch terminals flanking the forecourt area. A similar pattern is suggested by deposits containing Peterborough Ware cut into the 'forecourt' side of Site I at Dorchester on Thames, arguably an oval mound similar to that at Radley in its first phase (Atkinson, Piggott and Sandars 1951). It seems likely that continued communication with the ancestors was achieved by ritual practices including feasting in the forecourt areas for many years after the burial area had been closed off. It is interesting that the same practices extended to Peterborough and Beaker pottery: a surprising degree of continuity. Furthermore, the depositional sequence of plain bowl/Peterborough/Beaker is also found at Holdenhurst, the Maiden Castle long mound, Wor Barrow and Fussell's Lodge, while plain bowl is succeeded by Beaker at Nutbane and Hambledon (Mercer 1980). In the study area, Grooved Ware is conspicuous by its absence from long mound contexts.

If the earthen long mounds of southern Britain began as a tradition whose homogeneity was owed to a unity at an ideational or conceptual level, the proliferation of rites and structural forms with which it ended implies the breakdown of this consensus. The coexistence of vast monumental works like the bank barrows (and hence the cursus monuments?), of small oval mounds closely linked to the round barrow burials of the period, and of complex multistage barrows which made use of spatial divisions to enforce social distancing from the burial deposit, indicates the simultaneous operation of a number of contrasting ideologies. These might emphasise the role of the community as a whole, or an aristocratic line, or of the individual, each for quite different reasons.

The patterns and processes which can be discerned in burial practices within earthen long mounds find parallels in the chambered long cairns of the Cotswold–Severn area. These monuments are broadly contemporary with the earthen mounds, and have three basic forms: those with multiple chambers set laterally in the body of the cairn, those with simple chambers in the terminal of the cairn, and those with transepted chambers leading from a single entrance in the cairn terminal (Thurnam 1869; Grimes 1960). Recent work suggests a broad chronological sequence in which the laterally chambered tombs precede those with terminal chambers, the latter dating to a horizon of around 3000 bc onwards (Darvill 1982; Thomas 1988b). These architectural differences are paralleled by differences in mortuary practice. In the case of the laterally chambered tombs, skeletal remains are generally found to be disarticulated (Fig. 6.8). However, at Hazleton North one complete and one semi-complete male skeleton were found in the entrance of the passage leading to the North Chamber (Fig. 6.9). With this in mind, Saville (1984, 22) suggested that 'the absence of intact inhumations in the passages and chambers, particularly in the sealed North Chamber, would suggest that bodies were left to decompose in the entrance and subsequently were taken through as bones to the interior'. Similar patterns are recorded at Lanhill (Keiller and Piggott 1938) and Pole's Wood East, where 'one skeleton was found undisturbed and surrounded by other human bones so disposed, and in such numbers, as to make it clear that the skeleton they had belonged to had been displaced to make room for it' (Greenwell 1877, 527). At a number of sites, including Eyford, Penywyrlod and Cow Common Long, skulls had been arranged in rows along chamber walls.

Thus, while it may have been normal for bodies to be placed inside the tomb entrance in a fleshed state, substantial reorganisation occurred once the flesh had decayed. The careful organisation of skulls, in particular, suggests that more was involved here than the pushing aside of bones to make way for fresh interments. The

Figure 6.8   Burials in the North Chamber, Hazleton long cairn, Gloucestershire (photo: Alan Saville)

transition from the newly dead person to the ancestral bones seems to have taken place within the confines of the monument, and the movement of individual bones up the passage to the chamber, where they were reorganised in groups, might symbolise this transformation. The passages themselves are typically subdivided by septal slabs or uprights containing 'portholes' (Clifford and Daniel 1940), which would have made dragging an entire corpse into the chamber difficult. In some cases, only individual bones could have been passed through to the innermost recesses. Rather than see these constrictions as a means of deterring intruders, they might be a means of conceptually dividing up the passage, and thereby of breaking up the journey into a number of definable stages.

As with the earthen long mounds, then, the laterally chambered long cairns show evidence for the movement and circulation of human remains. Empty or almost empty chambers in several tombs indicate that this included the removal of bones from the tombs as well as their movement within the monument.

Having gained some impression of the practices which were associated with the laterally chambered tombs, it is possible to show change through time by focussing on the terminally chambered mounds. In all types of Cotswold–Severn tomb the representation of particular body parts may be uneven. In the laterally chambered variety skulls or longbones are frequently underrepresented. In equally many cases, however, there are too many skulls and mandibles. This is not the case in transepted tombs. At these sites, skulls or longbones may be 'missing', but are not overrepresented.

One conclusion which could be drawn is that, while the earlier tombs were part of a system of bone circulation which might involve bones being transported from one tomb to another, in the transepted tombs only removal from the burial deposit took place. In the transepted tombs the interment of fleshed corpses again appears to have been the norm. Crawford writes of the 'original posture' at Hetty Peggler's Tump (Uley) as having been 'sitting or rather squatting' (1925, 104), while Daniel (1937, 76) says that at Parc le Breos Cwm 'the bodies had all originally been placed in a sitting or crouching position'. It seems that the rite involved the immediate placement of the corpse in the chamber, a contrast with the multistage treatment in earlier tombs.

In both the earlier and later tombs space seems to have been used in order to emphasise certain divisions within the community, specifically those which relate to gender and age differences (Kinnes 1981, 85). Distinctions between male and female are sometimes found, as in the case of the predominance of females in the South Chamber and males in the North Chamber at Lanhill, or the six males in Cist 2 at Eyford. At Lugbury, no males were found in Cist A and only males were found in Cist C (Thurnam 1857), while at Notgrove an adult male was placed in a separate cist behind the transepted chambers, with female bones scattered over the surface of its revetment (Clifford 1936). It seems, however, to have been divisions between old and young which were especially stressed, and this particularly in the case of transepted tombs. Furthermore, the body treatment afforded to young people often tends to separate them out, as in the case of the cremated children in separate cists in Chamber C at Nympsfield (Clifford 1938).

Figure 6.9  Articulated skeleton in the north entrance at Hazleton long cairn (photo: Alan Saville)

Since the essence of ritual practice lies in the division and demarcation of bound-aries between elements of the social world (Turner 1969), the greater division of space inherent in the design of transepted tombs allows for more complicated rituals. Far more striking, however, is the similarity in the patterns of deposition which are found at the transepted tombs of Burn Ground, Notgrove and West Kennet. This suggests not only that a potential existed for the use of space in a classificatory manner, but that quite definite rules were applied to this process.

Rather less is known about arrangements within cairns with simple terminal chambers, as a result both of the quantity and quality of excavations. One pattern which may be of importance is the emphasis upon disarticulation within these tombs. If in the transepted tombs one is dealing with the interment of whole bodies, it may be worth considering pre-interment excarnation in the case of simple terminal chambers. The contrast between the two (presumably contemporary) tomb types has to be explained. Bloch and Parry (1982, 20) suggest that

> it would seem that those systems which make a distinction between kin and affines are the ones which are most likely to pick up on the common contrast between male bones and female flesh, and to be concerned to separate them at death; while the systems which allow no such distinction are much more likely to be concerned with the corpse as a whole.

It might be stretching ethnographic analogy to its limits to suggest that transepted and simple terminal chambered tombs constitute the monuments of endogamous and exogamous groups respectively. However, it is quite reasonable to suggest that on the one hand the combination of articulated bodies and high degree of ritual classification, and on the other bones in the 'utmost confusion' (Vulliamy 1921) and a single spatial unit relate to differences in the organisation of society.

In the early third millennium in the Cotswold–Severn region it seems that mortuary ritual began to emphasise two different strategies for coping with internal stress and contradiction. These were the transepted tombs with their attendant feasting, ritual classification, rigid definition of social ranks and insistence on the integrity of a genealogical (élite?) line; and the simple terminal chambers, where all internal divisions were broken down by the disarticulation and intermixing of a great mass of bones (Fig. 6.10).

For many years a debate has raged in megalithic studies as to whether 'extra-revetment' material, the jumbled mass of stone found beyond the outer revetment wall, represented an intentional construction or the product of cairn decay. At Hazleton, the answer to the problem seems relatively clear: 'this material was evidently the product of the collapse of the façade wall' (Saville 1981, 2). The downward and outward gravitational thrust of the cairn body resulted in the overbalancing of both the inner and outer revetment walls, the collapse of their upper courses, and the slippage of loose cairn material from above (Saville 1982, 6 and his Fig. 3). It is difficult to assess how long this process of decay would have taken; however, it is to be assumed that the earliest tombs would have reached a state of dilapidation within the span of the Neolithic. This fact is important, for at Gwernvale Britnell suggests that the act of blocking the tomb and placing extra-revetment material against the revetment walls was a conscious act aimed at 'the "instant" production of an archaic form – a tomb which had clearly ceased to be used for formal mortuary activities' (Britnell and Savory 1984, 150).

The implication of this observation is that at a time in the early to mid-third millennium bc (suggested by the terminal date for Hazleton, the dates for pits associated with the blocking at Gwernvale, and Peterborough Ware from the blockings at Lanhill and Gwernvale), laterally chambered tombs were being blocked, closed off and in some cases structurally altered in order to suggest great antiquity. At Hazleton, an estimate has been made that the entire period of use of the tomb was probably less than three hundred years (Saville *et al.* 1987, 115). An attempt was being made to create a distance between the past and the present, to constitute an ideal and unassailable past. Henceforth the skeletons within the tombs would be a remote and unchanging community of ancestors.

It must have been at about the same time that the terminally chambered tombs were being built. It is in the techniques employed in the construction of these tombs that the confusion over extra-revetment originates. At Burn Ground, Grimes (1960, 76) suggested that the outer revetment wall had been built within a V-shaped trench, so as to give the impression of a wall already nearing a state of collapse. Indeed, at Hazleton a similar feature had been caused by the gradual outward pressure of the cairn (Saville 1984). But at Burn Ground no slumping was visible in the inner revetment (Grimes 1960, 62, Fig. 27), indicating that the trench setting of the outer wall may indeed have been artificial. It is interesting that the most convincing parallels which Grimes could cite for this feature were at Notgrove and Nympsfield, both also transepted terminal-chambered tombs. Darvill (1982, 47) separates those cairns at which extra-revetment was a product of erosion and decay from those at which it seems to have been a deliberate construction. All the transepted tombs considered fell into the latter category. Furthermore, the blocking in the forecourt of transepted tombs appears always to have been disturbed during Neolithic times (Darvill 1982, 59). If the cairns of laterally chambered tombs were altered in order to suggest great age, the transepted tombs were actually *constructed* in such a way as to indicate antiquity. As with the lateral tombs, the burials may have been considered as a group that must not be added to or subtracted from, and that was remote from the day-to-day world of the present. Yet the fact that the forecourt blocking had always been tampered with suggests that this was not the case: burials were still being inserted.

In the transepted tombs there appears to have been some emphasis on the maintenance of the entire body. Hence it is significant that the last acts carried out inside the laterally chambered tombs were often the 'reconstitution' of individuals from the scattered parts available. At Ascott-under-Wychwood, bones from different individuals were articulated together (Chesterman 1977, 26), while in Chamber II at Pipton seven piles of bones had been separated out, although each might contain bones from several individuals (Savory 1956). In Chamber I at Ty Isaf, bones had been arranged in groups consisting of skull, mandible and one or two longbones placed against the orthostats (Grimes 1939), while at Lanhill, Keiller and

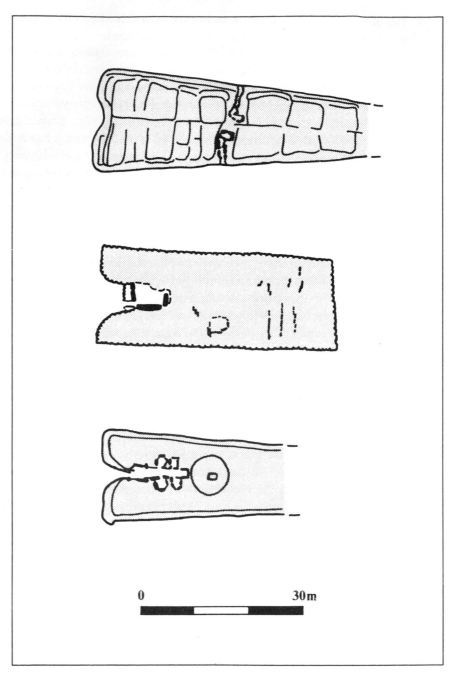

Figure 6.10    Comparative plans of Cotswold–Severn long cairns, from top: laterally chambered (Hazleton, after Saville 1982); with simple terminal chamber (Tinkinswood, after Ward 1915); with transepted terminal chambers (Notgrove, after Clifford 1936)

Piggott (1938, 125) noted that each skull 'was furnished with a lower jaw placed in approximately the correct position, but it was subsequently proved that one of the jaws could not have originally belonged to the skull in association with which it was found'.

I would suggest that the blocking of the tombs placed their contents in an unassailable position as regards the outside world, at the same time rendering unquestionable the claims to legitimacy of those most closely associated with the ancestors. This could be challenged on the grounds that the shutting off of a burial deposit could equally be a means of negating its influence upon the affairs of the living. That this is not the case is indicated by the way in which the tombs continued to be foci for activity long after they had been blocked. Secondary burials are often hard to date, and are thus not always of much consequence to the argument. Examples which clearly are of relevance are the child burial in a cist in the horn of Penywyrlod (Britnell and Savory 1984), the burials with leaf arrowheads in the mound at Sale's Lot (O'Neil 1966), and the female skull with Peterborough Ware sherds in front of the false portal at Gatcombe Lodge (Crawford 1925, 98–100; Clifford 1936, 45; Passmore 1938). Intrusive deposits of pots occurred in the cases of the Beaker at Sale's Lot (O'Neil 1966) and a Peterborough vessel inserted into the horn at Pole's Wood South (Rolleston 1876, 165–71; Greenwell 1877, 521–4). The deposition of a stone axe butt in the forecourt at Ty Isaf may or may not have postdated the blocking (Grimes 1939).

## Individual burials before Beakers

Until relatively recently it was universally accepted that the practice of burying individuals beneath round mounds was an innovation of the Beaker phase. However, as Burgess and Shennan (1978) pointed out, the round mound tradition stretched back before this. Sites like Westbury 7, with numerous disarticulated skeletons inside a round barrow with causewayed ditch (Hoare 1812, 54), could easily be contemporaneous with the long barrows. Other sites, like Mere 13d (Piggott 1931, 94–5) or Launceston Down (Piggott and Piggott 1944, 47–80), could be placed in the earlier Neolithic on artefactual grounds. It was left to Kinnes (1979) to demonstrate the scale of both individual burial and the use of round mounds in the Neolithic. Kinnes drew attention to the work of Mortimer and others on the Yorkshire Wolds. Here a singular sequence of individual burials exists, from Towthorpe Ware-associated sites like Huggate 230 and Duggleby Howe phase 1, through to the cremation burials of Duggleby 4 (Kinnes *et al.* 1983, 95). While the Yorkshire sites represent the largest concentration of such burials in Britain, there are significant groups in the south of the country.

In the south of England, the emergence of individual burials with grave goods can be seen within a late stage in the long mound tradition. Later long barrows might contain either one or two individuals in a grave or a small number of articulated burials in a chamber. These monuments were built at a time of profound social and cultural change, when many material and ritual institutions were being abandoned, replaced or augmented (*c.* 2700–2400 bc). Particular individuals were being singled out for preferential treatment in death.

The most prolific group of Neolithic individual burials in southern Britain is to be found in the Upper Thames Valley. Here also, there are late long barrows with articulated burials. At Radley a multiphase oval mound covered a primary interment of two articulated skeletons, one with a polished flint blade and jet belt slider, the other with a lozenge arrowhead. The site provided radiocarbon dates in the mid-third millennium bc (Bradley, Chambers and Halpin 1984). Nearby is the largely Bronze Age cemetery of Barrow Hills, which includes at least three ring ditches of Neolithic date, although the details of their primary interments are not known (*ibid.*, 9).

Downriver at Dorchester on Thames, Bradley has suggested that Site XI was originally a similar oval mound (Bradley and Holgate 1984, 118), aligned on Site VIII, the long mortuary enclosure. Site I has also a rather oval plan, with a line of later Neolithic recuts along one edge which would correspond to the forecourt area. The remains of a primary crouched inhumation were present on the old land surface (Atkinson, Piggott and Sandars 1951, 12). Here again, the oval mound served as a focus for later Neolithic mortuary activities. The cluster of monuments at Dorchester on Thames consists of a variety of round mounds and pit circles, into which secondary cremations had been dug. Presumably, some of these may have had primary inhumations on the old land surface which had not survived until the time of excavations.

As Figure 6.11 demonstrates, pre-Beaker individual burials were quite limited in their distribution. They are quite absent from the important areas of Neolithic settlement in the Cotswold and Mendip Hills, and rather rare in the Avebury district. Yet in each of these areas large numbers of round mounds of Bronze Age date have been excavated. The pattern of absence is not a consequence of lack of research.

Still more perplexing are the cremation burials which according to Kinnes' seriation (1979, Fig. 6.2) represent the culmination of the indigenous sequence of individual burial. It is possible that the spread of the rite of cremation at the end of the third millennium bc is an aspect of the development of new networks of contact between privileged groups in separate regions of Britain (Bradley and Chapman 1984). Cremation burials with skewer pins are, after all, known from mid-third millennium contexts in the Boyne Valley passage graves (Piggott 1954, 202), while a cremation cemetery with miniature cups, bone pins and polished edge knives is known at Ballateare on the Isle of Man (*ibid.*, 347). In the north of England these cremations are associated with oblique arrowheads (Kinnes *et al.* 1983, 98), and to a lesser extent with Grooved Ware (Kinnes 1979, Fig. 6.1). A plain Grooved Ware vessel was found with a cremation inserted into the remains of the post-circle in the terminal of the Dorchester on Thames cursus (Bradley and Holgate 1984). Cremations have been located in henge and hengiform monuments at Stonehenge (Atkinson 1956, 27–9), Barford (Oswald 1969), Llandegai (Houlder 1968), Woodhenge (Cunnington 1929, 29), Dorchester on Thames (Atkinson, Piggott and Sandars 1951) and Coneybury (Richards pers. comm.). However, it would be unwise to cast the cremations as the mortuary deposits of Grooved Ware users. Cremation, together with passage grave art, Grooved Ware, maceheads and indeed Beaker pottery, was merely one element which moved relatively independently in these expanded networks of contact.

While cremations have repeatedly been found in henge contexts, they are uniformly

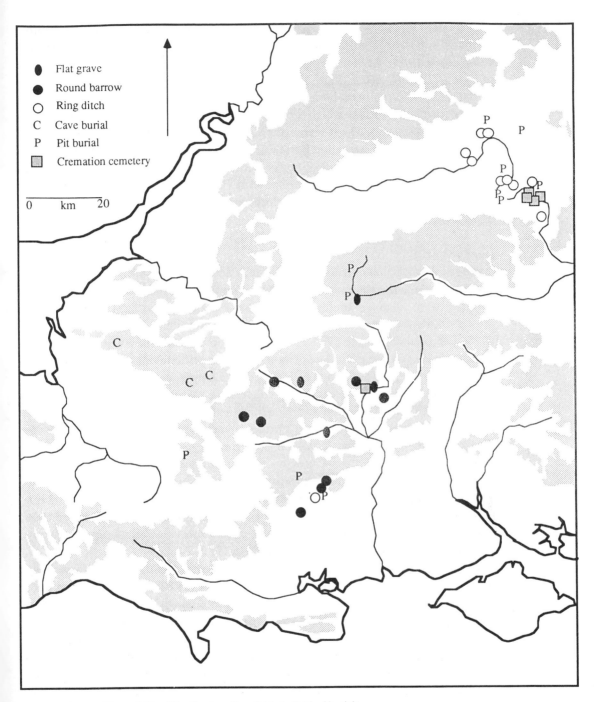

Figure 6.11    Distribution of neolithic individual burials

in secondary positions. In the case of the Dorchester on Thames post-circle, the cremated bone had percolated down through the void left by a burnt-out post (Bradley and Holgate 1984). At Stonehenge, the cremation in Aubrey Hole 32 provided a date of 1848±275 bc (C-602) (Smith 1974, 136), in contrast with the twenty-fifth century bc dates for the primary monument (Pitts 1982). It seems likely that the cremations were cut through a turfline which formed after an abandonment of the site (Richards 1982, 99; Evans 1983, 23). It seems, then, that in the south of England the development of a tradition of cremation burials associated with transverse arrowheads, flint fabricators and bone skewer pins is to be connected with the systematic reuse of old (and even overgrown) communal monuments. This would clearly seem to be related to an appeal to the past, although almost certainly a past which was either poorly understood or deliberately misrepresented.

## Beaker burials

Since the Beaker phenomenon was originally seen in ethnic terms (a model which survived even Clarke's analysis: 1970), the assumption was made that Beaker funerary practices were relatively uniform throughout Britain. In the light of views which present the Beaker assemblage as a 'package' of prestige items (Burgess and Shennan 1978; Thorpe and Richards 1984), closer scrutiny of the material is warranted in order to consider the context and nature of its adoption. In undertaking this task, I have used the scheme of Beaker development outlined by Lanting and Van der Waals (1972). Disquiet has recently been expressed concerning existing chronologies of Beaker development (Kinnes, Gibson and Needham 1983), and it is emphasised that the scheme is used here as no more than a broad guide to sequence. Lanting and Van der Waals envisaged a situation in which only the very earliest Beakers – European Maritime and some All-Over-Corded – were introduced to Britain direct from the continent. Even these need not have arrived as a consequence of folk movements: they could equally well be the result of gift exchanges between spatially remote élite groups. For while these earliest Beakers are found in graves like that at Hilton 2 (Grinsell 1959, 164), they persistently lack the characteristic continental associations of amber beads, battle axes and Grand Pressigny flint (Harrison 1980, 74).

The use of Lanting and Van der Waals' classification has a number of important advantages. It works at a tangent to Clarke's corpus (1970), allowing his groups to be split up temporally. Both systems are concerned with decoration, position of decoration, and vessel shape. However, the Lanting and Van der Waals scheme concentrates on the last two variables, and, rather than assuming the presence of a number of incoming human populations, allows for the mutual influence of insular and continental regional traditions at all stages of the sequence. Hence the two systems are grounded in different models of Beaker society and its relationship to its ceramics. Both are hypotheses, and have yet to be properly evaluated in the light of a sufficiently large number of independent radiocarbon dates. The excavations at Mount Pleasant (Longworth in Wainwright 1979a) have demonstrated the possibility that particular Beaker styles may have had very long periods of use.

The 'classic' Beaker-associated rite of burial involves the inhumation of a single individual, crouched or flexed and lying on one side. Grave goods generally include the Beaker pot itself, and sometimes one or more other items drawn from a fairly standardised repertoire. A good example of such a burial is Hemp Knoll in north Wiltshire (Robertson-Mackay 1980). Here, a grave pit 2.4 × 2 metres was dug to a depth of 1.5 metres, and the turf stripped from the surrounding area (Fig. 6.12). The grave itself formed the focus for a small round barrow thrown up on the site once the burial had been made. The body of a male individual aged 35 to 45 was placed tightly flexed inside a coffin 1.75 metres long, possibly of wickerwork. A European Bell Beaker was at its feet, an archer's wristguard on the left wrist, and a bone toggle at the waist, perhaps attached to a belt. Outside the coffin but within the grave pit were a tine of antler and, unusually, the head and hooves of an ox.

While such inhumations in some senses represent the culmination of tendencies present in indigenous traditions of individual burial, it is evident that they draw upon a more closely defined set of rules for procedure. A relatively restricted group of items can be included in the grave, and the body itself is treated in a way which suggests strong convention. Case (1977) observed that the grave assemblages are often indicative of persons who are in some senses 'specialists': warriors, smiths or leatherworkers. This may be less a direct reflection of status in life than a representation of persons in an idealised or stereotyped manner in death. One of the most significant changes which took place in burial ritual over the whole period discussed here is the shift from a focus on a large monument, within which human bones were secondary elements to be deposited, removed or moved around, to one on the human body itself. Barrett (1988b) aptly links this with a change from 'ancestor rituals' to funerals *per se*. This would involve also a change from a repeated experience of coming into contact with the ancestral remains to a single episode of deposition. This might mean that there was less potential for the 're-reading' or misinterpretation of the mortuary deposit, but at the same time it would dictate that any signification which the living wished to achieve through the medium of the dead would have to take place in a relatively short time, before the burial itself. It is thus significant that Beaker and other Early Bronze Age burials often do involve either coffins or biers. During any ceremonial preceding the burial, the body would have been visible, and would indeed have been carried to the grave under the view of onlookers. In this short time, a certain impression of the dead person would have to be created, which might or might not have anything to do with his or her nature in life. The grave goods might have a 'value' in themselves, but in the context of the funeral their function was symbolic, and lay in the production of a desired 'reading' of the body. Given these conditions, the message expressed by the body and its clothing and accompaniments might not be too subtle a one: the dead person had to be seen to be important, possibly in an extremely stereotyped way.

Lanting and Van der Waals would themselves admit that the seven steps of their sequence probably overlap in time (1972, 35). Despite this, comparing the various stages does allow a modicum of control over change through time. Through the successive steps there is a gradual rise in the number of items found with the body in the grave and a greater distinction between the richest and poorest graves (Fig. 6.13). This might not be a direct indication of the 'wealth' or 'status' of the dead, so much as

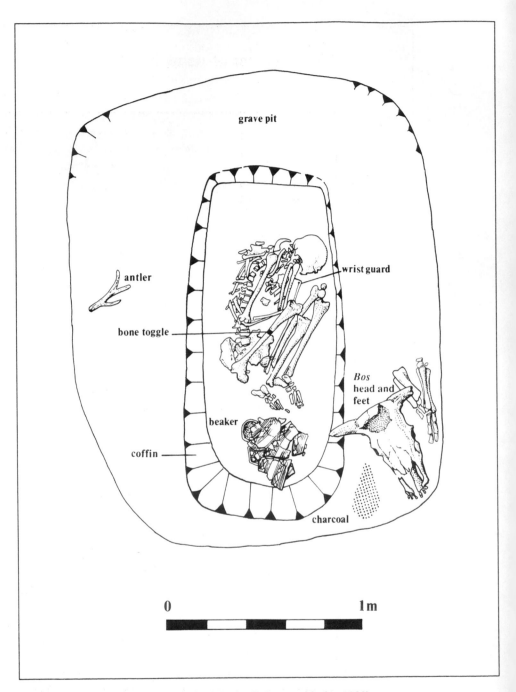

Figure 6.12    Hemp Knoll, Wiltshire, burial (after Robertson-Mackay 1980)

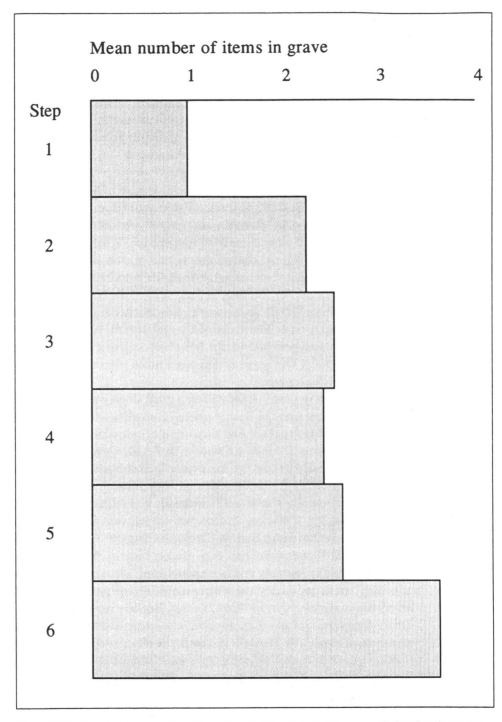

Figure 6.13    Beaker graves: number of items found with each body (Steps according to Lanting and Van der Waals 1972 – Step 7 burials have been omitted on account of the introduction of flat grave cemeteries, which distort numerical comparisons)

a reflection of how much investment the living would undertake in creating a certain image of the deceased. These phenomena peak in Step 6, while Step 7 sees a dramatic decline in the 'wealth' of Beaker burials. What seems to have taken place is that Beakers entered Britain as a scarce and highly sought-after item, but that, once they began to be produced locally, other items of the 'Beaker package' – barbed and tanged arrowheads, archers' wristguards, basket earrings, flint and bronze daggers, belt rings and buttons – had to be brought in to augment the exclusivity of the grave assemblage. This might be seen as a process in which it gradually became necessary to employ more symbols to ensure the correct reading of the corpse.

The styles of vessels themselves may have undergone a process of 'slippage' of meaning, which may explain the rapid development of decorative design in Beakers. Certain of Clarke's Beaker types seem to have lasted through a number of Lanting and Van der Waals' steps. In south Wessex, only 37 per cent of the Step 2 burials with a single Beaker and no other items in the grave have W/MR Beakers (while 50 per cent have E Beakers). Sixty per cent of the 'richer' graves, like Mere 6a, with its tanged copper dagger, two gold button caps, bone spatula and stone bracer (Hoare 1812, 44), have W/MR Beakers. By contrast, in Step 3, all of the burials in south Wessex with a single Beaker have W/MR (excepting a plain Beaker at Frampton 4). Richer burials have newer Beaker types, like the N/MR vessel with the Jug's Grave burial, which also had another Beaker, gold button cap, bone belt ring, four arrowheads and a flint blade (Clarke 1970, 502). This suggests that at any given point the richest Beaker graves had the most novel Beaker types.

Regionally, there seems to have been a great degree of continuity from Neolithic mortuary practices into the Beaker phase. The areas where early Beaker burials are found are those which already had a tradition of individual burial: the Thames Valley, Salisbury Plain and Cranborne Chase (Fig. 6.14). Often, old funerary monuments seem to have formed a focus for these early Beaker burials, as they had the burials of the later Neolithic. At Linch Hill, Stanton Harcourt, a male burial with Step 2 N/MR Beaker, bone belt ring and seven arrowheads was added to the Neolithic ring ditch (Grimes 1944, 39). Two Step 2 secondary burials with E Beakers were inserted into the Thickthorn Down long barrow (Drew and Piggott 1936).

However, in Wessex the richest early Beaker burials, like Mere 6a and Roundway 8 (Hoare 1812, 44; Annable and Simpson 1964, 38), seem to be in outlying areas, 'avoiding' the major communal monuments (Thorpe and Richards 1984). This has led to the suggestion that in south Wessex Beakers were first used by 'big men' of subservient status, rather than the élite who organised ritual activities in the henge monuments (*ibid.*, 79). Hence it is that in the Stonehenge area, early Beaker burials cluster in the Wilsford/Normanton area south of the cursus. The spatial proximity of this early nucleus of Beaker activity to the Winterbourne Stoke long barrow and the nearby Neolithic round mounds is, of course, significant.

By contrast, in the Upper Thames Valley rich Beaker burials were centrally located from the first (Fig. 6.15). There is a particularly dense concentration of early Beaker graves in the Stanton Harcourt area, within 2 km of the Devil's Quoits henge monument. The distribution is rather thinner around Dorchester on Thames – perhaps

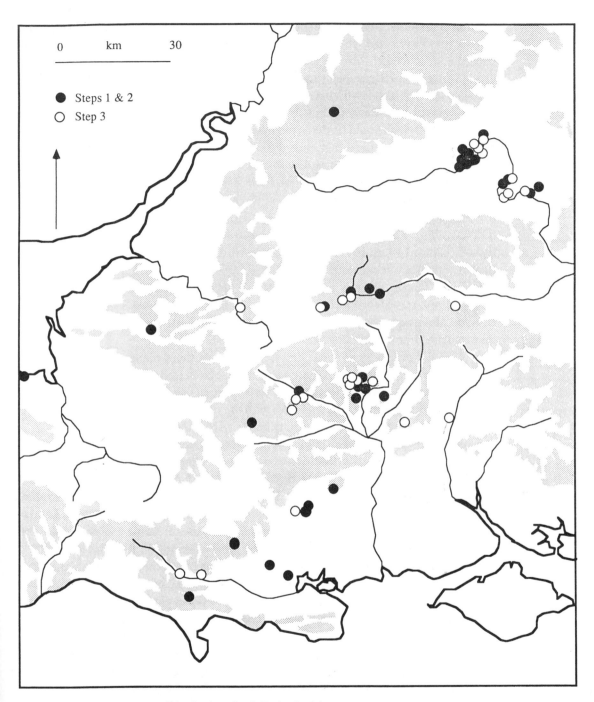

Figure 6.14    Distribution of early Beaker burials

because cremation burial was still being practised in the area. The end of that phase of activity may have come when the richest early Beaker burial in the area, a male with tanged copper dagger, bronze knife, slate wristguard and W/MR Beaker (Step 3), inside Dorchester XII, a small ring ditch outside the entrance to the Big Rings henge, signalled the 'closing-down' of a ritual and funerary complex.

If we accept that Beakers and their attendant paraphernalia were a package of prestige items which could be deployed in various ways in individual power struggles, we should not be surprised that quite different patterns emerged in different regions. The Avebury district, the Cotswolds, the Mendips and the south of Dorset each had little or no tradition of individual burial. Early Beaker graves are almost entirely absent from both the Cotswolds and Mendips, the exception being a male burial with E (Step 2) Beaker and possible earring inserted into the mound of Sale's Lot long cairn (O'Neil 1966). Early Beaker pottery was also found in the cairns at Notgrove and Eyford (Clifford 1936; 1937, 161). In other words, in the Cotswolds, the early use of Beaker ceramics was restricted to traditional funerary contexts. Likewise, in Mendip the earliest Beaker grave is the BW (Step 4) Beaker at Blackdown T5 (ApSimon 1969). However, no less than twelve Mendip caves have produced Beaker pottery, and at Bone Hole and Charterhouse Warren Farm Swallett, this was associated with disarticulated human remains (Levitan *et al.* 1988).

Around the periphery of these limestone uplands there are several conventional Beaker burials. However, all of these seem to have been quite remote from centres of population. It was not until Beakers of Step 6 were in use that burials were found on the uplands. Significantly, this coincides with the deposition of Beaker pottery, lithics and animal bones at the Gorsey Bigbury henge (ApSimon *et al.* 1976, 178).

A similar pattern can be seen in the Avebury area, where early Beaker (AOC) pottery has been recovered from the 'traditional' contexts of Windmill Hill (Smith 1965a, 80), West Kennet long barrow (Piggott 1962), Knap Hill (Connah 1965) and the stone-holes of the Sanctuary (Cunnington 1931, 323). Beaker burials do occur around Avebury, but many of them seem to have been incorporated into the Avebury monumental landscape. A Step 2 Bell Beaker was found beneath Stone 29a of the Kennet Avenue, and a multiple burial with N2 Beaker next to Stone 25b (Smith 1965a, 209). Possibly the new practice of burial with Beakers was being contained and related to the corporate whole through an integration with the communal monuments. However, by Steps 5 and 6 a change seems to have taken place, and rich burials like that at West Overton G6b are found in barrows in the Avebury area (Smith and Simpson 1966).

In south Dorset another variation can be seen. Beaker burials of any sort are rare before Steps 6 and 7. However, Beaker pottery seems to have been in use at the henge monument of Mount Pleasant from perhaps as early as the nineteenth century bc (Wainwright 1979a, 87). Perhaps, then, Beakers had 'taken over the role of Grooved Ware' (Bradley 1984a, 80) in this area.

The burial of an individual with a Beaker and other prestigious items was probably at no point a 'normal' way of treating the dead. As Metcalf (1981) points out, the lavishing of wealth and effort on a dead person may only take place when it is

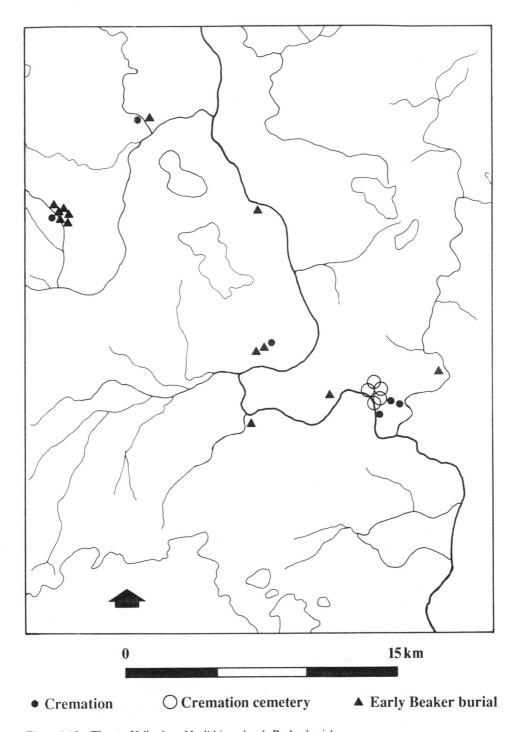

0                                                                    15 km

● Cremation        ○ Cremation cemetery        ▲ Early Beaker burial

Figure 6.15    Thames Valley later Neolithic and early Beaker burials

considered worth while by the living. In Metcalf's Borneo example this is usually when some degree of contact with the ancestors is thought necessary in order to improve the well-being of the community. However, when the burial of individuals with rich grave goods constitutes a means of bolstering the authority of living individuals through their descent from esteemed ancestors, these burials may be more necessary at times of social stress. If we compare the distribution of known Beaker burials through the steps of Lanting and Van der Waals' sequence (Fig. 6.16), it is clear that they were not deposited at a uniform rate. Nor were the 'peaks' of burial activity synchronised from one area to another.

A particularly clear contrast exists between Salisbury Plain, where peaks occur in Steps 3 and 5, and the Upper Thames, where the peaks are in Steps 2 and 7. It is important that in some areas (Mendip and Salisbury Plain, for instance) this increased burial activity coincides with the first use of Beaker pottery on henge monuments. Beaker burials may thus have been more important at times when some change was overtaking the structure of authority and ritual. Where new forms of authority were at their most fragile, more effort may have been expended in creating links with a 'legitimate' past.

These findings seem to be in sympathy with some observations made by Shennan (1982) concerning the Beaker phenomenon in central Europe. There also the Beaker assemblage was more easily adopted in areas which already had a tradition of individual burial. However, we should ask how these traditions came to be founded. In the Upper Thames, Neolithic monuments (causewayed enclosures, cursus, henges) are both more numerous and built on a smaller scale than in equivalent areas of Wessex. Possibly, then, smaller social units were responsible for these monuments. With social action taking place at a lower level of organisation, and the area composed of a number of small social groups, mortuary practices which emphasised the role of the individual may have developed more easily. In Salisbury Plain and Cranborne Chase the reverse was the case. Social units large enough to create Durrington Walls, the Dorset Cursus or Hambledon Hill may have involved a hierarchy of several social levels or ranks. Those occupying the lower of these levels may have been attracted to individualising trends, as Thorpe and Richards (1984) suggest. The picture which emerges is one of continuity within, but contrasts between, areas. One simple factor which may have been important is that of communication: the Upper Thames, Salisbury Plain and Cranborne Chase are all at the head of river networks communicating with the English Channel and hence with the continent. The Mendip and Cotswold Hills are naturally more insular. But at base these contrasts in mortuary tradition must relate to contrasts in social relations.

The Beaker package brought a standardised set of symbols and meanings to Britain, together with an accepted way of deploying them in a funerary context. In the Neolithic, traditions of individual burial in Britain had been extremely heterogeneous. In the Thames, women seem to have been afforded prestigious burial, perhaps because the female line was important to the integration of small, relatively mobile communities. In Wessex, males appear to have been treated preferentially, although the goods by which they were accompanied were by no means standardised. The

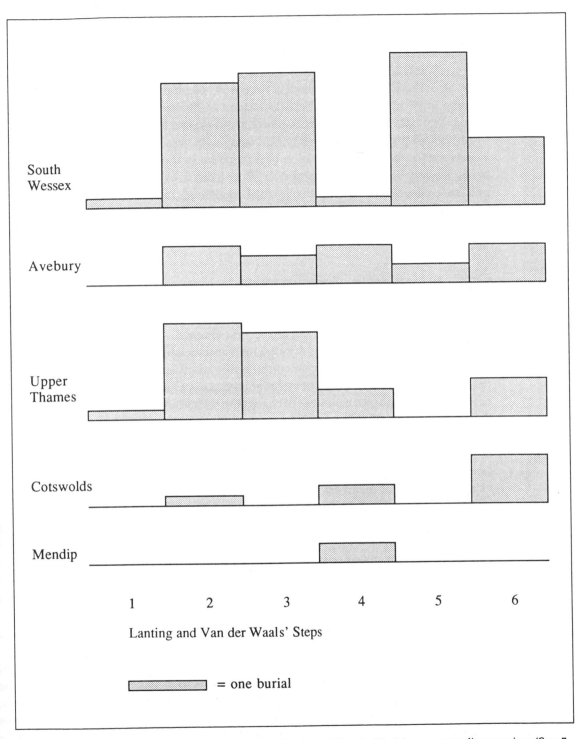

Figure 6.16    Beaker burials divided by Lanting and Van der Waals' stages, according to regions (Step 7 burials have been omitted on account of the introduction of flat grave cemeteries, which distort numerical comparisons)

arrival of Beakers set in motion a process through which these diverse regions began to become more alike. In areas which already had individual burials, the package was adopted in its entirety: in more traditional areas Beakers were first used in 'traditional' contexts. Only by the end of the Beaker sequence was the idea of individual burial beneath a round mound universally accepted. Gender relations, too, may have become more standardised. The orientations of Beaker burials in the study area (Fig. 6.17) indicate a rigid distinction between male and female space.

The culmination of the Beaker period came with vessels of Steps 5 and 6. These vessels are found in a concentration of rich graves in the immediate area of Stonehenge. By Step 7, the burials were poorer, more likely to be in flat graves than barrows, and less concentrated on Stonehenge. In all likelihood, the process of emulation and inflation had continued. In the effort to maintain the exclusivity of its mortuary symbols, the privileged social group located near to Stonehenge had moved on to new media.

### Conclusion: strategies of representation

This chapter has reviewed 1,500 years of mortuary practice in the south of England. In coming to terms with the development of cultural institutions over this depth of time, many of the preoccupations of the first chapter – the role of the subject in historical processes, the 'making' of individuals and social groups – are highly relevant. This is especially the case when we concede that mortuary practice does not merely reflect society, but is composed of values and symbols which are constitutive of social practice. We can discern a number of changes in the nature of funerary ritual through the period, and these changes can be attributed to changing 'strategies of representation', or ways of projecting the individual in death. This proposition could be taken in two very different ways, depending upon theoretical orientation. On the one hand, one could consider that trends towards the monopolisation of ancestors, or the individual interment of members of aristocratic descent groups were long-term power strategies devised by dynastic lines. Considering that some of these practices took millennia to emerge in their mature form, this is unlikely. On the other hand, one could consider that changes in mortuary representation were effectively 'strategies without strategists'. As new power relations, or new technologies of power developed, so did new roles and practices to which individuals adapted themselves.

I should like to adopt a point of view somewhere between the two extremes. In these terms, mortuary practice represents a structure which is in part responsible for the creation of the individual as a social being. At the same time, this structure is not fixed, but changes through the operation of the individual strategies of people. It is pointless to suggest that persons living in 2700 bc intended a form of mortuary practice which emphasised the individual at the expense of the collectivity to be dominant a millennium later. That process was the net result of innumerable individual strategies and actions played out over an enormous depth of time. Possibly, then, the central position which has been given to the concept of ideology in recent discussions of prehistoric funerary activity (e.g. Shanks and Tilley 1982; Shennan 1982) should be surrendered to that of hegemony.

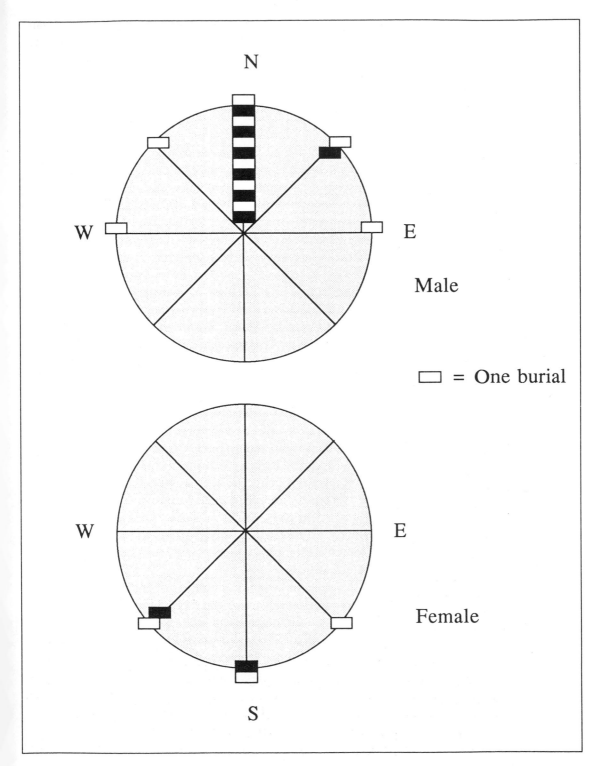

Figure 6.17   Beaker burials in the study area: grave orientation according to gender

> Hegemony contributes to or constitutes a form of social cohesion not through force or coercion, nor necessarily through consent, but most effectively by way of practices, techniques, and methods which infiltrate minds and bodies, cultural practices which cultivate behaviours and beliefs, tastes, desires, and needs as seemingly naturally occurring qualities and properties embodied in the psychic and physical reality (or 'truth') of the human subject.
> (Smart 1986, 160)

In these terms, mortuary ritual can be considered as hegemonic practice which serves to reproduce society and maintain relations of dominance. Most importantly, it provides a direct link between the manipulation of power and the representation of the human body. Clearly, the treatment of the body in death is connected with the power relations which determine the treatment of the body in life. The body as a symbolic force must be related to the body as a physical force. Thus funerary ritual is one of a set of physical practices which form a given community's expectations of what it is to be a person.

Through the period under study, a 'genealogy' of mortuary practice reveals a fundamental shift in the way in which the body is represented in death. In both the earthen long barrows and the Cotswold–Severn chambered tombs the body was broken down into its constituent bones. This was achieved through the operation of a series of rites of passage, which served to signal a change in the nature of the body. These rites of passage were spatially expressed, either in the movement of bones from one type of site to another, or in the progressive disarticulation of the body as it was moved down the segmented sections of a passage towards a chamber. These rites marked a major boundary between the condition of a person in life and that in death. Living and dead persons were both social beings, but it was necessary to make a rigid distinction between the two. Bloch and Parry (1982) gain the generalised impression from societies practising secondary burial that life as an individual is seen as a temporary state of affairs. The bones are clothed in flesh for a while, before returning to the tomb. Only in this transient phase is the person a 'subject'. Ancestors, by contrast, exist as a collectivity, whose location is ambiguous and whose bones represent a store of fertility for the community, which can be used like relics to exert an influence over the physical world.

Through the course of the third millennium a number of changes overcame the treatment of the dead. Firstly, a greater distance was created between the living and the dead. Fully enclosing ditches were dug around long mounds; a separation took place between burial and forecourt areas; burial deposits in Cotswold–Severn tombs became less accessible; old tombs were blocked; skeletal remains ceased to be circulated between sites. Secondly, perhaps partly as a result of the above, the emphasis on protracted rites of passage declined. The bodies of the dead were whole and articulated (Fig. 6.18). These two features between them meant that the dead ceased to have an 'interactive' role in society, yet maintained their individual identity. Possibly this greater distance between living and dead allowed the intercession between the two to be carried out by privileged individuals. Equally, such a distance

Figure 6.18    Beaker burial at Barrow Hills, Radley, Oxfordshire (photo: Claire Halpin)

may have been necessary given the erosion of the boundary between living and dead bodies. The body of the dead individual had ceased to be something which the community as a whole had any claims upon. Even the eventual shift towards cremation appears (from what evidence there is) to have been concerned less with the destruction of the individual than with the purification of the bones. These bones were not split up or mixed, but were deposited in such a way as to ensure the maintenance of identity. A mound located them in space, while grave goods (perhaps items which had gained a reputation of their own through a history of important exchange transactions, dowry payments, etc.) expressed an image of a person's nature. This association with physical things created a stronger memory of an important person, but in ways chosen by their descendants or kin.

Certain elements of the use of the dead remained stable throughout the period: they formed a resource of authority, and a means for ensuring continuity between generations. Their importance was probably always greatest when authority was most threatened or social changes were most severe. But within these parameters can be discerned a major change in the perception of the subject, from being a temporary transformation of materials held in common by the community to being an isolated thing, indivisible in perpetuity.

# 7

# Regional sequences of change

**Introduction**

The strategy which has been employed in the past five chapters has been to emphasise change through time. The phenomena which have been highlighted as significant have been those which demonstrate significant contrasts across time. In this chapter, the spatial axis is added to the temporal, in order to create a further dimension of contrast. While Piggott's (1954) masterly survey of the British Neolithic was organised on a regional basis, and a distinction was drawn between primary and secondary areas of colonisation on the part of the Windmill Hill culture, the period has largely been seen as geographically undifferentiated. This is particularly so in the case of lowland southern England. It is the purpose of this chapter to consider in detail the deployment of the various cultural media discussed in the previous chapters within three different areas, in order to demonstrate that aspects of material culture might have a quite different significance in different places.

This project immediately raises the question of how one should define a 'region' for the purposes of study. A simple solution would be to rely upon purely physiographic features, but such an approach is almost certain to bias the account in favour of environmental determinism. Having defined one's units of analysis on environmental criteria, it would be all too easy to argue that developments within these units were different because they were ecologically distinct.

How, then, do we define *social* units in prehistory? Renfrew (1973, 552) delimited five 'chiefdoms' within Neolithic Wessex on the basis of the distributions of ceremonial monuments. However, this assumes a set and constant relationship between monuments and society. While clusters of monuments may indeed relate to social units, it has to be considered that some groups may not have built monuments at all.

It seems most unlikely that the societies of the southern British Neolithic were entirely isolated from each other, considering the widespread nature of the distributions of certain items of material culture (stone axes, particular types of pottery, etc.). Nevertheless, as Barth (1969, 9) emphasises, boundaries between groups persist despite flows of material and personnel across them. The recent interest in the uses of material culture to define social boundaries (e.g. Hodder 1978; 1982a) provides some hope of the possibility of detecting social groups from the distribution of material culture. It is with this aim in mind that DeAtley and Findlow (1984, 2) suggest that 'the groups with which people identify can often be characterised by a modal cluster of material culture and behavioural traits as well as with a central geographical, and often organisational focus'. However, this again assumes a fixed relationship between people and material culture. Boundary maintenance through the use of material culture is not a universal, but a strategy which arises within particular historical circumstances (Hodder 1979). Moreover, although the boundaries concerned may be those between communities, they may equally well connote age- or sex-related interest groups which transcend the local area (Hodder 1982a, 84–6; Larrick 1986).

In the specific instance of Neolithic southern Britain, the same material items seem to have been in use across quite wide areas. Particular styles of pottery (Windmill Hill, Whitehawk, Ebbsfleet, Mildenhall, Abingdon, etc.) seem to have become increasingly localised towards the middle of the third millennium, but this one horizon of cultural difference hardly seems a sufficient basis for the division of the study area into local units. It seems more often to have been the case that material items were manipulated in within-group rather than between-group strategies. With these points in mind, it may be wise to consider that the role of material culture in making statements about social difference is best left as an object of study, rather than taken for granted.

Nevertheless, we are left with the problem of the definition of units of analysis. Bearing in mind the European experience of Neolithic settlements clustered into *Siedlungskammer* or settlement cells, the procedure adopted is the recognition of clusters of traces of settlement activity (largely lithic scatters, but also distributions of pit sites and ceramics), combined with distributions of field monuments. Having said this, I recognise that it may lead to a certain circularity of argument, since areas lacking settlement evidence cannot be assumed to be unoccupied; it may be that areas with impressive monuments have preferentially attracted the attentions of flint collectors. All that can be done with regard to this problem is to recognise that it is those areas between these concentrations which should be considered for future fieldwork (see Shennan 1985).

## Problems of the evidence

The comparison of the different areas as they have been defined is complicated by differences in their histories of research. Since much of the interpretation which follows depends both on differences between areas and even on the absence of particular features in some areas, it is as well to make the reader aware of some of these variations. The first area which is to be considered, Salisbury Plain, received considerable attention in the nineteenth century from Cunnington, Colt Hoare (1812) and Thurnam (1869) as regards barrow digging, but seems not to have been a major focus for flint collectors prior to the activities of Laidler and Young (1938). This can be contrasted with the Avebury area, which was successively combed for flints by Kendall, Passmore, Young and numerous individuals who sold specimens to Keiller while he was in residence in the village. However, the two major absences from the Avebury area in the later Neolithic, Grooved Ware pits and individual burials, cannot be put down to sample bias. The history of the digging of pipe trenches and similar excavations is at least as extensive around Avebury as near Durrington, while the area has been well served by barrow diggers (Thurnam 1860; Grinsell 1959).

The combination of extensive gravel extraction and the presence of the extremely active Oxford University Archaeological Society between the wars can doubtless be held partly responsible for the unusually rich record of Beaker and earlier burials and of small pit sites with pottery in the Upper Thames Valley. This does not affect the fact that earlier Neolithic funerary monuments are relatively rare in the area, or that traces of earlier Neolithic activity are minimal north of Oxford, or that the later Neolithic monuments of the area are conceived on a smaller scale than those of Wessex. So while one should be aware that quite major differences exist in the ways in which archaeology has been undertaken in the various parts of the study area, it is likely that the contrasts which are drawn here relate to genuine differences between the material practices of the communities which inhabited those regions in the Neolithic.

### Salisbury Plain: Stonehenge area

In the earlier part of the Neolithic, settlement seems to have been established on the low country on the west bank of the River Avon (Fig. 7.1). The traces of this activity 'occurred as small, essentially nucleated scatters of worked flint' (Richards 1982, 100). This would seem to accord with the pattern of small social groups engaged for at least part of the year in fixed-plot horticulture suggested in Chapter 2. Concentrations of worked flint have been located to the west of the Great Cursus and immediately outside Robin Hood's Ball (Richards 1984). Despite this, the many finds of earlier Neolithic pottery in the area are tightly concentrated in a swathe of country within two kilometres of the Avon. This distribution of evidence which might potentially relate to domestic activities contrasts somewhat with the location of long barrows. Two separate groups of barrows are to be found in the immediate area of Stonehenge (Richards 1984, 182), one in the same vicinity as the lithic scatters, and one concentrated in the immediate environs of the causewayed enclosure of Robin Hood's Ball.

Both of these groupings include barrows which appear to be, typologically speaking, late in date. The only excavated barrow which gives an indication of being 'early' is Amesbury 14 (Thurnam 1869, 183–4), situated near Normanton Down and containing disarticulated burials. In the southern group, later barrows include the oval barrow Wilsford 30, which contained four individuals 'strangely huddled together' (Hoare 1812, 206), and Winterbourne Stoke 1, with its single articulated male burial (Thurnam 1869, 184–6). The mounds near to Robin Hood's Ball include Figheldean 31 (*ibid.*, 180), which contained a single articulated individual, and the recently excavated oval barrow at Netheravon Brake, whose primary ditch silts provided a radiocarbon date of 2810±90 bc (OxA-1407). An arguable interpretation is that the former of these groups of barrows is connected with settlement activities, and grew up over a lengthy period of time, while the latter developed later, associated with the activities practised at and bound up with the connotations of the causewayed enclosure.

Elements of the long mound tradition appear to have continued to be deployed for many centuries after the barrows themselves were built. The Normanton Down 'mortuary enclosure' (Vatcher 1961) and the Lesser Cursus at Winterbourne Stoke both appear to date to the middle of the third millennium, while the Great Cursus is rather later. In the case of the latter monument the manipulation of the long mound repertoire is particularly clear, in that a bank-like mound (Amesbury 42) closes off its eastern end (Richards 1984, 182), while the western terminal was constructed so as to resemble a barrow (Christie 1963, 370). The destruction layer of the Lesser Cursus, dated to 2050±120 bc (OxA-1406), seems to indicate that this monument was replaced by the much larger Great Cursus in the later third millennium. The location of the two cursus monuments may be significant, since they are both situated between the two groups of long barrows already mentioned. Possibly, this deployment of emphatically linear structures may represent an act of separation between the two zones of the landscape and their increasingly conflicting practices: domestic activity on the one hand, the enclosure and its association with the exotic, the distant and the marginal on the other.

Significantly, it would have been at roughly the same time as this division of the landscape took place that a new group of monuments was being constructed, the first henges. At Stonehenge, the first phase of activity consisted of an earthen bank and ditch. The early monument bears a certain similarity to the causewayed enclosures, having a causewayed ditch (Braithwaite 1984, 101) and internal, timber-revetted bank (Berridge pers. comm.). The building of Stonehenge I (*c.* 2460±60 bc, BM-1583; 2440±60 bc, BM-1617) seems to be roughly contemporary with that of the henge at Coneybury Hill (2420±90 bc, OxA-1409). Both of these sites are located in the 'settled' area away from Robin Hood's Ball, thereby representing more focal locations rather than being peripherally sited. There is some indication that Coneybury was built in a location which already held some significance, since adjacent to the henge was a very large pit, dating to the end of the fourth millennium, and containing unabraded pot sherds deliberately spread across its bottom and sides (Richards 1982, 99), together with large quantities of animal bones.

This hint that henge monuments fitted into a landscape already composed of locales saturated with meanings and significance is corroborated by the evidence for numerous timber uprights in alignments and circles which have been found in the area around Stonehenge and Durrington Walls. Within Stonehenge itself there was an early phase of timber structures, including a central circle and an avenue leading to an entrance in the south-east of the monument (Hawley 1926, 3; Burl 1987, 55). Alignments of posts have been found under the north and south sectors of the bank of the Durrington Walls henge (Stone, Piggott and Booth 1954; Wainwright and Longworth 1971, 15, 17), under the bank at Woodhenge (Cunnington 1929, 10–11), in Stonehenge Bottom (Annable 1969, 123) and outside Stonehenge (Vatcher and Vatcher 1973, 59). Over this limited area of the landscape, then, an extensive form of control appears to have been exercised. These, presumably interlinked, timber structures would have had both a profound visual impact and a physical influence over movement within the area. Both the Stonehenge Bottom postholes and the primary ditch fill of Coneybury henge produced sherds of Grooved Ware, indicating that this phase of construction can be connected with the introduction of that ceramic tradition to the locality.

At some time around the twenty-second century bc the penannular bank of

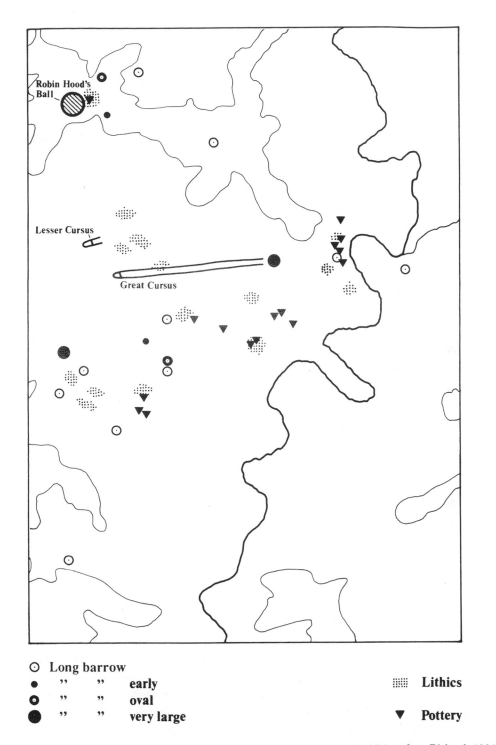

Figure 7.1   Salisbury Plain: earlier Neolithic activity (author's data with additions from Richards 1984)

Stonehenge I was pushed back into the ditch, and the circuit was replaced as a barrier by the Aubrey Holes. Atkinson claims that these were pits, not containing uprights (1956, 28). His reasons for this diagnosis have never been documented (Pitts 1982, 127), although parallels do exist in the Wyke Down henge (Barrett, Bradley and Green 1991) and, more broadly, Maumbury Rings. A number of recuts were made into the ditch, and at least one of these (Crater 2) contained sherds of Grooved Ware (Piggott 1936b, 221). Evidently, at this stage activities to which Grooved Ware was appropriate were carried out across a wide area of the landscape, in Stonehenge and Coneybury, but not in the area around Robin Hood's Ball, as far as evidence allows. Yet at Stonehenge the site was abandoned following this activity, and shrubs or even trees allowed to grow over the monument (Evans 1983, 27).

By the end of the third millennium bc, the particular set of practices which made use of Grooved Ware became more spatially restricted, with the abandonment of Stonehenge and Coneybury (Richards 1982) and possibly also other small henges at Fargo (Stone 1938) and Winterbourne Stoke 44 (Green and Rollo-Smith 1984, 316). The separation of different areas of the landscape in which separate social discourses were enacted, which had begun in the mid-third millennium, was intensified and elaborated at this point. In the area around Wilsford, Normanton and the west end of the Great Cursus, surface flint finds are dominated by a heavy, industrial assemblage (Richards 1984, 183) (Fig. 7.2). In this area, later Neolithic pottery finds are exclusively of Peterborough Ware (Stone 1938; Longworth 1959; Vatcher 1961; Grimes 1964). However, occupation evidently took place in this area, to judge from a scatter of 'domestic' flintwork with chisel-shaped arrowheads and polished flint adzes located immediately to the west of Stonehenge (Richards 1984, 185). In this same area are found a number of individual burials of Neolithic date, from the long barrow at Winterbourne Stoke 1 through to the causewayed ditched round barrows at Normanton Down and Amesbury 22 (Vatcher 1961, 167; Hoare 1812, 199) and the single burial with fine flint leaf-shaped projectiles at Winterbourne Stoke 35a (Thurnam 1869). This accords with the hypothesis already advanced that activities involving the use of Grooved Ware and the burial of individuals with grave goods respectively were mutually incompatible aspects of later Neolithic ritual discourse.

To the west of this zone, on the King Barrow Ridge and Stonehenge Bottom, is an area rich in surface flintwork. Fine items like arrowheads, polished discoidal knives and edge-polished axes have been found in profusion, together with relatively crude extraction tools (Laidler and Young 1938). In this area both Peterborough Ware and Grooved Ware have been found, but never in closed association in the same feature (Annable 1969, 394; Richards 1984, 183). Grooved Ware features on the King Barrow Ridge show a degree of formality in their depositional characteristics: a pit containing only the foot bones of pigs, for instance (*ibid.*), or the chalk plaques decorated with lozenge designs redolent of Grooved Ware and passage grave art (Vatcher 1969; Harding 1988). It could, indeed, be suggested that the formal quality of deposition in pit deposits increases with proximity to the Durrington Walls henge. It is the Grooved Ware from the pits near the monument which has most in common with the pottery located in the henges in terms of design complexity. Equally, marine

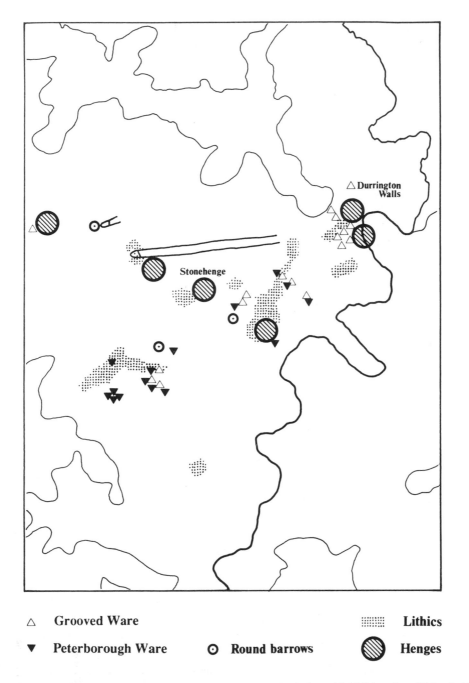

△    **Grooved Ware**                                                    **Lithics**

▼    **Peterborough Ware**        ⊙  **Round barrows**                   **Henges**

Figure 7.2    Salisbury Plain: later Neolithic activity (author's data with additions from Richards 1984)

shells have been found in the pits at Woodlands, Ratfyn and Larkhill (Stone 1935; 1949; Wainwright *et al.* 1971), yet not further west. Given the connotations of the exotic and distant imputed to Grooved Ware itself, the symbolic significance of shells brought to central Wiltshire from the coast might be considerable, in creating a manifest presence of the alien. The deliberate nature of these same deposits is further emphasised by the appearance of Woodlands Pit 4 as 'a basketful of material deliberately placed upside down' (Stone 1949, 123) and the capping of Pit 1 with a flint cairn (Stone and Young 1948, 289).

The intra-site analysis of materials within the Durrington Walls henge revealed a massive emphasis on the division of material items into conceptual categories (Richards and Thomas 1984). Durrington displays in microcosm a set of rules of classification which was applied to the landscape as a whole. Particular practices which could no longer be reconciled were separated into different areas of the landscape. The dead were excluded from the henge, together with the wild. All the later Neolithic pottery which has been found within two kilometres of Durrington Walls is Grooved Ware. It may be that only some members of society had access to this pottery, to the other associated items, and indeed to this part of the landscape. However, this may have been less because these objects represented 'prestige items' than because individuals gained access to them by virtue of eligibility to engage in the practices for which they were intended. Merely owning a Grooved Ware pot may have been less significant than being in a position to use Grooved Ware vessels within a particular discourse.

The raising of the bank and ditch at Durrington Walls to create a huge henge monument seems to have been a relatively late development. The dates for the primary silting of the ditch fall around 2000 bc, but by then the site had already been important for some time, possibly as a consequence of its status as a natural amphitheatre (Wainwright and Longworth 1971). Thorpe and Richards (1984) suggest that the change at Durrington from a series of free-standing timber structures to an enclosed space is roughly synchronous with the arrival of Beaker pottery in the area: surely more than a coincidence. It is probably equally significant that the earliest evidence for the use of Beaker ceramics in the area is found in the area around Wilsford and Normanton. That is to say, the initial use of Beakers was confined to locations where Grooved Ware was not appropriate.

If the construction of the bank and ditch at Durrington Walls, enforcing the distinction between those with access to ritual activities and those without (Braithwaite 1984, 99), was the initial response to the development of forms of discourse based upon a new set of material symbols, a more intensive expression can be seen at the later site of Woodhenge. For all its architectural complexity, Woodhenge is much smaller than Durrington, and for this reason Thorpe and Richards cite it as evidence of the failing power of an élite to control corvée labour (1984, 79). An equally important point is the increased formality of the monument. In the alignment of the timber rings towards the axis of the midsummer sunrise (Cunnington 1929, 9) is seen an attempt to extend control across space from a single point, in social circumstances in which the construction of extensive timber alignments was no longer practical. Both Durrington Walls and Woodhenge represent the contraction of a particular discourse back into a small area, yet give the impression that the order of classification which they embodied extended across the entire landscape.

Thorpe and Richards (1984) suggest that in the eighteenth century bc 'traditional authority' was finally eclipsed in the Stonehenge area, with the rise to dominance of the continentally based 'prestige goods hierarchy' connected with the use of Beakers. It was at this point that Beaker sherds first came to be deposited at Durrington Walls, and ceremonial activities at the site seem to have ceased. More cautiously, we might suggest a slow shift within the priorities of the society concerned, away from one aspect of its ritual life and towards another, leaving the henge monuments obsolete. The extent of the area in which Beaker burials were deposited seems to have expanded at this time, and a number of inhumations took place in the immediate vicinity of Durrington Walls.

The early second millennium bc appears to have been a period of cultural confusion and *bricolage* in the Stonehenge area. The traditional separations between different spheres of practice were blurred and broken down. The introduction of the Beaker system disrupted the division between corporate ritual and funerary practice, whilst the reuse of Stonehenge itself as a cremation cemetery redefined the monument as a space of death rather than of life. The Stonehenge cremations, and similar deposits found in a number of monuments in the immediate area, are arguably contemporary with the earlier Beakers. Their presence underlines the collapse of a system of classification and division which allowed contradictory elements (the corporate and the individual) to exist side by side within the same social formation.

The burial of the cremations at Stonehenge may roughly coincide with the first phase of construction in stone at the site. Stonehole 97 (Pitts 1982) is cut by the Heel Stone ditch, which is in turn postdated by the Avenue bank (*ibid.*, 93). Pottery from the stonehole of the Heel Stone is of Beaker fabric (Atkinson 1956, 70). Beyond this its date is uncertain. On stratigraphic grounds it is essential to postulate a stone phase prior to the arrival of the bluestones, using the 'substantially natural builders' (*ibid.*, 78), the unworked sarsens of the Heel Stone, Station Stones, Portal Stones and a presumed stone avenue of which Stone 97 was an element. Such an early lithic phase would have coincided temporally with the construction of Woodhenge.

The location of this monument in an area where individual burials were being deposited, and where both Beaker and Peterborough vessels were in use is an indication of the increasingly contradictory nature of society. References to the exotic and to the traditional were being made and mixed at random, presumably in the effort to maintain order in a situation where the resources which might guarantee stability had been undermined.

## The Upper Thames Valley

A striking contrast with the Salisbury Plain Neolithic sequence can be found on the gravel terraces of Oxfordshire and Gloucestershire. Here, earlier Neolithic settlement seems to have been sparse (Fig. 7.3). The only monument in the Upper Thames Valley which has provided radiocarbon dates in the fourth millennium bc is the Abingdon causewayed enclosure, and even in this case the earlier dates, from charcoal samples,

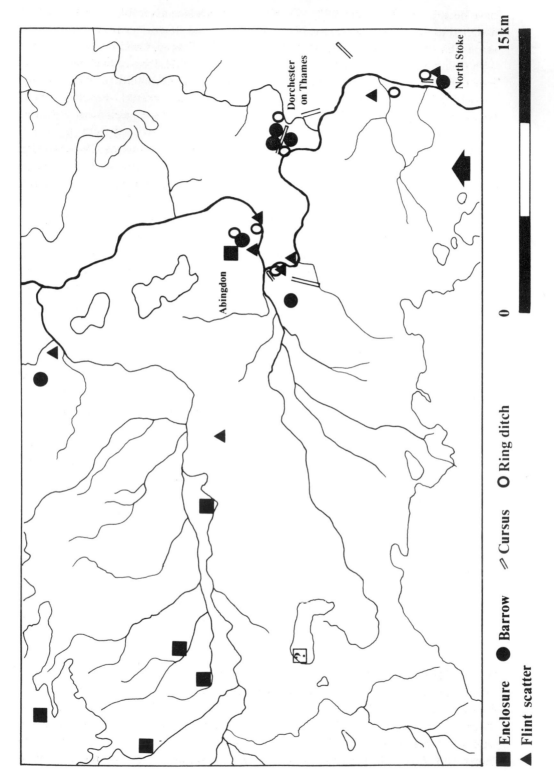

■ **Enclosure**  ● **Barrow**  ⚬ **Cursus**  ○ **Ring ditch**

▲ **Flint scatter**

Figure 7.3   Upper Thames Valley: earlier Neolithic activity

North Stoke

Dorchester on Thames

Abingdon

0            15 km

have been queried (Avery 1982, 49). Most of the surface assemblages which can be assigned to the earlier part of the Neolithic are located downriver from Oxford. The same area also contains all burials of Kinnes' (1979) Stages A and B, all ring ditches with Abingdon Ware associations, and the great bulk of the long or oval barrows and mortuary enclosures. It was on the extreme northern edge of this cluster of activity that the Abingdon enclosure lay. It is thus arguable that the stretch of gravel terraces between Abingdon and North Stoke represents the primary nucleus of Neolithic settlement in the Upper Thames Valley.

The Abingdon site itself seems to have been a two-phase construction, the outer ditch having been added to enlarge the area enclosed (Avery 1982, 15). In the first phase the ditch and bank appear to have been relatively insubstantial structures, while the filling of the ditch consists of deliberately placed deposits of fully rotted organic material (*ibid.*, 17). The closest parallel for this is from Wessex, in the organic deposits carefully placed in the ditch segments at Hambledon Hill (Mercer 1980, 30). If the ditches at Abingdon were essentially quarry pits for a simple dump rampart, it seems likely that their filling with organic layers alternating with sterile lenses is a consequence of the periodic, or cyclical, collection and burial of material which derived from activities which took place, also on a cyclical basis, within the enclosure. The ceramic assemblage at Abingdon is dominated by open bowls and cups (Case in Avery 1982, 30), while the faunal assemblage contains examples of articulated skeletal elements (Cram in Avery 1982, 46).

This evidence suggests that the Abingdon enclosure began its life as a relatively minor monument used for periodic activities by scattered communities living downriver as far as North Stoke. However, with the digging of the more substantial outer ditch and the construction of the associated turf-revetted rampart (Case 1956, 14), it is arguable that the character of the monument changed. The more reliable of the radiocarbon dates, ranging from 2760±135 bc (BM-352) to 2500±145 bc (BM-354) are from bone and antler from the upper levels of the inner ditch, and appear to relate to this phase of activity. At the very end of the period of use of the enclosure, to judge from a date of 2550±60 bc (BM-2392), an oval barrow with two articulated adult burials, one with jet slider and polished flint blade, the other probably with kite-shaped arrowhead, was built nearby at Barrow Hills (Bradley, Chambers and Halpin 1984, 2). This is a direct parallel for mid-third millennium mounds at Hambledon Hill, Whitesheet Hill, Maiden Castle and Robin Hood's Ball. The combination of a shift to a fortified enclosure and a prestigious monumental burial seems to indicate that, as elsewhere, the enclosure had become intimately connected with the activities of an élite group.

Of the other monuments within the long mound tradition in the Upper Thames Valley, almost all fall typologically into the later part of the sequence. Several of the monuments at Dorchester on Thames (Atkinson, Piggott and Sandars 1951) can be interpreted as oval mounds (Bradley and Chambers 1988). The bank barrow at North Stoke, dated to 2622±49 bc (BM-1405) appears to run between a 'mortuary enclosure' similar to that at Dorchester and a peculiar arrangement of ditches at the north end (Case and Whittle 1982). The one site which is outside the 'core area' of settlement is that at New Wintles, Eynsham (Kenward 1982), which can be interpreted as a simple mortuary structure similar to those under Wayland's Smithy I (Atkinson 1965) and Haddenham (Hodder and Shand 1988).

These long and oval structures do not form a homogeneous group, and the great variability of earlier Neolithic mortuary practice is emphasised by the presence of ring ditches with Abingdon Ware in their primary ditch fills at Corporation Farm (Bradley and Holgate 1984, 120) and Thrupp Farm (Thomas and Wallis 1982, 184). A ring ditch at Newnham Murren, Wallingford, with a crouched female burial, is perhaps dated by a sherd of Abingdon Ware in the grave fill (Moorey 1982).

A further element of mortuary practice which seems to have persisted throughout the Neolithic in the Upper Thames was the deposition of human skeletal remains in pits. At Dorchester on Thames, near the south-east end of the cursus, a pit with human bones (largely cranial) was excavated, and dated to 2850±130 bc (OxA-119). Similarly, Pit F at Sutton Courtenay contained the bones of a woman and two children (Leeds 1923, 151–2), and Pit V ten skulls, all but one of which may have been male (Leeds 1934, 267). The chronological relationship of these pits to the cursus is unclear. At Tolley's Pit, Cassington, a pit containing six skeletons appears to be of rather later date, as maggot-decorated sherds were found in the fill (Leeds 1940). At Barrow Hills, F483 contained two fragmentary bodies, with transverse and barbed and tanged arrowheads in the fill (Bradley, Chambers and Halpin 1984, 21). The analogy with pit graves in Cranborne Chase (Pitt Rivers 1898) suggests that some of these sites may have been involved with the process of bone circulation, rather than simple inhumation, and it is suggested that the use of human bones as artefacts of symbolic power was of particular importance in the Upper Thames area. Sutton Courtenay V and Dorchester both show the deposition of skulls in areas which would later be the sites of cursus monuments. Skull fragments have also been reported from the inner ditch at Abingdon (and also from the enclosure at Staines, downriver; Kinnes 1979, 120), in the ditch of the Barrow Hills over the mound (Bradley, Chambers and Halpin 1984, 5), in one pit and one ditch segment at New Wintles (Kenward 1982, 51), in the ditch of Dorchester Site VIII (Ashmolean Museum), with later Neolithic material in Sutton Courtenay Pit Q (Leeds 1934), and with Fengate Ware in pits at Astrop, Northants (Ashmolean Museum). In addition, a human pelvis was found in the outer ditch at Abingdon (Case 1956). It seems unlikely that all of these cases can have been the result of carelessness on the part of the Neolithic population. The interpretation which is suggested here is that the deposition of parts of ancestral human bodies, and particularly the skull, in auspicious locations was regarded as a means of 'presencing' the dead in the landscape.

A peculiarity of the distribution of earlier Neolithic monuments in the Upper Thames is the cluster of causewayed enclosures some way upstream from Oxford, around Lechlade. These include Aston Bampton (Benson and Miles 1974, 39), Little Clanfield (*ibid.*, 33), Signet Hill, Westwell (R. Hingley, pers. comm.), Eastleach (Palmer 1976), Down Ampney (R. Hingley, pers. comm.) and Langford (Palmer 1976). Yet aside from these monuments, traces of earlier Neolithic activity in the area are comparatively scarce. This might be explained by the lesser degree of gravel extraction further up the Thames (Benson and Miles 1974, 76). However, while scatters of lithics seem to be absent from this area, flint and stone axes are present in large numbers, many from river and stream contexts. This might indicate that the upper reaches of the Thames were less an area of intensive settlement than one which was visited at particular times of year, perhaps for seasonal grazing. This rests well with the suggestion that the enclosures in the area are to be connected with a broader pattern of settlement, perhaps including the Cotswold uplands (Holgate 1988a).

The later third millennium in the Upper Thames saw a marked expansion of settlement from this 'core' area, taking in new areas of river gravels upriver and also moving onto heavier soils (Fig. 7.4). This expansion of settlement has an interesting relationship to the development of monuments. Cursus monuments are common in the 'core area' of earlier Neolithic settlement, yet are entirely absent from the more northerly stretch of the Thames which includes the important areas of later Neolithic activity at Eynsham, Cassington and Stanton Harcourt. These linear monuments often incorporate earlier sites or places of importance within their plans: the Dorchester cursus ditch cuts across those of Site VIII, a rectangular 'mortuary enclosure' (Atkinson, Piggott and Sandars 1951), the North Stoke bank barrow butts onto a similar enclosure and narrowly avoids a presumably earlier ring ditch (Bradley and Holgate 1984, 102), whilst the Drayton/Sutton Courtenay cursus was built over an area which may already have held two or more pit graves. This linking and incorporation of venerated places was taking place within the settled landscape at the same time as some elements of the community were breaking off to farm the land upriver. It betrays a similar desire for control to that which is seen in the deposition of human remains, possibly indicating a degree of social instability related to changing residence patterns. The contrast between the 'parent' zone and the area of secondary settlement is one which underlies several others which develop in the later Neolithic.

Bradley (in Bradley and Holgate 1984, 130) emphasises the small scale of monuments in the Thames by comparison with Wessex. To this must be added the consideration of number. Cranborne Chase, for instance, has one very large cursus while the Thames has at least seven small ones. This may relate in some way to the abilities of the societies concerned to mobilise labour: it need not mean that there were fewer people in the Thames Valley. Furthermore, the entire population may have considered themselves a single political unit. The implication of the presence of numerous small monuments clustered into a number of separate foci within the Thames Valley is that a less centralised form of social organisation existed there than in other parts of southern England. Social action was circumscribed at a lower level.

Mortuary sites of later Neolithic date are plentiful in the Upper Thames Valley (Fig. 7.4). The Dorchester complex contains a great proportion of these, yet examples are also known from Barrow Hills and Mount Farm (Case 1986). The presence of later Neolithic burials further to the north-west is shown by the Linch Hill Corner site, near Stanton Harcourt. There a double ring ditch contained a central grave, holding a female burial with jet slider and flint knife (Grimes 1944, 34). Ring ditches with Peterborough Ware associations have been excavated at Stanton Harcourt and Cassington (Case 1963).

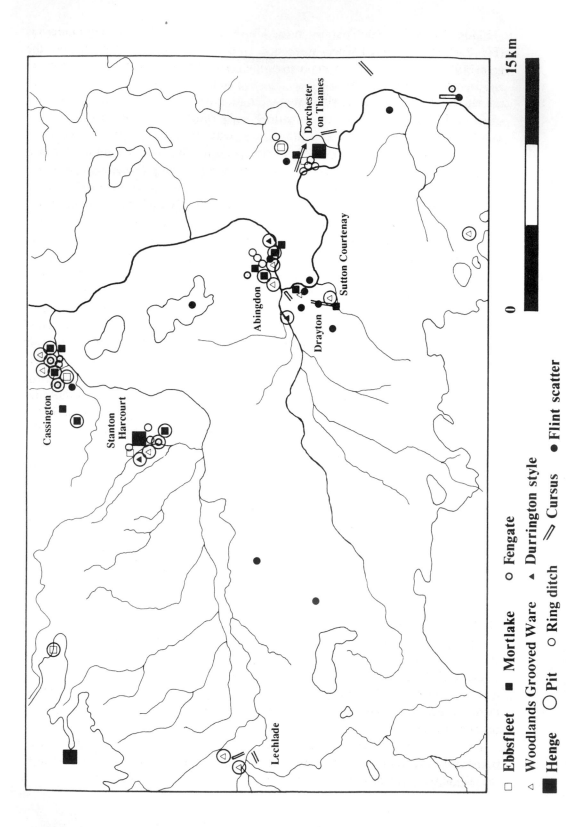

Figure 7.4 Upper Thames Valley: later Neolithic activity

□ Ebbsfleet  ■ Mortlake  ○ Fengate

△ Woodlands Grooved Ware  ▲ Durrington style

▣ Henge  ◯ Pit  ○ Ring ditch  ⫽ Cursus  ● Flint scatter

0                    15 km

Finds of later Neolithic pottery in the Upper Thames Valley are very numerous (Fig. 7.4). Peterborough Wares are frequently found in mortuary contexts, but the great bulk of finds comes from pits cut into the gravel subsoil. Grooved Ware finds are almost entirely from pits. As in Wessex, the two ceramic traditions are never found in the same context, but the lack of spatial separation between them is more akin to the situation in East Anglia, where pits with Peterborough, Beaker or Grooved Ware sherds are frequently found on the same site (Healy 1984, 104). It is possible that in the small, competitive and unstable communities of the later Neolithic, different subgroups supported their claims to power through access to a variety of external exchange systems and contacts.

All the Grooved Ware in the area falls into Longworth's Woodlands and Durrington Walls subclasses (Wainwright and Longworth 1971), and largely the former. Close association between Grooved Ware and henge monuments is not found in the Thames Valley, although it may be that the depositional practices associated with Durrington Walls-style pottery were rather more formal. For instance, at Abingdon Common a pit was located isolated from any other prehistoric material, lined with stones and containing very large sherds of six Durrington Walls Grooved Ware vessels (Parrington 1978, 31–3). Stanton Harcourt Pit A (Thomas 1955, 4) contained a highly decorated Durrington vessel inverted on the floor of the pit, in a matrix of dark loam. The only other finds were six flint flakes. Nearby pits contained much smaller sherds in the Woodlands style (Case and Whittle 1982, 103). Another isolated pit containing Durrington Walls sherds was excavated at Thrupp Farm (Thomas and Wallis 1982, 184). Particularly in the case of pits containing Woodlands-style sherds, it is possible to discern a relationship between Grooved Ware pits and standing monuments in the Upper Thames. At Barrow Hills, a number of highly ornate Woodlands sherds, and also less diagnostic sherds with spiral motifs, have been recovered from pits in the vicinity of a barrow group which has its origins in the Neolithic (finds with Oxford Archaeological Unit). Near Cassington Mill (Case and Whittle 1982) a series of pits, some with Woodlands Grooved Ware, was excavated in an area rich in ring ditches and Beaker graves. At Lechlade (Jones 1976) pits with Woodlands sherds, burnt soil, charcoal, flints and animal bones were found at the Loders and Roughground Farm, close by two cursus monuments, a pit alignment and posthole arrangements (*ibid.*, 2). The relationship between Grooved Ware pits and earlier monuments is particularly close at Sutton Courtenay (Leeds 1923; 1927; 1934), where it seems that the richest pits are those *between* the cursus ditches. Two consistent elements can be detected in the filling of pits with Woodlands pottery: burnt organic soil and animal bones. At Blewbury 'the animal bone had evidently been deposited as joints, as articulated shaft and knuckle bones were apparent' (Halpin 1984, 1). These bones (kindly shown to me by Claire Halpin) include roughly equal proportions of pig and cattle, and are largely from the meat-rich parts of the animals. At Cassington (Jackson 1956) pig bones predominated.

The essential features of the use of these pits were the consumption (and sometimes perhaps the intentional wasting) of meat, the breaking of pottery, the burning of fires, the digging of a pit and the burial of sherds, bones, fire debris and various items of exotic material culture. It may be that activities connected with the use of Durrington Walls pottery were less concerned with the consumption of meat, and more with the deposition of complete vessels. As was suggested in Chapter 4, these deposits can be seen as a means of re-socialising locations of importance.

The rite of individual inhumation with grave goods had already been practised in the Upper Thames for some centuries, before the appearance of Beakers. Early Beaker graves are common throughout the Upper Thames Valley, but it is striking that a concentration of very rich Step 2 burials exists at Stanton Harcourt, within two kilometres of the Devil's Quoits. By contrast, no Step 1 or 2 burials have been found within two kilometres of the Dorchester complex: the radiocarbon dates suggest that the cremation burials are contemporary. So it seems that by the nineteenth century bc two ceremonial sites in the Upper Thames, each with a major henge monument, were operating mutually exclusive mortuary rites. At Stanton Harcourt, in the newly colonised zone, Beaker burials expressed the wealth of a few individuals, while at Dorchester on Thames a much greater proportion of the population was afforded burial, yet the relative distribution of grave goods and the spatial organisation of the cemeteries suggest that status differences were expressed in this rite.

Beaker burials in the Upper Thames reached a peak with Steps 2 and 3, in contrast with more conservative areas of southern Britain. It is interesting that the richest Step 3 burial of all, a male with tanged copper dagger, bronze knife, slate wristguard and W/MR Beaker, came from Dorchester Site XII, a small ring ditch outside the south entrance of the Big Rings henge (Clarke 1970; R. J. C. Atkinson's notes, Ashmolean Museum). It is the only Beaker burial in the entire complex. By 1700 bc fewer Beaker burials were being interred in the Upper Thames Valley, and there are no Step 5 burials in the area at all. There are only three Step 6 burials, of which two are extremely rich: Radley 203, a male with S2(W) Beaker, ten flint flakes, five barbed and tanged arrowheads, an antler spatula and a bronze awl (Bradley, Chambers and Halpin 1984, 15), and the rather remote Lambourne 31, with S2(W) Beaker, jet button, six arrowheads, scraper, strike-a-light and two knives (Clarke 1970). The great renaissance of Beaker burial in the Upper Thames Valley did not come until Step 7, with the flat grave cemeteries at Cassington and Eynsham (Case 1977, 82). So, while the Upper Thames possesses one of the most complete sequences of Beaker burials in the south of England (Bradley and Holgate 1984, 128), these burials were by no means deposited at a uniform rate throughout. It cannot be claimed that privileged burial with exotic grave goods was a normal way of disposing of the dead at any stage; it seems more likely that this increased investment of effort was a form of conspicuous consumption in itself. The chronological 'waves' of Beaker burials seen in the Upper Thames and elsewhere can thus be interpreted as a response to periods of social instability or transition, in which claims to land or authority were in need of clarification. The first of these horizons, constituted by Steps 2 and 3, commenced contemporary with the floruit of indigenous burial rites at Dorchester on Thames, and ended with the interment of a spectacularly rich burial outside the Big Rings henge.

The interrelation of these various cultural elements through the later part of the Neolithic sequence in the Upper Thames can perhaps be clarified by considering one particular set of sites in more detail. The complex of monuments at Dorchester on Thames was constructed over a period of hundreds of years, and hence its structure must be considered as the outcome of a series of acts of building rather than as a unitary design (Atkinson, Piggott and Sandars 1951; Bradley and Chambers 1988). The earliest structural phase of the complex consists of a cemetery of oval monuments (Fig. 7.5). Site VIII, the long mortuary enclosure, was recognised by Atkinson (1948, 66) as an early element, since its ditch had entirely silted up by the time that the cursus had been dug across it. Bradley (in Bradley and Holgate 1984, 118) points out that Ditch II of Site XI, its earliest structural unit, is markedly oval in plan, and that it and Site II share a common alignment with Site VIII. When the first ditch of Site II is separated from the plan it too is markedly ovoid, its long axis aligned on Site I. It was originally claimed that Site II Phase I had never been finished, and that the ditches had been refilled before any silting had taken place (Atkinson, Piggott and Sandars 1951, 23). However, this assumes that the material on the ditch bottom (a fine black soil) was the product of the destruction of the monument. Were this so, one might expect the material which filled the ditch segments to be similar to that which had been taken out. However, if the ditch segments were the source of material for a central mound, Zeuner's findings (in Atkinson, Piggott and Sandars 1951, 121) that 'the dark fillings of the pits and ditches are debris from fires mixed with other organic refuse and varying proportions of natural soil' are illuminating. It may be that at these sites, and at others like the round mount at Newnham Murren (Moorey 1982), the mound itself served as a platform for activities involving the burning of fires, at a time before silting had taken place into the ditches. It could thus have been some time later that the circular ditch of Phase II was cut.

Site I, upon which Site II is aligned, is also oval in plan. The original ditch was U-sectioned and produced sherds of Abingdon Ware. Later recuts containing Peter-borough sherds are concentrated on the west side of the ditch, in a manner which recalls the deposition of Peterborough Ware in long mound forecourts. Despite the distortions in plan which have resulted from this recutting it is possible to suggest that this edge originally constituted a façade trench. A parallel for such a monument might be found in Grendon, Northants, a subrectangular ring ditch with façade, dated to the earlier third millennium bc (Gibson 1985). At Site I, the remains of a crouched burial were found on the old land surface (Atkinson, Piggott and Sandars 1951, 12). This indicates a similarity to the Barrow Hills, Radley oval mound, also with crouched burials. At the east end of the complex, a D-shaped enclosure pre-dating the cursus is presumably roughly contemporary with this phase of activity (Bradley and Chambers 1988, 279). This enclosure in turn cuts a pit containing human bones, dated to 2850±130 bc (OxA-119) (*ibid.*, 280). This effectively provides a commencement date for the entire complex.

A second major phase of activity at Dorchester came with the construction of a series of circular mounds. At both Sites II and XI an oval monument was 'converted' into a round one, and later enlarged. The break in the cursus south-west ditch to avoid the outer ditch of Site XI indicates that all of this must have occurred before the construc-tion of the cursus. At Site XI the greasy black soil was again found directly on the

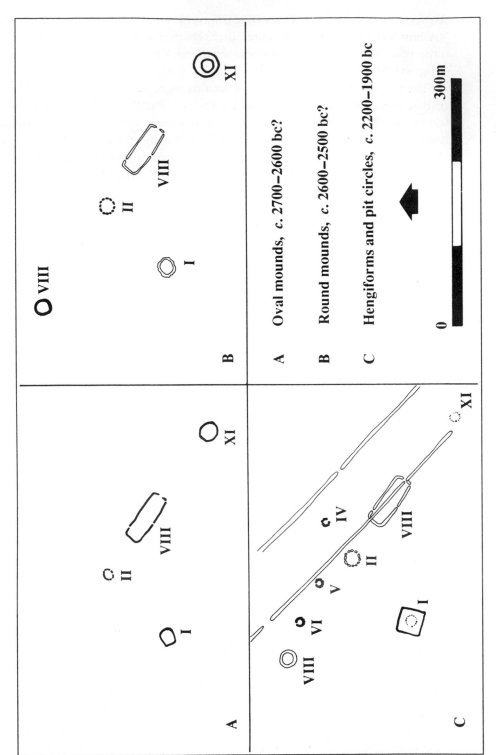

Figure 7.5 The Dorchester on Thames complex: sequence

bottom of Ditch I (that is, Phase II); a transverse arrowhead was found in this material (Ashmolean Museum). In the outer ditch, Ditch III, Ebbsfleet sherds were found in a layer of dark soil which overlay a primary silting. Ebbsfleet sherds were also recovered from the upper silting of Site VIII.

The cutting of the cursus ditch, on an alignment slightly different from that of the earlier sites, is dated by antler from the ditch base at 2560±100 bc (BM-2443). The ditch cuts through Site VIII and up to the perimeter of Site XI, incorporating these minor monuments into a greater structure in a manner also seen at North Stoke and Drayton. One interpretation of this incorporation is as a reassertion of the social collectivity, repudiating the significance of dissonant social trajectories and their monumental expression.

At some point in the later third millennium the ditch of Site I was recut, most extensively on the south-west side. The large sherds of Fengate Ware in these recuts, contrasting with the small scraps of pottery elsewhere in the monument, indicate that this was an act of purposeful deposition, laying claim to the ancestral influences of the site. Still later, the mound must have been flattened to enable a circle of posts or pits to be dug, changing the alignment from NE/SW to E/W. The small sherds of pottery from these holes are perhaps of Beaker affinity (Atkinson *et al.* 1951, 9). The square ditch which encloses the site shares the alignment of the circle of holes, and hence, despite the Abingdon Ware in this ditch, it can be suggested that it too was dug at a late date. Allen's mention of a round barrow within a square ditch at Limlow Hill, Cambridgeshire, indicates that the feature need not be early in date (Allen 1938, 170). A similar circle of holes was cut at Site IX, while a circle of posts inside the south-east end of the cursus has provided radiocarbon dates of 2110±110 and 2170±120 bc (BM-2161R and BM-2164R). This may also be the approximate date of construction for Sites IV, V and VI. Site V at least appears to have had an external ditch, although IV and VI may have been causewayed-ditched round barrows. As with the earlier monuments, deposits of burnt soil have been found in the ditches of these sites, frequently interdigitated with layers of sterile grave (Atkinson *et al.* 1951, 38).

By the start of the second millennium, then, a number of small monuments, pit- or post-circles, some with external banks, had been constructed in and around the cursus. The next phase of activity consisted of the reuse of these sites as cremation cemeteries. At the end of the cursus the secondary nature of the cremation deposits has been demonstrated by the date of 2120±130 bc (BM-2163R) for deposits associated with the post-circle. On Site IV, cremation deposits in the ditch are high in the sections (Atkinson *et al.* 1951, 38). In all, 128 cremations were recovered from the sites excavated by Atkinson, Piggott and Sandars, with others located in more recent excavations by the Oxford Archaeological Unit. T. H. Gee's notes (Ashmolean Museum) indicate that a cremation in a pit was located ten yards south-east of Site I in 1956. Others might have been present. Some form of spatial expression of differences between the burials is certainly indicated at Site II. The burial with the richest artefacts, Cremation 21, equipped with bone skewer, pin, flint fabricator, flint flake and stone macehead, was found in the centre of the monument, presumably having been cut from the crest of a still surviving mound. The other cremations were arranged

around the edge of the mound in a semicircle, the burials to the east being predominantly young and including females, those to the west largely old and male. Grave
goods were restricted to the burials in the western part. In view of the observation that
the later Neolithic saw an increased interest in astronomical phenomena, and particularly in efforts to link monuments to heavenly movements and alignments, it may
be that these burials indicate a link between human existence and the diurnal cycle of
eastern sunrise and western sunset. The inequalities of this community were thus
being reconciled by their portrayal as a part of a natural cycle (Bourdieu 1977,
143–58).

The Dorchester on Thames monuments can be seen as an expression of the tension
between power invested in the individual or in the collectivity. The ebb and flow of
local social arrangements resulted in shifts in a strategy of representation. Sites XI and
II were 'converted' from oval into round mounds, although it is to be assumed that the
rite of burial was articulated interment throughout. The building of the cursus
distorted the meaning of all previous monuments, yet another series of small
monuments pre-dated it. These in turn became the foci for a rite of burial which was
much less exclusive, but which through its use of space drew distinctions between
individuals and imposed a particular interpretation upon the nature of social relations.
The place of the Dorchester Big Rings henge monument in this sequence seems
unclear. The pottery from Atkinson's excavation was Beaker (Clarke 1970, 493),
which may indicate a late date for its construction. However, at the other major henge
of Stanton Harcourt Devil's Quoits, Gray (1973; 1974) indicates that finds were very
scarce, the ditches having been distorted by continual cleaning out. The date of
1640±70 bc (HAR-1888) for bone trampled into the silting agrees with dates for
Beaker secondary activity at the henges of Condicote and Gorsey Bigbury. Thus the
date of 2060±120 bc (HAR-1887) may relate to the primary use of the site. This being
the case, it remains to be explained why so little activity is evidenced at either of these
large henge monuments in the pre-Beaker era. It should be noted that Big Rings lies
in what was defined earlier in this chapter as the primary core of Neolithic settlement,
while the Devil's Quoits is situated in the area which was utilised only in the later
Neolithic. It has already been implied that these two areas were in some way separate
social units in the later Neolithic. Perhaps each symbolised its corporate identity
through the construction of a large henge monument, but the perennial presence of
deposits of burnt organic material, animal bones and broken pottery at the *smaller*
monuments indicates that ritual practice was more often carried out at a more local
level.

### The Avebury district

The north Wiltshire downs have been one of the most intensively studied areas of
Neolithic Britain. Keiller's excavations at Windmill Hill and Avebury, Cunnington's
at the Sanctuary, Piggott's at the West Kennet long barrow and Atkinson's at Silbury
Hill have between them done much to create our image of what constitutes the British
Neolithic. Observations made in the immediate vicinity of Avebury have been turned
outward and used as the yardstick by which the Neolithic is measured. However, this

should not be allowed to create the impression that the area is typical of Neolithic southern Britain.

To begin with, however, earlier Neolithic activity in the area may have had much in common with other landscapes. In much the same way as on Salisbury Plain, the flint scatters of earlier Neolithic date in the Avebury area are small, and localised (observation based on fieldwalking 1983–4). Scatters are often situated at the junction of chalk uplands and wet lowlands. This is particularly the case with the sites along the south-facing escarpment of Milk Hill/Tan Hill/Golden Ball Hill and the Bishop's Cannings Downs, overlooking the greensand Vale of Pewsey (Fig. 7.6). The pattern suggested is one of spatially discrete habitation sites clustered around the headwaters of the Kennet, located on the hillslopes of the Upper and Middle Chalk. The massive spread of clay-with-flints around the Savernake Forest seems to have been avoided (as far as can be told from fieldwork, which has been scanty in that area), yet already on the hill country of Hackpen and the Aldbourne Downs activity seems to have started on the interstice of the clay-with-flints and Upper Chalk. Passmore (n.d., 19) held that the 'Ewin's Down, Stock Close and Stock Lane ridge of down has yielded more and better specimens of worked flints than any place I know' and that 'this is one of the most extensive flint manufactories in England' (*ibid.*, 20). While the bulk of the material from these sites is later Neolithic, a sizeable proportion is Mesolithic and earlier Neolithic (Holgate 1984). Passmore (*n.d.*) believed that indentations in the ground on Hackpen and around Barbury Castle were flint workings, a suggestion which gains credence in the light of the excavation of flint 'grubbing pits' at Hambledon Hill (Mercer 1982). The pits on Hackpen can still be seen in suitable lighting conditions. Moreover, fieldwalking conducted by R. Holgate and the author in 1983–4 indicated that a belt of debitage followed the contour of Hackpen precisely where the chalk and clay-with-flints meet, and where particularly high-quality flint might be expected to be located.

The faunal remains from earlier Neolithic contexts confirm that, as elsewhere in southern England, cattle were the predominant species. By comparison with the figures for southern Wessex sheep are more heavily represented, which may indicate that intensive clearance had taken place west of the Winterbourne and Kennet (Smith 1984, 103), although the usual reservations that few of these sites represent typical domestic assemblages apply. Molluscan faunas in old land surfaces at West Kennet, Horslip, Silbury Hill, Beckhampton Road and South Street give the impression of an extensive cleared area, yet with a variety of forms of ground cover, perhaps including small cultivated plots (Evans 1971, 65–6; Evans *et al.* 1988). At the enclosures of Windmill Hill and Knap Hill, woodland prevailed before the construction of the monuments (*ibid.*). However, even at Millbarrow, north of Windmill Hill, there are hints of extensive clearance (Whittle 1989, 7). The extreme density of settlement throughout the Neolithic in the Avebury area possibly entitles us to consider it as a single political unit, and this evidence of a large expanse of cleared country may indicate that some aspects of economic activities were organised on a large scale.

From early on in the sequence a degree of cultural heterogeneity is evident in the

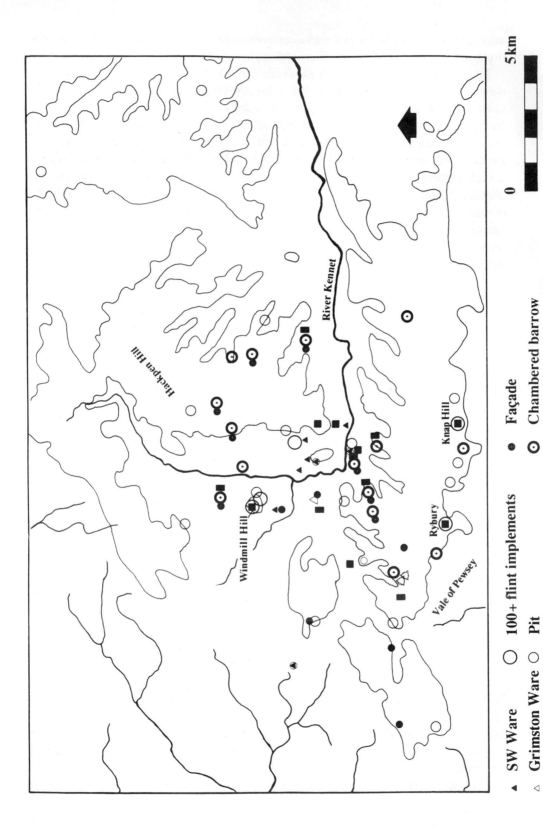

▲ SW Ware      ○ 100+ flint implements      ● Façade

△ Grimston Ware      ◉ Pit      ◎ Chambered barrow

■ Decorated ware      ■ 200+ ft      ● Earth barrow

Figure 7.6    Earlier Neolithic Avebury: pottery (those in small open circles represent assemblages from pits), lithic scatters (open circles) and long mounds (filled

area. The pottery from the pre-enclosure activity at Windmill Hill is closely related to the south-western group, as exemplified by the Maiden Castle and Hembury assemblages (Smith 1965a, 28). Similar undecorated pottery with lugs and featureless rims was found in a pit on Waden Hill (Thomas 1956), beneath the barrow Avebury G55 (Smith 1965b), in the ditches of Horslip Barrow (Ashbee, Smith and Evans 1979, 223), beneath the Avebury bank (Smith 1965a, 224), on the West Kennet Avenue (*ibid.*, 232) and picked up on the surface by W. E. V. Young at the foot of Avebury Down (Avebury Museum). However, pits located beneath barrows G61 and G62a on Roughridge Hill, Bishop's Cannings (Proudfoot 1965), contained vessels with heavy carinations and everted rims more akin to the Grimston tradition (M. Pitts, pers. comm.). Similar vessels were recovered from the old land surface beneath the South Street long barrow (Ashbee, Smith and Evans 1979, 270). Two traditions of plain pottery were thus current in the Avebury area in the earlier third millennium bc. It is worth recording at this point Howard's (1981, 25) conclusions on the basis of a petrological study of the earlier Neolithic wares at Windmill Hill, that the local pottery was made by two social groups exploiting the clays of the Marlborough Downs and the Kennet Valley respectively. The presence of decorated vessels in the ditches at Windmill Hill, but not in the pre-bank pits, may indicate that the idea of pottery decoration was actually introduced in the course of the earlier Neolithic, from the east. Windmill Hill itself, with its widely spaced multiple ditch rings, is more akin to the causewayed enclosures of the Thames Valley than those of Wessex (Palmer 1976). The preferential deposition of decorated sherds at mortuary sites like West Kennet (Piggott 1962) and enclosures like Windmill Hill, Knap Hill (Connah 1965, 11) and Rybury (Smith 1965c) indicates that such pottery may have been of special significance in the Avebury region.

One of Smith's (1965a; 1966) most interesting conclusions from the Windmill Hill excavations was that the huge dumps of animal bones in the ditches, including articulated limbs and associated with unweathered sherds of pottery, implied that communal feasting had taken place. Deposits of waste and organic material would have been placed in the ditches and immediately covered over with raked-down bank material (Smith 1971, 97). More recent excavations (Whittle 1988b; 1990) have shown the deliberate nature of these deposits. One group of material on the top of the primary rubble of the outer ditch consisted of a human child's skull and the butchered skull of a young ox, associated with two cattle horn cores and bones of deer (Whittle 1988b, 2). Other deposits consisted of bundles of bones either tied up or perhaps placed in the ditch in bags (*ibid.*, 5). The 1988 excavations also demonstrated the sheer density of cattle bones in the ditches, a feature not immediately clear from the earlier reports. Re-study of the site records in the Avebury museum added to this impression of formality in deposition – bones from feet, legs and skulls of cattle dominated deposits in the outer ditch, while the meat-rich parts of the carcases were more heavily represented in the innermost of the three ditch circuits. As at the other causewayed enclosures in Wessex, pottery vessels of open, uncarinated form more suited to the consumption than the storage of food dominate the earlier Neolithic ceramic assemblage from Windmill Hill. All of these points add to an impression of activities at the site which involved the consumption of vast quantities of food, and which could not be described as 'domestic'.

The Windmill Hill site also appears to have had a lengthy and complex history. Pre-enclosure features include not only the pits located by Keiller (Smith 1965a), but also postholes and an adult male burial in a pit below the outer bank (Whittle 1990). The comparatively greater scale of the outer bank and ditch over the inner two circuits, and the location of Ebbsfleet sherds well down in the sections of the former, may indicate that this is a later addition to the monument (Whittle 1988b, 5). If so, the increase in the scale of the site fits both with the elaboration of certain other causewayed enclosures in the early/mid-third millennium bc (see Chapter 3 above), and with a particular tendency to monumental aggrandisement notable in the Avebury area.

A remarkable concentration of earthen long mounds, both unchambered and with orthostatic chambers, is focussed on the headwaters of the Kennet (Barker 1984). The record of burials within these barrows is very uneven, and it is difficult to generalise on the available evidence. Nevertheless, an exceptional series of burials was located in the large barrow with transepted terminal chamber at West Kennet (Piggott 1962), and it may be possible to employ the findings from this site to interpret some of the others. The West Kennet barrow appears to have been built at the beginning of the third millennium bc (Atkinson and Piggott 1986). Initial burial deposits included both articulated bodies and clean bones, and it appears that bones were taken out from the chambers as well as placed in them (Thomas and Whittle 1986). It has been argued that access to and knowledge of the contents of the chambers at West Kennet con-stituted a restricted form of social knowledge, granted to a pre-eminent group within society (*ibid.*, 138). Over a period of some hundreds of years, the chambers were entered, experienced, and the contents reinterpreted and placed in new spatial con-figurations. From the start, it seems that the five individual chambers leading off from the central gallery were judged appropriate for the deposition of the bones of different classes of person. Adult males predominated in the westernmost chamber, young persons in the south-east, and so on. It can be argued that this initial connection between particular bounded areas of space and age and gender categories served to bring into being a conceptual order which was both reproduced and transformed by subsequent depositional events.

Over the centuries, highly patterned deposits of human and animal bones, lithics and a great quantity of pottery were placed in the chambers at West Kennet (Thomas and Whittle 1986). Layers of clean chalk and burnt matter provide the matrix for this material. The burnt soil, the animal bones, and the possibility that pottery vessels were deliberately smashed against the portals of the passage all indicate that the context of deposition might have been one of 'feasting with the ancestors'. Interestingly, the bones, pots and flints appear to become more spatially concentrated over time, eventually coming to emphasise the north-east chamber. It may be no more than coincidental that the original burials in this chamber had been of mature individuals. In any case, this spatial restriction of the material 'play' within the tomb interior may be indicative of a further restriction of access to ritual knowledge within the wider community. This argument finds some support in the other tombs of the area.

Of the other barrows, only King's Play Down (Cunnington 1909) bears comparison with the rite of single inhumation practised in later long mounds elsewhere in Wessex. At Oldbury Hill, a male and two female adult skeletons were recovered from chalk-digging (Cunnington 1872), and at Shepherd's Shore five disarticulated burials were excavated (including three adults and one child) (Cunnington 1927). Easton Down also contained disarticulated burials, two adult males and two children (Thurnam 1860). At two sites it is likely that burials had been removed: the chamber at Temple Bottom contained only a few teeth and hand and foot bones (Lukis 1867), whilst that at West Woods was empty save for a deposit of 'black material' (Passmore 1923). By comparison with either southern Wessex or the Cotswolds, these numbers of inter-ments appear rather low. It might be ventured that long mound burial in the Avebury area was always a rite which was relatively exclusive. One might also mention the peculiarity that the earthen long mounds at Beckhampton and South Street contained no primary burials whatsoever (Ashbee, Smith and Evans 1979). This might indicate that these mounds were merely exploiting the outward form of the long mound concept (Thomas 1984), or indeed that in north Wiltshire the fact of being buried in such a mound was of less importance than access to knowledge concerning their construction and contents.

West Kennet appears to have been blocked, and a series of enormous stones erected across its entrance, at a relatively late date (Piggott 1962). Sherds of Beaker pottery came from the upper levels of the filling. The tomb at Manton Down also appears to have been blocked, but excavation showed no signs of later Neolithic activity in the chamber (Barker 1984, 29). Millbarrow Chamber reputedly had been filled with material similar to that at West Kennet (*ibid.*), and indeed stoneholes on the site of the chamber excavated in 1989 produced sherds of Peterborough Ware (Whittle 1989, 5). The mound at West Kennet appears to have been lengthened at some time in its history (Thomas and Whittle 1986, 138), while Millbarrow proved on excavation to have two concentric pairs of flanking ditches, the outer pair presumably having provided material for the enlargement of the mound (Whittle 1989, 4). The peristalith surrounding the mound was interpreted as a secondary feature (*ibid.*). The parallel here with Wayland's Smithy, enlarged from a small mound with timber chamber to a larger monument with stone chamber and peristalith, is very clear (Atkinson 1965). Some of the tombs in the Avebury district seem to have been blocked off comparatively early, others to have been elaborated externally and to have continued to be used. As with the evidence from the West Kennet chambers, this seems to indicate a gradual reduction of the number of 'important' monuments, and of the number of privileged spaces within which restricted knowledge related to the ancestors could be revealed and reproduced. This suggests a slow process through which the number of people having access to this information declined.

By the middle of the third millennium bc, a number of presumably interrelated social groups had firmly established themselves on the headwaters of the Kennet. Their basic repertoire of material culture was that shared by the inhabitants of the south-west of England, yet to this had been added pottery decoration inspired by eastern sources and a class of chambered tomb which is more common on the

Cotswolds. The megalithic tombs of the Avebury region are all terminally chambered, whether simple or transepted, and thus relatively late in date, indicating that they had been inspired by the parent zone to the west. Contacts with the Cotswold and Mendip regions are further emphasised by the oolitic rock and shell-tempered pottery found at Windmill Hill and other sites. The possibility that the vessels imported into the causewayed enclosure contained some archaeologically invisible burden has something of the connotation of tributary relations to it. Inevitably, one is brought back by these considerations to the question of the exchange of lithic items. It is likely that the Marlborough and Lambourne Downs were being exploited for flint from a relatively early date, and these were clearly the nearest sources of high-quality flint to the Mendips, Cotswolds and Upper Thames Valley. The complex of monuments around Avebury may in part owe its existence to communities who were able to exploit their geographical position on the extreme edge of the chalklands. The ability to extract, centralise and mobilise enormous quantities of flint of a much higher quality than could be obtained from pebble beds further west might have provided the Avebury community with the ability to extract exotic goods, social knowledge (including methods of tomb building), personnel and corvée labour from their western contacts. Hence Windmill Hill, placed on the north-west edge of the district, became the premier emporium of Neolithic England. While Hambledon Hill with its outwork systems is a larger monument than Windmill Hill, at that site it is the functions connected with the management of cattle and the disposal of the dead which strike one as of greatest importance. At Windmill Hill it is the sheer bulk of exotica and feasting debris with which the site was associated that seems more significant.

In the later Neolithic, one of the major features which seems to mark Avebury out from the rest of Wessex is a quite different pattern of depositional practices. Both individual burials and pits containing Grooved Ware are rare or absent. Grooved Ware is known from nine sites in the Avebury area, but in almost all cases it has been found in association with other wares. The separation of Grooved Ware from Peterborough pottery is not evident in the region. In southern Wessex, Grooved Ware was the ceramic most often recorded in isolation; around Avebury it is the style least often found unassociated (Fig. 7.7). Indeed, eight sites have Grooved Ware, Peterborough Ware, Beaker and earlier Neolithic pottery all in some kind of association. It can be argued that some of these sites were settlements, yet others are rather peculiar deposits. The material from under the barrow of West Overton G.6b, close to the Sanctuary, included sherds of fifteen Windmill Hill vessels, twenty-four Grooved Ware pots, twenty Peterborough bowls and thirteen Beakers, yet the total lithic assemblage amounted to only one leaf arrowhead, one borer, four scrapers and 125 flakes (Smith and Simpson 1966, 152–5). A similar assemblage of over seventy vessels came from beneath Avebury G.55, again with a relative lack of lithic material (Smith 1965b). These circumstances have led to the suggestion that these sites in some way represent formal deposits, perhaps of intentionally smashed pots, a practice for which continental parallels are not unknown (Thomas and Whittle 1986). One can also cite the pit beneath West Overton G6a, containing sherds of nine Fengate vessels, but absolutely no lithics whatsoever (Smith and Simpson 1964, 82–4). Surely it can be no

coincidence that the former two sites were later chosen for the construction of round
barrows? It is important, however, to draw a distinction between these deposits and
the Grooved Ware pits of southern Wessex and the Thames Valley. In the latter case
the evident care with which the material was deposited can leave little doubt that a
precise set of rules was being followed in the process of deposition. With G.55 and
G.6b one is confronted with something more akin to the residues of a potlatch: an area
set aside for the gratuitous destruction of a particular form of material culture.

Grooved Ware, then, might have represented little more than another form of exotic
material suitable for the expression of prestige. Most of the Grooved Ware in north
Wiltshire is of Durrington Walls type; at Windmill Hill and West Kennet, the Clacton
style was present. Patterning does *not* appear to relate to design structure (as it does in
south Wessex), yet this restricted distribution of pottery of East Anglian affinity may
indicate that its exotic character was of more consequence. Grooved Ware thus seems
to have had an entirely different role in north Wiltshire from that which it held in
southern Wessex. While it may have been accessible only to a minority, it was
eventually treated in much the same way as other pottery. The point is further
emphasised by the absence of large deposits of Grooved Ware and feasting debris from
the Avebury henge (Gray 1935; Smith 1965a).

The museum collections of surface lithic material give some impression of later
Neolithic activity in the Avebury area: more and larger assemblages (Fig. 7.8). This is
especially notable in the low-lying areas surrounding the Avebury monument itself.

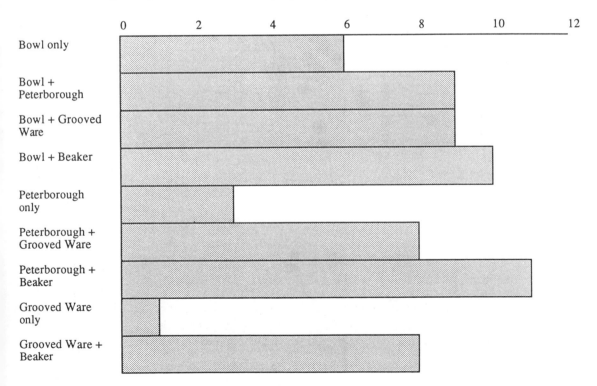

Figure 7.7   Avebury ceramic associations

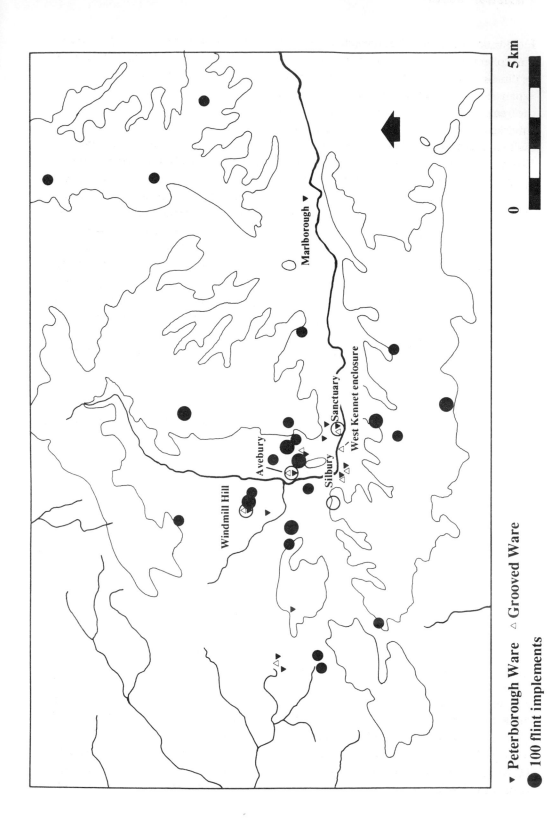

▼ **Peterborough Ware** △ **Grooved Ware**

● **100 flint implements**

Figure 7.8  Later Neolithic Avebury. Solid dots represent lithic scatters

Fieldwalking suggests that the extent to which the locations indicated by the various flint collectors, Young, Kendall, Passmore and the rest, constitute separate 'sites' may be illusory. Rather than the small high-density scatters of the earlier Neolithic, great expanses of worked flint are spread out across the fields. In the immediate vicinity of the henge these scatters actually run up to the banks of the monument. There is thus a marked contrast with the spatial organisation of activity in south Wessex, where the main concentrations of population were remote from the larger henge monuments. Likewise, there is little hint at Avebury of cemeteries of rich burials developing in opposition to the henge monument.

The later Neolithic also seems to have seen the expansion of lithic extraction on Hackpen and the Aldbourne Downs. Polished discoidal and plano-convex knives are present in the material from Hackpen, yet the numerous arrowheads and axes from Stock Lane and Stock Close mentioned by Passmore (n.d., 19) are little in evidence, suggesting that only a proportion of the original collections has reached the various museums. Certain forms of material culture show quite restricted distributions in the later Neolithic. Petit tranchet derivative arrowheads are more concentrated on the Kennet–Winterbourne confluence than leaf shapes had been. This applies to oblique arrowheads far more than chisel forms, conforming to the observation that the oblique type had a socially restricted distribution in Wessex and Mendip. Maceheads also appear to have been restricted, turning up in contexts like the Avebury henge stone-holes, the Kennet Avenue, the West Kennet long barrow and at Windmill Hill. If there is some evidence that the exchange of flint expanded in the later Neolithic, the same may be true of stone axes. At Windmill Hill the great majority of axes and axe flakes deposited in the ditch are from the terminal silts (Smith 1965a, 111), although the increased rate of *deposition* may not be directly related to the number of axes passing through the enclosure. Where complete axes are deposited in such numbers it is assumed that this is a deliberate act, analogous to the wasting of meat demonstrated by the faunal remains. As with the pottery deposits already discussed, it seems that conspicuous consumption and destruction were of great importance to the society of later Neolithic Avebury.

A variety of monument-building strategies was followed in the Avebury district in the later third millennium. The restriction of depositional practices to a smaller number of tombs (possibly only West Kennet, but conceivably also East Kennet) and the blocking and filling of others (Thomas and Whittle 1986) may indicate that particular groups were gaining a monopoly over intercession with the supernatural.

It would have been this period which saw the construction of Avebury and the Sanctuary. It has generally been accepted that the stones and the earthwork enclosure at Avebury must be contemporary with each other (Smith 1965a, 248). Originally, it was held that a third stone circle, matching the two inner ones, spanned the northern bank and ditch, thus pre-dating them. This has since been shown not to have existed (*ibid.*). Smith (*ibid.*) perceptively suggested that it would have proved difficult, if not impossible, to erect the stones of the outer circle if the great ditch had already been cut. However, it seems that the bank of the enclosure was a two-phase structure: a turfline within the bank can just be made out in the section from Gray's excavation (Gray

1935, 130), but is far better seen in photographs from the Vatchers' Avebury School site excavation (unpublished; material Avebury Museum). Any ditch associated with this bank would have been considerably less monumental than the later one (or indeed may not have been internal), and would have left a quite sufficient space for the erection of the stones. The date and nature of this first enclosure are open to interpretation, since material listed as having been found 'under the bank' could pre-date *either* bank. However, economy of hypothesis leads one to the conclusion that it was similar in form and chronology to Mount Pleasant or Durrington Walls.

On the south slope of Overton Hill, at the end of the Hackpen ridge, was situated the Sanctuary. Piggott's (1940) interpretation of the site as a series of timber buildings, eventually with stones *inside* the hut, can now be seen to be an unnecessary elaboration. If some of the timber circles of *c.* 2000 bc could not possibly have supported roofs (Mercer 1981b, 157), it is unlikely that any did. Late Beaker sherds came from the postholes of the Ten Foot and Bank Holiday Rings (Smith 1965a, 245), but these are consistently high up the profile (in weathering cones?), while sherds of Windmill Hill and Mortlake Ware were found at the bottoms of the posts (Cunnington 1931, 322–3). Ebbsfleet and Early Beaker sherds were found in primary positions in the outer stone ring. W. E. V. Young, employed as foreman on the site, noted in his diary that the (Step 4) Beaker burial in the circle probably pre-dated (although perhaps only by hours) the insertion of Stone 12 of the Stone and Post Ring (Young 1930). Cunnington (1931, 309) pointed out that if the lithic and timber elements were contemporary, the Stone and Post Ring would have had only a three-foot-wide entrance, with the rather untidy arrangement of an orthostat on one side, and a post on the other. All these observations lead to the conclusion that the Sanctuary was a two-phase structure, in which stones followed a setting of concentric timber circles. This falls into line with the sequences at Stonehenge and Mount Pleasant Site IV.

The argument which has been developed so far suggests that the rivalry between the groups which made up the Neolithic political units of the Avebury area resulted in a continual quest for exotic items to be used in prestige competition. Monumental architecture, raw materials and ceramic and lithic artefacts had already been used for this purpose. It follows that the response of such a social formation to contact with the Beaker network would be quite different from that of the 'conservative' system in south Wessex. Sure enough, early Beakers are not found in individual graves remote from the large monuments so much as incorporated into the monuments themselves. All-Over-Cord Beakers are recorded from Windmill Hill (Smith 1965a, 80), the West Kennet long barrow (Piggott 1962), Knap Hill (Connah 1965) and in the stone sockets at the Sanctuary (Cunnington 1932, 323). Step 1 burials are unknown. Beaker ceramics appear to have been used in the first instance in much the same way as any other ceramics, as their inclusion in the deposits beneath G.55 and G.6b indicates. Nevertheless, one or two relatively early Beaker burials are present: the Step 2 flat graves at West Lockridge and Smeath Ridge, Ogbourne Down (Grinsell 1957) and the barrow Roundway 8, which contained an elderly man with W/MR Beaker, tanged copper dagger, copper racquet pin, stone wristguard and two barbed and tanged arrowheads (Annable and Simpson 1964, 38). It seems that the full Beaker inhumation tradition was extant in the Avebury area. The early predominance of flat graves, as opposed to barrows, *might* be taken as evidence that this inhumation was a relatively covert practice. However, it can also be pointed out that a high proportion of the burials of Steps 2 to 4 are on 'monumental' sites. That is, they are often at the foot of one of the stones of the later monuments. These include a burial with a Step 2 European Bell Beaker beneath Stone 29a of the West Kennet Avenue, and a multiple burial with a Step 4 N2 Beaker near Stone 25b (Smith 1965a, 209). In addition, Stone 18b had a burial with no pot, and 22b had one with a vessel of vague Grooved Ware affinity (*ibid.*). Stoneholes 41 and 102 of the Avebury henge also had human bones associated with them, and the former of these had Beaker sherds: both had been disturbed by stone destruction (*ibid.*, 204). The skeleton with a Step 4 'Barbed-Wire' Beaker from the Sanctuary has already been mentioned, and there is also a Step 3 N/MR burial from the Longstones Cove, on the Beckhampton Avenue (Clarke 1970, 501). These are conceptually rather different from burials like that at Woodhenge, say, which could be seen as a means of distorting the 'message' of an established monument, or of laying claim to the past. In most of these cases the burial is arguably contemporary with the erection of the stone. Their interpretation as 'dedicatory' burials of sacrificial offerings (Burl 1979, 197) is inevitable. But an alternative is possible. It is somewhat illogical to see burials with Beakers in flat graves or barrows as privileged individuals, but burials with Beakers at the foot of stones as sacrifices. The integration of Beaker burials into the grand design of the Avebury monuments is more an expression of the interdependence of individual and group power. The Grooved Ware under the (second phase?) bank at Avebury (Smith 1965a, 224) and these Step 2 to 4 burials, the running of the West Kennet Avenue across an 'occupation site' characterised by Grooved Ware and Fengate pottery (*ibid.*, 233), and the Beaker and Mortlake pottery in the stoneholes at the Sanctuary all indicate that a reasonable date for all the stone elements of Avebury, the Avenues and the Sanctuary could be postulated in the nineteenth century bc.

Another monument which would have been significant within the early second millennium milieu is the massive mound of Silbury Hill. As with the rather earlier barrows at Beckhampton Road and South Street, Silbury appears to have had no primary burial. The existing radiocarbon chronology for the site is confusing, and suggests an extremely long history of construction. This sits uneasily with the excavator's observation that the monument had been built in a single unbroken process, on the grounds that turflines had not formed at any stage before the completion of the mound (Atkinson 1970). It may be admissible to disregard the experimental radiocarbon dates from vegetable matter in the primary mound of Silbury I (Whittle pers. comm.). This could still leave a relatively long process of construction, stretching between *c.* 2100 bc and the dates from antler picks associated with Silbury IV of 1899±43 bc and 1802±50 (BM-842; BM-841). Over such a period the various phases of construction might represent changes of design imposed by subsequent generations or consecutive power groups, even if construction was continuous yet sporadic. When completed, Silbury would have had an imposing appearance, with stepped concentric revetment walls of chalk blocks (Atkinson 1970, 314).

Nevertheless, its location next to Waden Hill results in its being hidden from view in many areas to the north. It is the case that several of the monuments of the Avebury area are not constructed so as to maximise their potential for visibility. Windmill Hill, for instance, appears to have been more impressively fortified on its northern side in its later phases (Whittle pers. comm.). This might be interpreted in a number of ways. Given the argument that the region was characterised by competition between rival local groups, it might be that each monument was intended to preside over only a certain area. Alternatively, individual sites might have been located in order to be visible from outside the immediate area of concern of those living in the Avebury district, in the case of Silbury along the Bishop's Cannings Downs. Finally, it might be that the combination of disclosure and hiddenness was an element intentionally built into the design of the monumental complex, such that the whole might not be appreciated from any one point. Thus the avenues of stones served to draw the onlooker in towards the Avebury henge, whose internal features might only be apprehended once one had passed through the entrance, while the scale and mass of Silbury might only be seen from particular directions. In consequence, the complex as a whole could only be experienced in the course of travelling through the valley, ensuring that each monument and its particular meaning would be fully appreciated in its turn.

In the particular case of Silbury, it is certainly possible to speculate on the significance of the architecture. Indeed, it could be that the subsequent remodellings might be attempts to draw upon quite different traditions. In this way the earlier mounds find parallels in the nearby Marlborough Mound, and perhaps the Conquer Barrow in southern Dorset and the large round mounds of Yorkshire. The final phase, by contrast, may be modelled on the passage tombs of the Boyne Valley and Brittany, a tradition whose use had already lapsed by the time that Silbury was completed. Once again, this demonstrates a desire to emulate exotic traditions whose significance might have been only partially understood.

At around the same time as Silbury was completed, a large double-palisaded enclosure was constructed nearby on the valley floor at West Kennet (Whittle and Smith 1990). The closest parallels for such a structure would be the enclosures at Meldon Bridge (Burgess 1976) and Mount Pleasant (Wainwright 1979a). Radiocarbon dates of 1860±50 bc (BM-2597) and 1670±50 bc (BM-2602) confirm that the monument fits into a general picture of a final enhancement of the monumental landscape of Avebury at the beginning of the second millennium.

By around 1800 bc all the major monuments of the Avebury area must have been complete. It is reasonable to presume that this last burst of monumental activity, in which the Avebury henge was linked into the landscape (and physically connected to the Sanctuary) by the West Kennet and Beckhampton Avenues, represents a massive mobilisation of corvée labour in an assertion of the 'higher unity' over the individual descent groups of the area. The two banks of the Kennet were drawn together by a single structure. Possibly this phase of activity saw the rise to dominance of a single small group, briefly controlling a proto-state social formation. This would indeed provide a context for the construction of a large defensive enclosure. But this did not last. In Steps 5 and 6 the deposition of Beakers changed markedly in its nature. No

Beaker burials were now put into the stone monuments or flat graves: all Step 5 and 6 burials were in round barrows (Fig. 7.9). One of these, West Overton G6b, contained an extremely rich burial and was placed on a location which had previously been of some significance for pottery deposition (Smith and Simpson 1966). As in the Thames Valley, S1 Beakers are absent, but the S2 Beakers from barrow burials at Bishop's Cannings S4 and Oldbury Hill (Hoare 1812, 93; Annable and Simpson 1964, 41) both have the everted necks characteristic of Step 5. At the same time as this increase in the number of barrow burials, Beakers are once again found in the earlier monuments of the region: at Knap Hill, Windmill Hill and the Sanctuary (Clarke 1970, 500–2), Step 5 and 6 Beakers are present. The presence of an S2(W) Beaker at the West Kennet long barrow (*ibid.*) seems to have been one of the last acts before its final blocking. In the years around 1700 bc the building of large monuments stopped, to be replaced by prestigious burials, as elsewhere in Wessex. The deposition of Beaker material on a variety of earlier sites none the less indicates that all links with the past had not been broken, even if the central authority had collapsed.

## Contrasts

At a certain level of generality, some trends can be discerned which are common to all three of the areas which have been considered here. In all three areas the later fourth millennium saw the establishment of Neolithic communities and the construction of the earliest field monuments. All three areas saw the development of more complex monumental landscapes in the later third millennium bc, and their eventual replacement by individual barrow burials in the earlier second millennium. However, it is the contrasts between these areas which are most instructive.

While all three areas saw an expansion of settlement in the later Neolithic, this appears to have been most profound in the Upper Thames Valley, where whole new areas may have been colonised for the first time after *c.* 2500 bc. In this case, the newly occupied areas may have 'budded off' from a core zone of settlement, developing a cultural identity of their own in the process. The distinctiveness of the Upper Thames is also recognisable in the use of monuments, where the multiple, small foci may denote a society less centralised than those in Wessex. This would certainly accord with the impression of a fluid, expansive settlement system. A more subtle contrast can be drawn between Avebury and Salisbury Plain. The monuments of the Avebury district seem to have acted together to transform a landscape, and at a certain point several sites were structurally unified by the construction of the avenues. Competition between groups may have been important here, but internal contradictions within the society less so. However, monuments like Stonehenge and Durrington Walls may have been primarily locations for particular practices. In the later third millennium, particular activities seem to have been separated out in the Salisbury Plain landscape, and this may have been in consequence of their mutually contradictory nature.

The introduction of the ostensibly homogeneous phenomenon of the Beaker package into these three areas gives an indication of quite how distinct their societies had become by the end of the third millennium. On Salisbury Plain, a cultural order already groaning under the weight of its own internal contradictions was sent into cri-

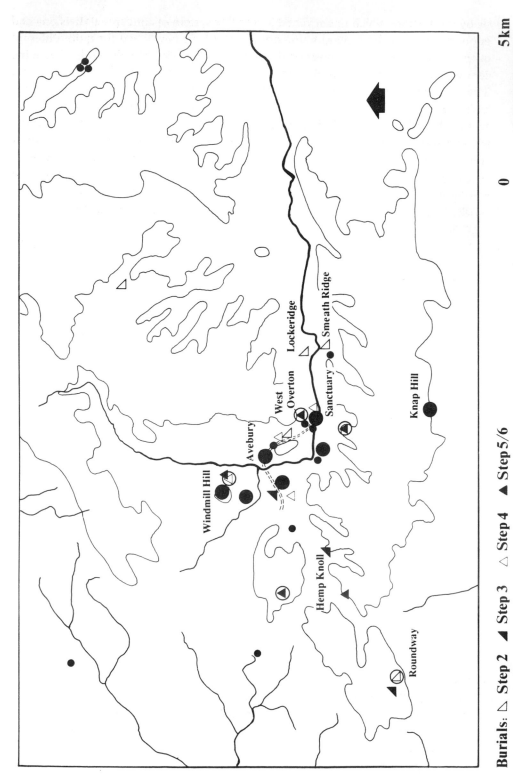

Burials: △ Step 2  ▲ Step 3  △ Step 4  ▲ Step 5/6

○ Barrow  ● Monument  • Stray sherds

Figure 7.9  Avebury Beaker burials

sis by innovations which undermined a complex system of conceptual divisions and oppositions. Neighbouring monuments seem to have been used for quite different purposes; quite different depositional practices existed side by side. Only after some centuries did a unified Early Bronze Age material order develop. Yet in the Upper Thames the transition to Beaker burial and the abandonment of monuments seems to have been more abrupt, possibly another consequence of a less rigid social fabric and an established tradition of individual burial. The Avebury area was different again, where a more centralised society was, initially at least, able to incorporate new material culture into its own traditional practices. The collapse of Avebury as a centre may have been less the consequence of the introduction of new ideas of individualism and hierarchy associated with Beakers, as of the eclipse of its position at the centre of a series of exchange systems, as metalwork became more important than stone and flint.

# 8

# Conclusion

The studies collected in this book have considered in turn a number of aspects of Neolithic culture in southern Britain: pottery, monuments, depositional practices, subsistence economy, funerary practice and regional variability. The separation between these phenomena has been enforced rather artificially, and it will already be clear that certain points of convergence can be identified. Part of the aim of this final chapter is to draw attention to these correlations. However, this design must be tempered with a degree of caution. The objective of the book as a whole is not a totalising one, and it makes no claim to present a full picture of what was doubtless an extremely complex past reality. Each chapter has approached the reality of Neolithic culture from a different angle, tracing a particular line of descent through time. These 'genealogies' skirt around the edges of a past reality, intersecting in places, yet never giving a full and undistorted access to the past. It follows that, in summing up, what can be presented is a collection of fragments rather than a unified whole: perhaps some advances on previous thinking about the Neolithic, but certainly not a new 'model of the Neolithic'. The most which the book can claim is to have moved a few degrees around the hermeneutic circle towards an understanding of the Neolithic.

## Subjects and social reproduction

One comment which could clearly be made upon the whole of what has been written so far is that it appears to be a history less of people than of practices. In a sense, this is a consequence of the proximal point that archaeologists study the material remains of human activities rather than the minds of the people concerned. That these remains relate to traditions of practice which may have been reproduced through many generations tends to erode the importance of individual actors. Before going on to discuss the substantive conclusions of the study, it might be as well to clarify the model of the human subject which is assumed in these findings. The philosophy which underlies this book could be described as a form of historical materialism, albeit one removed from either economic determinism or structuralism. It is materialist in asserting the primacy of social being over consciousness, and historicist in resisting the subjection of the specific to the general. Clearly, such a position brings into question what role one affords to the individual in history, especially if one has already rejected any necessary baseline for human identity. In twentieth-century social thought, extreme solutions have often been put forward for this problem, ranging from the meaning-giving transcendental ego to the totally decentred subject, the *Träger* (or carrier) of determining relations. When Hodder says that 'the acts of individuals are not determined by a cultural code because the culture is itself constructed in these acts' (1985, 4), he comes close to the position of Husserlian phenomenology. Here, the subject is the source of all meaning and form in the world (Eagleton 1983, 58–60). The problem with adopting such a point of view is that this act of creation actually takes place *within* language: 'I would not be able to have an experience in the first place unless it took place in the terms of some language within which I could identify it' (*ibid.*, 60).

To isolate the individual from shared systems of signification is to decontextualise (Barrett 1987, 471). Furthermore, the stress which has been placed upon the autonomy of the individual in some schools of thought can be quite as dehumanising as the anti-humanism of Lévi-Strauss or Althusser. The individual becomes not the agent but the psychologically programmed actor (Lloyd 1986, 279).

The decentring of the subject in structuralist and post-structuralist thought (the denial of the meaning-giving individual as a given) has provided a fundamental challenge to Western thought. In Saussurian linguistics, language is revealed as a system of differences, relationships between signifiers. Hence ' "cat" has meaning not "in itself", but because it is not "cap" or "cad" or "bat" . . . the relation between the whole sign and what it refers to (what Saussure called the "referent", the real furry four-legged creature) is therefore also arbitrary' (Eagleton 1983, 97).

It follows, then, that according to this view when one uses the word 'I', one is using a sign which is only given its meaning through its relation to other signs. Similarly, the individual subject is given his or her identity through being the 'bearer' of a set of social relationships. Applied to history, such a perspective has the salutary effect of displacing the 'great man theory', since no one subject is central to history, and there is no point outside history from which we can look back and define it as being 'about' a particular individual. However, Althusser's claim that history is a process without a subject is ingenuous. Clearly, the timeless subject of *his* history is structure, the endless framework of the Mode of Production, running through its countless transformations into infinity.

Here it was that Foucault superseded Althusser, by seeing neither a constant subject nor an eternal structure: both are historical effects (Hoy 1986, 128). It would seem that the advance which has been achieved by structuralism and post-structuralism is that subjectivity has been recognised as a problem (Giddens 1987, 98). However, having dissolved both subject and structure and insisted upon their historicity, Foucault none the less tends to see individuals as impotent (*ibid.*). It may be more helpful to move beyond the de-centred subject to a perspective of the individual as agent. An agent is 'made' by his or her social circumstances, yet experiences these circumstances (Thompson 1978, 199) and in turn acts upon them. Thus history, the process of social life, consists of structures and agents continually 'making' each other. This returns us to Marx's oft-quoted statement that 'men make their own history, but they do not make it just as they please; they do not make it under circumstances chosen by themselves, but under circumstances directly encountered, given and transmitted from the past' (Marx 1968, 96).

This is highly significant to the way in which we write the archaeological past. If we accept a dialectical relationship between structure and agency, we can begin to consider the question of social reproduction. Conventionally, a systems model adopted by archaeologists has given the impression that societies exist ordinarily in homeostasis, until driven into pathology by exterior forces, principally the environment (Clarke 1968, 42–148; see Hodder 1982b for critique). Once we reject this, and recognise that conflicts and contradictions of one sort or another inevitably divide the individuals within any group, a different kind of question becomes important. How is it that any kind of continuity is possible from one generation to the next? How is it that customs, modes of practice, and forms of authority are reproduced? Why is it that social life has any pattern at all, and why does it not dissolve into a multiplicity of unrelated, random acts?

Probably the most adequate treatment of this problem is that presented by Bourdieu (1977). Bourdieu rejects the 'realism of the structure', which sees structure as 'given' outside history (the Althusserian position). Both structure and the subject are recognised as historically contingent, yet Bourdieu goes further, in presenting a mechanism for the interaction of the two. Born into a particular cultural and historical setting, individuals internalise rules of language use and behaviour in the course of their upbringing. This learned yet unreflected-upon body of codes and norms which forms the basis for instinctive day-to-day practice Bourdieu calls the *habitus*. The *habitus* is 'The immanent inner law, laid down inside each agent by his earliest upbringing, which is the precondition not only for the coordination of practices, but also for practices of coordination' (Bourdieu 1977, 81).

The internalisation of *habitus* is achieved in the context of the home: the basic cultural categories which make up the social division of labour are learned within the culturally constructed environment. Hence it follows that material culture, created routinely as an expression of particular accepted views of reality, comes by its materiality to help build the *habitus* of the individual. By being a part of the constructed world which is to be internalised, material culture frames the construction of what is taken for granted.

It is through the construction of a nexus for habitual action in each individual that the basis for social reproduction is laid down. Such habitual practices always tend to reproduce the objective structures of which they are the product (Bourdieu 1977, 72). Social institutions like gender relations, age sets, kin relations and positions in the productive process are arbitrary, yet by being bound up with habitual practice they ensure that this arbitrariness will not be recognised (*ibid.*, 164).

**Narratives of the Neolithic**
Each of the chapters, in following one strand of the evidence, has been constructed as a narrative, and in consequence each has demanded a degree of rationalisation in the process of ordering the available evidence. The evaluation of these accounts, which can be considered almost as 'parallel texts' relating the same events from different points of view, is clearly problematical. As much as the points of agreement between the different 'stories', we should perhaps be interested in places where they contradict each other, and the reasons why this comes about. However, while a degree of

autocritique may be implicit in this chapter, this may be as much a task for the reader as for the author.

In the next few pages the main conclusions of the book will be reconsidered, with the hope of drawing out the points upon which the arguments constructed in each chapter accord or conflict. This process is not intended as a 'test' of the hypotheses constructed in any deductive sense, since the same set of assumptions on the part of the author is likely to underlie the whole. Instead, the aim is to clarify some of the issues which have emerged in the course of the work, and to come to terms with some of the weaknesses of the arguments.

One issue which came to dominate much of the discussion was the question of whether the orthodox view that the Neolithic constituted an essentially economic phenomenon could any longer be upheld. The alternative of considering the Neolithic to be an integrated conceptual and classificatory system, something 'to think with', which bore with it by implication a particular set of social relations and a particular means of social reproduction, forms a central element of this final discussion.

In beginning the analysis with the question of subsistence practice, I identified several separate sources for the present dominant interpretation of the Neolithic lifestyle as one of settled mixed farming. These included the romantic nostalgia for an 'eternal' British countryside and an idealised bucolic way of life; the semantic difficulties which arise from the use of the word 'Neolithic' itself; the palaeoeconomic (and, indeed, culture-historical) insistence on food-getting as a universally primary aspect of human behaviour; and the periodic feeling of unease over the state of the world's resources experienced in the 1960s and '70s, and again in the late 1980s. While certain assumptions are virtually universal (sedentism; the primacy of the economic base; the nature of the Neolithic as an 'economic' phenomenon), particular contradictions can be recognised between points of view. Thus Case (1969a) talked of the maturity and stability of the Neolithic farming system, while others (Bradley 1978b; Whittle 1978) hypothesised catastrophic agricultural failures. The issue of 'intensification', also, remains a vague one within an agriculture seen as largely full-blown from its inception (e.g. Barker 1984, Chapter 8). The lack of evidence for permanent settlements, field systems and cereal agriculture is generally presented as something to be argued around rather than explained.

The alternative proposed here has been that the *idea* of a way of life which separates humanity from nature may be more important than the material reality. The appropriation of nature may have been conceptual as much as it was physical. Certainly, domestic animals had an important part to play in the lives of Neolithic people in Britain, and their existence may have at times been organised around the movement of beasts between upland and lowland pastures. Yet precisely how often meat was eaten may be questioned, and even the issue of whether dairy products were consumed is one clouded in doubt. Still more ambiguous is the question of vegetable food production, where almost all carbonised Neolithic plant assemblages in Britain are dominated by wild species. In both the earlier and later Neolithic the lithic assemblages give the impression of people attuned to a mobile lifestyle, and it may be largely the patterning of this mobility which separates the two periods.

These ambiguities in the evidence, it is argued, support an interpretation in which 'the Neolithic' is less a particular economy than a system of social reproduction, a set of structured social relationships which were organised about an interlocking series of binary oppositions: us/them, in/out, culture/nature, tame/wild. The significance of domesticated species, and in particular cattle, might thus be more symbolic than nutritional. However, the division between wild and tame would be only a part of an overarching structure of classification organised about division and homology, and one might venture that the separation of classes of *person* might always be one of its most important aspects.

If the consideration of subsistence practice leads one to qualify the role of agriculture in Neolithic Britain, the reverse is the case with monument building. The extreme paucity of evidence for economic practice presents a sharp contrast with the ubiquity of Neolithic field monuments. The suggestion that monuments are a feature of a mature, surplus-producing economy (Case 1969a; Zvelebil and Rowley-Conwy 1986) does not accord with the available radiocarbon evidence. On the contrary, it seems that in many areas the construction of monuments may have been the first act of 'Neolithisation'. For example, in Brittany the large menhirs may date to the earliest Neolithic (Giot 1988). The decoration of several such stones with representations of hafted axes, cattle, shepherds' crooks and possibly boats may indicate that the attributes of a new way of life were being 'presenced' in the landscape (Thomas forthcoming), much as the early megalithic tombs employed the presence of the ancestors as a medium for the transformation of space. This use of monuments to transform the landscape indicates that they were as fundamental to the Neolithic way of life as was the use of domesticates, at least by the time of the first Neolithic presence in the British Isles. Once again, culture was being employed as a means of imposing a certain conceptual scheme upon the world.

While the settlement history of Neolithic southern Britain seems to reveal a degree of discontinuity in the changes in landuse which can be discerned in the middle of the third millennium bc, such a uniform temporal contrast is not evident in monumental architecture. At the local level monument building was a highly discontinuous process, and the regional sequences in Chapter 7 demonstrate that each act of construction was tied to power strategies being played out between and within communities at the micro level. However, these individual actions drew upon an architectural repertoire which, at the gross regional level, shows a high degree of continuity. Thus a major and synchronised temporal shift from long mounds and causewayed enclosures to henges and other large constructions (Renfrew 1973), which would indeed correlate with expansion of settlement, is far too simple a representation of the evidence. The pattern which can be recognised at this higher level is one of growing architectural complexity effecting an increased control on bodily movement through the internal space of the monument. This can be linked to an effort to influence the perception and 'reading' of space on the part of the individual.

Locally, we can also discern the way in which individual monuments acquired 'histories' of their own, as subsequent acts of construction and deposition added new connotations and transformed the way in which the structures could be experienced. While we talk of 'monuments' as an undifferentiated class of phenomena, it seems that a given site could function in quite different discourses at different times in its history. Very different activities might have been appropriate to the monument at these different junctures. Some of the depositional episodes that are evident at these sites may have constituted acts of 'translation', by which a monument was redefined. Hence the introduction of burials into a monument hitherto used for feasting or exchange transactions might introduce the location into a new sphere of practices defined as being 'of the dead'.

These episodes bring us to the question of depositional practices as such. While monuments, mortuary practice, material culture studies and so on are all recognised areas of discourse within Neolithic archaeology, the question of deposition is one that has been neglected; indeed, it has rarely been recognised as an object of study in itself. It is instructive to consider deposition in the context of monumentality. Both phenomena appear to have been caught up with the process of transforming the landscape and the 'fixing' of location. The act of placing items and materials into the ground apparently served as a contextualised classificatory statement. A number of different context types (pits, causewayed enclosure ditches, long barrow ditches, henge ditches and interiors, etc.) were employed, each having attributed to it a distinctive repertoire of items which could legitimately be deposited. The practice of fixing classificatory schemes in the space made use of both direct association and of segregation *within* association. A number of items brought into a closed space or set of spaces might be manipulated to highlight either similarity or opposition, along a variety of axes dictated by a conceptual structure. Thus the act of burying a set of items might be at once a means of transforming and/or commenting upon the character of a particular place, and of disposing of particular artefacts (or removing them from circulation), and, in addition, of presenting a statement about the nature of certain metaphysical relationships, and of making those relationships manifest in space.

Of particular significance is the suggestion that these practices of deposition changed through time. From the beginning of the Neolithic, the act of placing items in the ground seems to have been a symbolically significant one. Nevertheless, the practice of digging pits specifically for the purpose is one which is temporally concentrated in the period 2200–1700 bc (the latest Neolithic). It follows that in this period, also that in which the definition of space and deposition of material culture within monuments reached its peak, a particular emphasis was being placed upon the creation of conceptual boundaries and their physical representation. In the succeeding Bronze Age, quite different depositional regimes came to dominate, largely concerned with the use of bronze artefacts. However, there do seem to be strands of continuity which link elements of these practices to the deposits of pottery and stone axes found in rivers and bogs in the Neolithic. In a sense, then, bronze metalwork came to fit into the pre-existing structures of classification established in the Neolithic, yet in the process transformed them.

That Bronze Age transformation had the effect of selecting one element of depositional practice and privileging it. However, in the Neolithic a very wide range of media had been employed. Items redolent of the domestic sphere, of the cooking and eating of food and of the transformative properties of fire are a major element of what was referred to in these practices, yet the effort was also made simultaneously to include and exclude the natural and the wild. Such an opposition was essential if a conceptual system was to be created which encompassed the world as it was experienced and understood. This overlapping and polysemous system of classification, in which particular items and substances might evoke different contrasts and qualities according to the contexts and associations into which they were brought, depended entirely upon the unstable nature of meaning. 'The Neolithic' represented a cultural frame within which social life and social reproduction could proceed, and the discussion in this book of a particular class of material items, namely pottery, came to concentrate on the way in which 'things' fitted into the conceptual order as objects to think with. This constitutes a contrast with the present, where things represent quantities (cf. money) rather than qualities (homologous to those of the world in general). In this sense the comparison between material culture and language is a more valid one in the case of the Neolithic than in the present day: things are so much more eloquent and their meanings so much more fluid where they cannot be identified as fossilised lumps of human labour.

Studying pottery provides a particular history of how a class of material items shifted in its use and significance through time. As Herne (1988) has suggested, pots may have been exclusively used in a restricted set of transactions in the earliest part of the Neolithic. The extreme similarity of Grimston bowls with contemporary continental pottery might indicate that part of their role was to bring the connotations of a novel and still alien way of life into the context of small-scale interpersonal interactions. Meals, rituals or exchanges might be 'framed' by the presence of the appropriate material items. While the proliferation of pottery vessels of a variety of forms and shapes in the earlier Neolithic probably does relate to its use in a wider range of practices, that use would still have been bound up with the maintenance of appropriate modes of conduct in interaction. Equally, the development of long-lived traditions of manufacture would have contributed to the reproduction of social relations by establishing routine patterns of production, distribution and especially use of ceramics. The application of decoration to some of these vessels itself related to the process of classification by separating classes of person (initially presumably on ethnic lines with the localised wares of the Abingdon/Whitehawk/Mildenhall/Windmill Hill series) and of practices, in that only particular kinds of vessels were decorated.

If anything, the range of purposes for which pottery was used seems to have become more restricted in the later part of the Neolithic, with a decline in the range of vessel forms and an emphasis on particular vessel volumes. The use of decoration on pots increased with the development of Peterborough Wares, yet these and Grooved Ware, rather later in its inception, were less closely connected with particular geographical areas. Instead, their deposition in distinctive ranges of context types might indicate that their use was restricted to particular classes of person or, as was suggested here, to particular spheres of practice. Indeed, not only the places in which pots or sherds could be deposited but the ranges of associations and connotations ascribed to

Peterborough Ware and Grooved Ware were quite distinct. It was argued that Peterborough Ware was redolent of the past, of tradition and of the natural and organic, yet that Grooved Ware presented a major contrast with all previously used ceramic traditions. Not only was its range of shapes, fabrics and volumes quite distinct, but its decoration employed exotic symbols, made manifest on mobile artefacts, which could then be deployed in discourse both within monuments and by their deposition in pits. This greater emphasis on the symbolic content of material culture was thus closely tied to the creation and reading of space. Equally important is the way in which Grooved Ware and Peterborough Ware between them constituted aspects of a unified conceptual scheme which related to different (and conceivably opposed or incompatible) aspects of social reality. By the later Neolithic, then, the use of ceramics can be read as indicating an intensification and/or transformation of the original Neolithic classificatory scheme, and this in turn might denote a more complex set of social circumstances. Such an interpretation would certainly harmonise with the contemporary increase in the complexity of monumental architecture, and the rise in frequency of pit deposits.

It was argued that this means of conceptually ordering the world under circumstances of growing contradiction between incompatible practices and strategies was disrupted by the introduction of Beaker pottery from Europe. The alien set of references and associations of the incoming tradition spanned the carefully separated spheres of practice of the old regime, and was instrumental in a shift of social orientation towards the circulation and inheritance of wealth objects. Nevertheless, the use of pottery remained a rarefied one, with vessels of the bucket and beaker forms of early second millennium bc traditions dominating the subsequent Collared Urn and Food Vessel styles, largely restricted to funerary and ritual contexts of use and deposition. Only with the profound social changes of the later second and early first millennia did pottery enter a wider range of spheres of practice (Barrett 1980).

The question which remains here is how different a story one would construct about a different class of items. It might be particularly interesting, for instance, to chart the use and associations of axes from stone and flint through to metal, since some continuity is indicated by their deposition in rivers and bogs. Both stone and bronze axes were also deposited in monuments as acts which seem teminatory or transformatory in character. Yet palstaves seem to carry this particular strand of use and deposition into the later Bronze Age. Thus different classes of material item might reflect different temporalities, relating to partially distinct aspects of social relations, rather than all being uniformly transformed by changes in social formation or mode of production.

It may be a somewhat obvious point, but the enhanced importance of the dead and of mortuary practice from the beginning of the Neolithic in Britain is a further example of culture as classification. That is to say, funerary rites are deeply concerned with the definition of different classes of person: alive, dead, ancestor. Furthermore, one of the tendencies which was identified in the analysis presented in Chapter 6 was the trend towards the 'distancing' of the ancestors from the living as the third millennium bc progressed, seen in the greater physical separation of the mortuary deposit from the outside world. Similarly, within tombs greater distinctions were drawn between old and young, male and female. These points echo the suggestion already made that the period from the earlier to the later Neolithic saw the elaboration and intensification of systems of social classification.

Perhaps the other main trend in mortuary practice which should be singled out at this stage is the odd combination of conservatism and change which characterises the shift towards individual burial. This shift itself may signify a changed conception of personhood towards individuation and/or a greater stress on inheritance. Yet at each stage the process appears to have been legitimated by reference back to the past, such that individual burials were inserted into long-defunct long barrows. Related to this process was a gradual diversification of mortuary practices as the Neolithic progressed, as the original uniformity of the long mound tradition was lost and new forms of individual inhumation began to be used. Again, this may be a further consequence of the emergence of a more internally differentiated society in which the dead were being put to quite diverse uses.

These points lead to one other important observation: that the consideration of mortuary practices should not necessarily be categorically separated from that of depositional practice in general. Many of the contexts discussed in Chapter 4 actually contained human remains, and in that study a change in the status of the dead was recognised, in the observation that human remains came over time to be classified with 'wild', 'natural' and 'outside' materials and locations instead of 'tame', 'cultural' and 'inside'. This adds a further significance to the spatial distancing of the dead already mentioned: the deceased may have become more problematic.

What has been said so far in this chapter makes a fairly clear methodological point: it is easier to add a further level of rationalisation when two separate narratives are brought together than it is to accept their contradiction. However, the consideration of the regional sequences dealt with in Chapter 7 makes a certain measure of auto-critique unavoidable. If the Neolithic represented more a conceptual system for ordering the world than an economy, the diversity of uses to which Neolithic material culture was put in different geographical areas is puzzling. It must be freely admitted that Chapters 2 to 6 are written at a fairly general level. If, as these studies seem to suggest, the aspects of Neolithic culture fitted together as parts of a means of classification, does it follow that the conceptual schemes employed in individual regions were quite distinct? One answer might be that if the system of classification functioned at the level of the *habitus*, in guiding day-to-day practice, distinct communities might start from the position of adopting a general cultural repertoire and yet slowly transform it in the historical process of social reproduction. The degree to which these individual schemes had diverged by the end of the third millennium is demonstrated by the differing effects of the arrival of the Beaker 'package'. It has been suggested that, by constituting a conceptual anomaly, Beaker pottery might have been disruptive of societies attuned to the separation of distinct spheres of practice. That this disruption was varied, and that the shift to a uniform social order based upon the circulation of prestigious material items was by no means synchronous across southern Britain, is thus a measure of this diversity. As in any cultural landscape which might be documented by a present-day ethnographer, Neolithic Britain can be seen as having been made up of a number of communities whose susceptibility to change varied. The character of this variability must surely be located in differences in social relations, and in particular in the traditions of practice which enabled these societies to reproduce themselves.

# REFERENCES

Adkins, R. and R. Jackson 1978 *Neolithic Axes from the River Thames*. London: British Museum.

Allen, G. W. G. 1938 Marks seen from the air in the crops near Dorchester, Oxon. *Oxoniensia* 3, 169–70.

Annable, F. K. 1969 Excavation and fieldwork in Wiltshire 1968. *Wiltshire Archaeological Magazine* 64, 123–7.

Annable, F. K. and D. D. A. Simpson 1964 *Guide Catalogue to the Neolithic and Bronze Age Collections in Devizes Museum*. Devizes: Wiltshire Natural History and Archaeological Society.

Appadurai, A. 1985 Introduction: commodities and the politics of value. In: A. Appadurai (ed.) *The Social Life of Things*, 3–63. Cambridge: Cambridge University Press.

ApSimon, A. 1969 1919–1969: fifty years of archaeological research. *Proceedings of the University of Bristol Spealeological Society* 12, 31–56.

  1986 Chronological contexts for Irish megalithic tombs. *Journal of Irish Archaeology* 3, 5–15.

ApSimon, A., J. Musgrave, J. Sheldon, E. K. Tratman and L. Wijngaaden-Bakker 1976 Gorsey Bigbury, Cheddar, Somerset: radiocarbon dating, human and animal bones, charcoals and archaeological reassessment. *Proceedings of the University of Bristol Spealeological Society* 14, 155–83.

Ashbee, P. 1966 Fussell's Lodge long barrow excavations, 1957. *Archaeologia* 100, 1–80.

  1970 *The Earthen Long Barrow in Britain*. London: Dent.

  1978 *The Ancient British*. Norwich: Geo.

Ashbee, P., I. F. Smith and J. G. Evans 1979 Excavation of three long barrows near Avebury. *Proceedings of the Prehistoric Society* 45, 207–300.

Atkinson, R. J. C. 1948 Archaeological notes. *Oxoniensia* 13, 66–87.

  1951 The henge monuments of Great Britain. In: R. J. C. Atkinson, C. M. Piggott and N. Sandars *Excavations at Dorchester, Oxon.*, 81–107. Oxford: Ashmolean Museum.

  1956 *Stonehenge*. London: Hamish Hamilton.

  1965 Wayland's Smithy. *Antiquity* 39, 126–33.

  1968 Old mortality: some aspects of burial and population in Neolithic England. In: J. Coles and D. D. A. Simpson (eds.) *Studies in Ancient Europe*, 83–94. Edinburgh: Edinburgh University Press.

  1970 Silbury Hill, 1969–70. *Antiquity* 44, 313–14.

Atkinson, R. J. C., C. M. Piggott and N. Sandars 1951 *Excavations at Dorchester, Oxon.* Oxford: Ashmolean Museum.

Atkinson, R. J. C. and S. Piggott 1986 The date of the West Kennet long barrow. *Antiquity* 60, 143–4.

Avery, M. 1982 The Neolithic causewayed enclosure, Abingdon. In: H. J. Case and A. W. R. Whittle (eds.) *Settlement Patterns in the Oxford Region*, 10–50. London: Council for British Archaeology.

Bakels, C. C. 1982 The settlement system of the Dutch Linearbandkeramik. *Analecta Praehistorica Leidensia* 15, 31–43.

Bakker, J. A. 1982 TRB settlement patterns on the Dutch sandy soils. *Analecta Praehistorica Leidensia* 15, 87–124.

Bamford, H. 1985 *Briar Hill*. Northampton: Northampton Archaeological Monograph 3.

Barker, C. T. 1984 The long mounds of the Avebury region. *Wiltshire Archaeological Magazine* 79, 7–38.

Barker, G. W. W. 1985 *Prehistoric Farming in Europe*. Cambridge: Cambridge University Press.

Barker, G. W. W. and D. Webley 1978 Causewayed camps and early Neolithic economies in central southern England. *Proceedings of the Prehistoric Society* 44, 161–86.

Barley, N. 1981 The Dowayo dance of death. In: S. C. Humphreys and H. King (eds.) *Mortality and Immortality*, 149–59. London: Academic Press.

Barrett, J. C. 1980 The pottery of the later Bronze Age in lowland England. *Proceedings of the Prehistoric Society* 46, 297–319.

1985 Hoards and related metalwork. In: D. V. Clarke, T. Cowie and A. Foxon (eds.) *Symbols of Power at the Time of Stonehenge*, 93–106. Edinburgh: National Museum of Antiquities.

1987 Contextual archaeology. *Antiquity* 61, 468–73.

1988a Fields of discourse – reconstituting a social archaeology. *Critique of Anthropology* 7 (3), 5–16.

1988b The living, the dead, and the ancestors: Neolithic and Early Bronze Age mortuary practices. In: J. C. Barrett and I. A. Kinnes (eds.) *The Archaeology of Context in the Neolithic and Bronze Age*, 30–41. Sheffield: Department of Archaeology and Prehistory.

1989 Conclusion: render unto Caesar . . . In: J. C. Barrett, A. Fitzpatrick and L. McInnes (eds.) *Romans and Barbarians in North-West Europe*. Oxford: British Archaeological Reports S471.

Barrett, J. C., R. J. Bradley and M. Green 1991 *The Archaeology of Cranborne Chase*. Cambridge: Cambridge University Press.

Barth, F. (ed.) 1969 *Ethnic Groups and Boundaries*. Boston: Little, Brown and Co.

Baudrillard, J. 1988 *Jean Baudrillard: Selected Writings*, ed. M. Poster. Cambridge: Polity.

Bell, M. 1982 The effects of land use and climate on valley sedimentation. In: A. F. Harding (ed.) *Climatic Change in Later Prehistory*, 127–42. Edinburgh: Edinburgh University Press.

Bender, B. 1975 *Farming in Prehistory*. London: John Baker.

Benson, D. and T. Miles 1974 *The Upper Thames Valley: An Archaeological Survey of the River Gravels*. Oxford: Oxford Archaeological Unit.

Bersu, G. 1940 Excavations at Little Woodbury, Wiltshire, part one: the settlement as revealed by excavation. *Proceedings of the Prehistoric Society* 6, 30–111.

Binford, L. R. 1962 Archaeology as anthropology. *American Antiquity* 28, 217–25.

1964 A consideration of archaeological research design. *American Antiquity* 29, 425–41.

1968 Post-Pleistocene adaptations. In: L. R. Binford and S. R. Binford (eds.) *New Perspectives in Archaeology*, 313–41. Chicago: Aldine.

1971 Mortuary practices: their study and potential. In: J. A. Brown (ed.) *Approaches to the Social Dimensions of Mortuary Practices*, 6–29. Society for American Anthropology Memoir 25.

Bloch, M. 1974 Symbols, song, dance and features of articulation. *Archives of European Sociology* 15, 55–81.

1982 Death, women and power. In: M. Bloch and J. Parry (eds.) *Death and the Regeneration of Life*, 211–30. Cambridge: Cambridge University Press.

Bloch, M. and J. Parry 1982 Introduction: death and the regeneration of life. In: M. Bloch and J. Parry (eds.) *Death and the Regeneration of Life*, 1–44. Cambridge: Cambridge University Press.

Bourdieu, P. 1973 The Berber house. In: M. Douglas (ed.) *Rules and Meanings*, 98–110. Harmondsworth: Penguin.

1977 *Outline of a Theory of Practice*. Cambridge: Cambridge University Press.

Bradley, R. J. 1971 Stock raising and the origin of the hillfort on the South Downs. *Antiquaries Journal* 51, 8–29.

1975 Maumbury Rings, Dorchester: the excavations of 1908–13. *Archaeologia* 105, 1–97.

1978a *The Prehistoric Settlement of Britain*. London: Routledge and Kegan Paul.

1978b Colonisation and land use in the late Neolithic and early Bronze Age. In: S. Limbrey and J. G. Evans (eds.) *The Effect of Man on the Landscape: The Lowland Zone*, 95–103. London: Council for British Archaeology.

1982 Position and possession: assemblage variation in the British Neolithic. *Oxford Journal of Archaeology* 1, 27–38.

1983 The bank barrows and related monuments of Dorset in the light of recent fieldwork. *Proceedings of the Dorset Natural History and Archaeological Society* 105, 15–20.

1984a *The Social Foundations of Prehistoric Britain*. London: Longmans.

1984b Studying monuments. In: R. J. Bradley and J. Gardiner (eds.) *Neolithic Studies*, 61–6. Oxford: British Archaeological Reports 133.

1985 *Consumption, Change and the Archaeological Record*. Edinburgh: Department of Archaeology.

1987a Flint technology and the character of Neolithic settlement. In: A. Brown and M. R. Edmonds (eds.) *Lithic Analysis and Later British Prehistory*, 181–6. Oxford: British Archaeological Reports 162.

1987b Stages in the chronological development of hoards and votive deposits. *Proceedings of the Prehistoric Society* 53, 351–2.

1989 Deaths and entrances: a contextual analysis of megalithic art. *Current Anthropology* 30, 68–75.

Bradley, R. J. and R. A. Chambers 1988. A new study of the cursus complex at Dorchester on Thames. *Oxford Journal of Archaeology* 7, 271–90.

Bradley, R. J., R. A. Chambers and C. Halpin 1984 *Excavations at Barrow Hills, Radley*. Oxford: Oxford Archaeological Unit.

Bradley, R. J. and R. C. Chapman 1984 Passage graves in the European Neolithic: a theory of convergent evolution. In: G. Burrenhult (ed.) *The Archaeology of Carrowmore*, 348–56. Stockholm: Institute of Archaeology.

Bradley, R. J., R. M. Cleal, J. Gardiner, A. Legge, F. Raymond and J. S. Thomas 1984 Sample excavations on the Dorset Cursus in 1984. *Proceedings of the Dorset Natural History and Archaeological Society* 106, 128–32.

Bradley, R. J., R. M. Cleal, M. Green, J. Gardiner and M. Bowden 1984 The Neolithic sequence in Cranborne Chase. In: R. J. Bradley and J. Gardiner (eds.) *Neolithic Studies*, 87–105. Oxford: British Archaeological Reports 133.

Bradley, R. J. and R. Holgate 1984 The Neolithic sequence in the Upper Thames Valley. In: R. J. Bradley and J. Gardiner (eds.) *Neolithic Studies*, 107–35. Oxford: British Archaeological Reports 133.

Bradley, R. J. and J. S. Thomas 1984 Some new information on the henge monument at Maumbury Rings, Dorchester. *Proceedings of the Dorset Natural History and Archaeological Society* 106, 128–32.

Braithwaite, M. 1982 Decoration as ritual symbol: a theoretical proposal and an ethnographic study in southern Sudan. In: I. Hodder (ed.) *Symbolic and Structural Archaeology*, 80–8. Cambridge: Cambridge University Press.

1984 Ritual and prestige in the prehistory of Wessex *c*. 2000–1400 BC: a new dimension to the archaeological evidence. In: D. Miller and C. Tilley (eds.) *Ideology, Power and Prehistory*, 93–110. Cambridge: Cambridge University Press.

Brewster, A. 1984 *The Excavation of Whitegrounds Barrow, Burythorpe*. Wintringham: John Gett.

Britnell, W. and H. Savory 1984 *Gwernvale and Penywyrlod: Two Neolithic Long Cairns in the Black Mountains of Brecknock*. Cardiff: Cambrian Archaeological Association.

Britton, D. 1963 Traditions of metalworking in the late Neolithic and Early Bronze Age of Britain. *Proceedings of the Prehistoric Society* 29, 258–325.

Brown, A. and M. R. Edmonds 1987 *Lithic Analysis and Later British Prehistory*. Oxford: British Archaeological Reports 162.

Bulmer, R. 1967 Why is the cassowary not a bird? A problem in zoological taxonomy. *Man* 2, 5–25.

1976 Selectivity in hunting and in disposal of animal bones by the Kalam of the New Guinea Highlands. In: G. de G. Sieveking, I. Longworth and K. Wilson (eds.) *Problems in Economic and Social Archaeology*, 169–86. London: Duckworth.

Burgess, C. 1976 Meldon Bridge: a Neolithic defended promontory complex near Peebles. In: C. Burgess and R. Miket (eds.) *Settlement and Economy in the Third and Second Millennia B.C.*, 151–80. Oxford: British Archaeological Reports 33.

1980 *The Age of Stonehenge*. London: Dent.

Burgess, C. and J. D. Cowen 1972 The Ebnal hoard and Early Bronze Age metal-working traditions. In: F. Lynch and C. Burgess (eds.) *Prehistoric Man in Wales and the West*, 167–88. Bath: Adams and Dart.

Burgess, C. and S. Shennan 1976 The Beaker phenomenon: some suggestions. In: C. Burgess and R. Miket (eds.) *Settlement and Economy in the Second and Third Millennia B.C.*, 309–31. Oxford: British Archaeological Reports 33.

Burgess, C., P. Topping, C. Mordant and M. Maddison 1988 *Enclosures and Defences in the Neolithic of Western Europe*. Oxford: British Archaeological Reports 403.

Burl, H. A. W. 1969 Henges: internal structures and regional groups. *Archaeological Journal* 126, 1–28.

1976 *Stone Circles of the British Isles*. Yale: Yale University Press.

1979 *Prehistoric Avebury*. Yale: Yale University Press.

1987 *The Stonehenge People*. London: Dent.

Burton, J. 1984 Quarrying in a tribal society. *World Archaeology* 16, 234–47.

Buxton, J. 1968 Animal identity and human peril: some Mandari images. *Man* 3, 35–49.

Calkin, J. 1947 Neolithic pit at Southbourne. *Proceedings of the Dorset Natural History and Archaeological Society* 69, 29–32.

Care, V. 1982 The collection and distribution of lithic raw materials during the Mesolithic and Neolithic periods in southern England. *Oxford Journal of Archaeology* 1, 351–65.

Case, H. J. 1956 The Neolithic causewayed camp at Abingdon. *Antiquaries Journal* 36, 11–30.

1963 Notes on finds and on ring ditches in the Oxford region. *Oxoniensia* 28, 19–52.

1969a Neolithic explanations. *Antiquity* 43, 176–86.

1969b Settlement patterns in the north Irish Neolithic. *Ulster Journal of Archaeology* 32, 3–27.

1977 The Beaker Culture in Britain and Ireland. In: R. Mercer (ed.) *Beakers in Britain and Europe*, 71–101. Oxford: British Archaeological Reports S26.

1982 Cassington, 1950–52: late Neolithic pits and the big enclosure. In: H. Case and A. Whittle (eds.) *Settlement Patterns in the Oxford Region*, 118–51. London: Council for British Archaeology.

1986 The Mesolithic and Neolithic in the Oxford region In: G. Briggs, J. Cook and T. Rowley (eds.) *The Archaeology of the Oxford Region*, 18–37. Oxford: Oxford University Department of External Studies.

Case, H. J. and A. W. R. Whittle (eds.) 1982 *Settlement Patterns in the Oxford Region*. London: Council for British Archaeology.

Catt, J. A. 1978 The contribution of loess to soils in lowland Britain. In: S. Limbrey and J. G. Evans (eds.) *The Effect of Man on the Landscape: The Lowland Zone*, 12–20. London: Council for British Archaeology.

Chadburn, A. and J. Gardiner 1985 A Grooved Ware pit and prehistoric spade marks on Hengistbury Head (Site 6), Dorset, 1984. *Proceedings of the Prehistoric Society* 51, 315–18.

Chapman, R. 1981 The emergence of formal disposal areas the the 'problem' of megalithic tombs in prehistoric Europe. In: R. Chapman, I. Kinnes and K. Randsborg (eds.) *The Archaeology of Death*, 71–81. Cambridge: Cambridge University Press.

Chapman, R. and K. Randsborg 1981 Approaches to the archaeology of death. In: R. Chapman, I. Kinnes and K. Randsborg (eds.) *The Archaeology of Death*, 1–24. Cambridge: Cambridge University Press.

Cherry, J. 1978 Generalisation and the archaeology of the state. In: D. Green, C. Haselgrove and M. Spriggs (eds.) *Social Organisation and Settlement*, 411–37. Oxford: British Archaeological Reports S47.

Chesterman, J. T. 1977 Burial rites in a Cotswold long barrow. *Man* 12, 22–32.

Childe, V. G. 1951 *Social Evolution*. New York: Schumann.

Childe, V. G. and I. F. Smith 1954 The excavation of a Neolithic barrow on Whiteleaf Hill, Bucks. *Proceedings of the Prehistoric Society* 20, 212–30.

Christie, P. 1963 The Stonehenge Cursus. *Wiltshire Archaeological Magazine* 58, 370–82.

Clare, T. 1987 Towards a reappraisal of henge monuments: origins, evolution and hierarchies. *Proceedings of the Prehistoric Society* 53, 457–78.

Clark, J. G. D. 1977 *World Prehistory*. Cambridge: Cambridge University Press.

Clark, J. G. D., E. S. Higgs and I. Longworth 1960 Excavations at the Neolithic site of Hurst Fen, Mildenhall, Suffolk, 1954, 1957 and 1958. *Proceedings of the Prehistoric Society* 26, 202–45.

Clarke, D. L. 1968 *Analytical Archaeology*. London: Methuen.
    1970 *Beaker Pottery of Great Britain and Ireland*. Cambridge: Cambridge University Press.

Clarke, D. V. 1983 Rinyo and the Orcadian Neolithic. In: A. O'Connor and D. V. Clarke (eds.) *From the Stone Age to the 'Forty-Five*, 45–56. Edinburgh: John Donald.

Clarke, D. V. and N. Sharples 1985 Settlements and subsistence in the third millennium B.C. In: A. C. Renfrew (ed.) *The Prehistory of Orkney*, 54–82. Edinburgh: Edinburgh University Press.

Cleal, R. 1984 The later Neolithic in the east of England. In: R. J. Bradley and J. Gardiner (eds.) *Neolithic Studies*, 135–58. Oxford: British Archaeological Reports 133.
    1986 The later Neolithic in eastern England. Unpublished Ph.D. thesis, University of Reading.

Clifford, E. M. 1936 Notgrove long barrow, Gloucestershire. *Archaeologia* 86, 119–62.
    1937 The Beaker folk in the Cotswolds. *Proceedings of the Prehistoric Society* 3, 159–63.
    1938 The excavation of Nympsfield long barrow. *Proceedings of the Prehistoric Society* 4, 188–213.

Clifford, E. M. and G. Daniel 1940 The Rodmarton and Avening portholes. *Proceedings of the Prehistoric Society* 6, 133–65.

Cohen, G. A. 1978 *Karl Marx's Theory of History: A Defense*. Oxford: Oxford University Press.

Cole, S. 1965 *The Neolithic Revolution*. London: British Museum Natural History.

Coles, J. and B. Orme 1976 The Sweet Track: Railway site. *Somerset Levels Papers* 2, 34–65.
    1979 The Sweet Track: Drove site. *Somerset Levels Papers* 5, 43–64.

Conkey, M. 1982 Boundedness in art and society. In: I. Hodder (ed.) *Symbolic and Structural Archaeology*, 115–28. Cambridge: Cambridge University Press.

Connah, G. 1965 Excavations at Knap Hill, Alton Priors, 1961. *Wiltshire Archaeological Magazine* 60, 1–23.

Corcoran, J. W. X. P. 1960 The Carlingford culture. *Proceedings of the Prehistoric Society* 26, 98–148.

1972 Multi-period construction and the origins of the chambered long cairn in western Britain and Ireland. In: F. Lynch and C. Burgess (eds.) *Prehistoric Man in Wales and the West*, 31–63. Bath: Adams and Dart.

Cosgrove, D. E. 1984 *Social Formation and Symbolic Landscape*. London: Croom Helm.

Crawford, O. G. S. 1925 *The Long Barrows of the Cotswolds*. Gloucester: John Bellows.

Cunnington, M. E. 1909 Notes on barrows on King's Play Down, Heddington. *Wiltshire Archaeological Magazine* 36, 311–17.

1927 Shepherd's Shore. *Wiltshire Archaeological Magazine* 43, 397–8

1929 *Woodhenge*. Devizes: Simpson.

1931 The 'Sanctuary' on Overton Hill, near Avebury. *Wiltshire Archaeological Magazine* 45, 300–35.

Cunnington, W. 1872 Notes on a long barrow at Oldbury Hill. *Wiltshire Archaeological Magazine* 13, 103–4.

Curwen, E. C. 1930 Neolithic camps. *Antiquity* 4, 22–54.

1934 Excavations at Whitehawk Camp, Brighton, 1932–1933. *Antiquaries Journal* 56, 11–23.

Daniel, G. 1937 The chambered barrow in Parc le Breos Cwm, South Wales. *Proceedings of the Prehistoric Society* 3, 71–86.

Darvill, T. C. 1981 Excavations at the Peak Camp, Cowley: an interim note. *Glevensis* 15, 52–6.

1982 *The Megalithic Chambered Tombs of the Cotswold–Severn Region*. Highworth: Vorda.

1987 *Prehistoric Britain*. London: Batsford.

Darvill, T. C., R. Hingley, M. Jones and J. Timbey 1986 A Neolithic and Iron Age site at the Loders, Lechlade, Gloucestershire. *Transactions of the Bristol and Gloucester Archaeological Society* 104, 24–48.

David, N., J. Sterner and K. Gavua 1988 Why pots are decorated. *Current Anthropology* 29, 365–89.

DeAtley, S. P. and F. Findlow 1984 Exploring the limits: introduction. In: S. P. DeAtley and F. Findlow (eds.) *Exploring the Limits: Frontiers and Boundaries in Prehistory*, 1–3. Oxford: British Archaeological Reports S223.

DeBoer, W. 1984 The last pottery show: system and sense in ceramic studies. In: S. van der Leeuw and A. C. Pritchard (eds.) *The Many Dimensions of Pottery*, 527–68. Amsterdam: University of Amsterdam.

de Man, P. 1978 The epistemology of metaphor. *Critical Enquiry* 5, 13–30.

Dennell, R. W. 1972 The interpretation of plant remains: Bulgaria. In: E. S. Higgs (ed.) *Papers in Economic Prehistory*, 149–60. Cambridge: Cambridge University Press.

1976 Prehistoric crop cultivation in southern England: a reconsideration. *Antiquaries Journal* 56, 11–23.

1983 *European Economic Prehistory*. London: Academic Press.

Derrida, J. 1978 *Spurs: Nietzsche's Styles*. Chicago: University of Chicago Press.

1986 Différence. In: M. C. Taylor (ed.) *Deconstruction in Context: Literature and Philosophy*, 396–420. Chicago: University of Chicago Press.

Dews, P. 1987. *Logics of Disintegration*. London: Verso.

Dincauze, D. and R. Hasenstab 1989 Explaining the Iroquois: tribalisation on a prehistoric periphery. In: T. C. Champion (ed.) *Centre and Periphery: Comparative Studies in Archaeology*, 67–87. London: Unwin Hyman.

Dixon, P. 1988 The Neolithic settlements on Crickley Hill. In: C. Burgess, P. Topping, C. Mordant and M. Maddison (eds.) *Enclosures and Defences in the Neolithic of Western Europe*, 75–88. Oxford: British Archaeological Reports S403.

Donley, L. 1982 House power: Swahili space and symbolic markers. In: I. Hodder (ed.) *Symbolic and Structural Archaeology*, 63–73. Cambridge: Cambridge University Press.

Douglas, M. 1957 Animals and Lele religious symbolism. *Africa* 27, 46–58.

    1966 *Purity and Danger*. London: Routledge and Kegan Paul.

Drew, C. D. and S. Piggott 1936 The excavation of long barrow 163a on Thickthorn Down, Dorset. *Proceedings of the Prehistoric Society* 2, 77–96.

Drewett, P. 1975 The excavation of an oval burial mound of the third millennium BC at Alfriston, East Sussex. *Proceedings of the Prehistoric Society* 41, 119–52.

    1977 The excavation of a Neolithic causewayed enclosure at Offham Hill, East Sussex. *Proceedings of the Prehistoric Society* 42, 201–41.

    1980 Neolithic pottery in Sussex. *Sussex Archaeological Collections* 118, 23–30.

    1982 Late Bronze Age downland economy and excavations at Black Patch, East Sussex. *Proceedings of the Prehistoric Society* 48, 321–400.

    1986 The excavation of a Neolithic oval barrow at North Marden, West Sussex, 1982. *Proceedings of the Prehistoric Society* 52, 31–51.

Duncan, J. and N. Duncan 1988 (Re)reading the landscape. *Society and Space* 6, 117–26.

Eagleton, T. 1983 *Literary Theory*. Oxford: Blackwell.

Easthope, A. 1983 *Poetry as Discourse*. London: Methuen.

Edmonds, M. R. 1987 Rocks and risk: problems with lithic procurement strategies. In: A. Brown and M. R. Edmonds (eds.) *Lithic Analysis and Later British Prehistory*, 155–80. Oxford: British Archaeological Reports 162.

Edmonds, M. R. and J. S. Thomas 1987 The Archers: an everyday story of country folk. In: A. Brown and M. R. Edmonds (eds.) *Lithic Analysis and Later British Prehistory*, 187–99. Oxford: British Archaeological Reports 162.

Edwards, K. 1979 Palynological and temporal inference in the context of prehistory. *Journal of Archaeological Science* 6, 255–70.

    1982 Man, space and the woodland edge – speculations on the detection and interpretation of human impact in pollen profiles. In: M. Bell and S. Limbrey (eds.) *Archaeological Aspects of Woodland Ecology*, 5–22. Oxford: British Archaeological Reports S146.

Ehrenburg, M. 1980 The occurrence of Bronze Age metalwork in the Thames: an investigation. *Transactions of the London and Middlesex Archaeological Society* 31, 1–15.

Entwistle, R. and A. Grant 1989 The evidence for cereal cultivation and animal husbandry in the southern British Neolithic and Bronze Age. In: A. Milles, D. Williams and N. Gardner (eds.) *The Beginnings of Agriculture*, 203–15. Oxford: British Archaeological Reports S496.

Evans, C. 1988 Excavations at Haddenham, Cambridgeshire: a 'planned' enclosure and its regional affinities. In: C. Burgess, P. Topping, C. Mordant and M. Maddison (eds.) *Enclosures and Defences in the Neolithic of Western Europe*, 127–48. Oxford: British Archaeological Reports S403.

Evans, J. G. 1971 Habitat change on the calcareous soils of Britain: the impact of Neolithic man. In: D. D. A. Simpson (ed.) *Settlement and Economy in Neolithic and Early Bronze Age Britain and Europe*, 27–73. Leicester: Leicester University Press.

    1983 Stonehenge – the environment in the late Neolithic and Early Bronze Age and a Beaker-Age burial. *Wiltshire Archaeological Magazine* 78, 7–30.

Evans, J. G., S. Limbrey, I. Máté and R. J. Mount 1988 Environmental change and land-use history in a Wiltshire river valley in the last 14000 years. In: J. C. Barrett and I. A. Kinnes (eds.) *The Archaeology of Context in the Neolithic and Bronze Age*, 97–103. Sheffield: Department of Archaeology and Prehistory.

Farrington, I. n.d. An alternative view on the transition to agriculture: American and Australian collectors compared. Paper read at the conference 'Early Man in America', Mexico City.

Farrington I. and J. Urry 1985 Food and the early history of cultivation. *Journal of Ethnobiology* 5, 143–57.

Field, N., C. Matthews and I. F. Smith 1964 New Neolithic sites in Dorset and Bedfordshire, with a note on the distribution of Neolithic storage pits in Britain. *Proceedings of the Prehistoric Society* 30, 352–81.

Field, N. and J. Penn 1981 A late Neolithic macehead from Kingston upon Thames. *Transactions of the London and Middlesex Archaeological Society* 32, 15–17.

Fisher, P. F. 1982 A review of lessivage and Neolithic cultivation in southern England. *Journal of Archaeological Science* 9, 299–304.

Flannery, K. V. 1968 Archaeological systems theory and early Mesoamerica. In: B. Meggers (ed.) *Anthropological Archaeology in the Americas*. Washington.

  1972 The cultural evolution of civilisation. *Annual Review of Ecology and Systematics* 3, 399–426.

Fleming, A. 1973 Tombs for the living. *Man* 8, 177–93.

Ford, S. 1987 Chronological and functional aspects of flint assemblages. In: A. Brown and M. R. Edmonds (eds.) *Lithic Analysis and Later British Prehistory*, 67–86. Oxford: British Archaeological Reports 162.

Forde-Johnstone, J. 1974 A hoard of flint axes from Moel Arthur, Flintshire. *Transactions of the Flintshire Historical Society* 21, 99–100.

Foucault, M. 1967 Nietzsche, Freud, Marx. In: *Nietzsche*. Paris: Cahiers du Royaumont.

  1977 *Discipline and Punish*. London: Allen Lane.

  1984a Nietzsche, genealogy, history. In: P. Rabinow (ed.) *The Foucault Reader*, 76–100. Harmondsworth: Peregrine.

  1984b Space, knowledge, and power. In: P. Rabinow (ed.) *The Foucault Reader*, 239–56. Harmondsworth: Peregrine.

  1988 Technologies of the self. In: L. Martin, H. Gutman and P. Hutton (eds.) *Technologies of Self*, 16–49. London: Tavistock.

Fowler, P. 1981 Wildscape to landscape: 'enclosure' in prehistoric Britain. In: R. J. Mercer (ed.) *Farming Practice in British Prehistory*, 9–54. Edinburgh: Edinburgh University Press.

Frankenstein, S. and M. Rowlands 1978 The internal structure and regional context of early Iron Age society in south-west Germany. *Bulletin of the Institute of Archaeology, London*, 15, 73–112.

Frere, D. H. S. 1943 Late Neolithic Grooved Ware near Cambridge. *Antiquaries Journal* 23, 34–41.

Friedman, J. 1975 Tribes, states and transformations. In: M. Bloch (ed.) *Marxist Analyses in Social Anthropology*, 161–202. London: Malaby.

Gamble, C. 1981 Social control and the economy. In: A. Sheridan and G. Bailey (eds.) *Economic Archaeology*, 215–30. Oxford: British Archaeological Reports S96.

Gardin, J. C. 1980 *Archaeological Constructs*. Cambridge: Cambridge University Press.

Gardiner, J. P. 1984 Lithic distributions and settlement patterns in central southern England. In: R. J. Bradley and J. P. Gardiner (eds.) *Neolithic Studies*, 15–40. Oxford: British Archaeological Reports 133.

  1987a Tales of the unexpected: approaches to the assessment and interpretation of museum flint collections. In: A. Brown and M. R. Edmonds (eds.) *Lithic Analysis and Later British Prehistory*, 49–66. Oxford: British Archaeological Reports 162.

  1987b The occupation 3500–100 bc. In: B. Cunliffe *Hengistbury Head*, 22–66. Oxford: University Committee for Archaeology.

Gell, A. S. R. 1969 Grooved Ware from West Runton, Norfolk. *Antiquaries Journal* 29, 81.

Gibson, A. 1985 A Neolithic enclosure at Grendon, Northants. *Antiquity* 59, 213–19.

Giddens, A. 1981 *A Contemporary Critique of Historical Materialism, Vol. 1: Power, Property and the State*. London: Macmillan.

 1984 *The Constitution of Society*. London: Polity.

 1987 *Sociology and Modern Social Theory*. London: Polity.

Gilbert, A. S. 1975 Modern nomads and prehistoric pastoralists: the limits of analogy. *Journal of the Ancient Near Eastern Society, Columbia University* 1975, 1–20.

Giot, P. R. 1988 Stones in the landscape of Brittany. In: C. Ruggles (ed.) *Records in Stone: Studies in Memory of Alexander Thom*, 319–24. Cambridge: Cambridge University Press.

Godelier, M. 1977 *Perspectives in Marxist Anthropology*. Cambridge: Cambridge University Press.

Goldsmitt, W. 1979 A general model for pastoral social systems. In: *Pastoral Production and Society*, 15–27. Cambridge: Cambridge University Press.

Gourlay, R. and J. C. Barrett 1984 Dail na Caraidh. *Current Archaeology* 8, 347–9.

Gray, H. St G. 1935 The Avebury excavations, 1902–1922. *Archaeologia* 84, 99–162.

Gray, M. 1973 Devil's Quoits. *Council for British Archaeology Group 9 Newsletter* 1973, 13.

 1974 Devil's Quoits. *Council for British Archaeology Group 9 Newsletter* 1974, 7.

Green, C. and S. Rollo-Smith 1984 The excavation of eighteen round barrows near Shrewton, Wiltshire. *Proceedings of the Prehistoric Society* 50, 255–318.

Green, F. J. 1981 Iron Age, Roman and Saxon crops: the archaeological evidence from Wessex. In: G. Dimbleby and M. Jones (eds.) *The Environment of Man*, 129–53. Oxford: British Archaeological Reports 87.

Greenwell, W. 1877 *British Barrows*. Oxford: Clarendon.

Grigson, C. 1982a Sexing Neolithic domestic cattle from skulls and horncores. In: B. Wilson, C. Grigson and S. Payne (eds.) *Ageing and Sexing Animal Bones from Archaeological Sites*, 25–35. Oxford: British Archaeological Reports 109.

 1982b Porridge and pannage: pig husbandry in Neolithic England. In: M. Bell and S. Limbrey (eds.) *Archaeological Aspects of Woodland Ecology*, 297–314. Oxford: British Archaeological Reports S146.

Grimes, W. F. 1939 The excavation of the Ty Isaf long cairn, Breconshire. *Proceedings of the Prehistoric Society* 5, 119–42.

 1944 Excavations at Stanton Harcourt, Oxon., 1940. *Oxoniensia* 8/9, 19–63.

 1960 *Excavations on Defence Sites, Vol. 1*. London: HMSO.

 1964 Excavations in the Lake group of barrows, Wilsford, Wiltshire in 1959. *Bulletin of the Institute of Archaeology, London* 4, 89–121.

Grinsell, L. V. 1957 Archaeological Gazetteer. In: *The Victoria County History of Wiltshire, Vol. 1(1)*, 21–279. London: HMSO.

 1959 *Dorset Barrows*. Dorchester: Dorset Natural History and Archaeological Society.

Halpin, C. 1984 Blewbury. *Oxford Archaeological Unit Newsletter* 11, 1–2.

Hansen, J. 1980 The palaeoethnobotany of Franchthi Cave, Greece. Ph.D. dissertation, University of Minnesota.

Hardin, M. 1984 Models of decoration. In: S. van der Leeuw and A. C. Pritchard (eds.) *The Many Dimensions of Pottery*, 573–614. Amsterdam: University of Amsterdam.

Harding, A. 1981 Excavations in the prehistoric ritual complex near Milfield, Northumberland. *Proceedings of the Prehistoric Society* 47, 87–135.

Harding, P. 1988 The chalk plaque pit, Amesbury. *Proceedings of the Prehistoric Society* 54, 320–6.

Harding, P. and C. Gingell 1986 The excavation of two long barrows by F. de M. and H. F. W. L. Vatcher. *Wiltshire Archaeological Magazine* 80, 7–22.

Harland, R. 1987 *Superstructuralism: The Philosophy of Structuralism and Post-Structuralism*. London: Methuen.

Harris, O. 1978 Complementarity and conflict: an Andean view of women and men. In: J. S. La Fontaine (ed.) *Sex and Age as Principles of Social Differentiation*, 21–40. London: Academic Press.

1982 The dead and the devils among the Bolivian Laymi. In: M. Bloch and J. Parry (eds.) *Death and the Regeneration of Life*, 45–73. Cambridge: Cambridge University Press.

Harrison, R. J. 1980 *The Beaker Folk*. London: Thames and Hudson.

Hawkes, C. F. C. 1931 Hillforts. *Antiquity* 5, 60–97.

1954 Archaeological method and theory: some suggestions from the Old World. *American Anthropologist* 56, 155–68.

Hawkes, T. 1972 *Metaphor*. London: Methuen.

Hawley, W. 1926 Report on the excavations at Stonehenge during the season of 1924. *Antiquaries Journal* 6, 1–16.

Healy, F. 1984 Farming and field monuments: the Neolithic of Norfolk. In: C. Barringer (ed.) *Aspects of East Anglian Prehistory*, 77–140. Norwich: Geo.

Hedges, J. and D. Buckley 1981 *Springfield and the Cursus Problem*. Essex County Council.

Hemp, W. 1930 The chambered cairn of Bryn Celli Ddu. *Archaeologia*, 80, 179–214.

Herne, A. 1988 A time and a place for the Grimston bowl. In: J. Barrett and I. Kinnes (eds.) *The Archaeology of Context in the Neolithic and Bronze Age: Recent Trends*, 9–29. Sheffield: Department of Archaeology and Prehistory.

Hertz, R. 1960 *Death and the Right Hand*. Aberdeen: Cohen and West.

Higgs, E. S. and M. R. Jarman 1975 Palaeoeconomy. In: E. S. Higgs (ed.) *Palaeoeconomy*, 1–8. Cambridge: Cambridge University Press.

Hillier, W. and J. Hanson 1984 *The Social Logic of Space*. Cambridge: Cambridge University Press.

Hillman, G. 1981a Reconstructing crop husbandry practices from charred remains of crops. In: R. Mercer (ed.) *Farming Practice in British Prehistory*, 123–62. Edinburgh: Edinburgh University Press.

1981b Crop husbandry: evidence from macroscopic remains. In: I. Simmons and M. Tooley (eds.) *The Environment in British Prehistory*, 183–91. London: Duckworth.

Hirst, P. Q. 1985 Constructed space and the subject. In: R. Fardon (ed.) *Power and Knowledge*, 171–92. Edinburgh: Scottish Academic Press.

Hirth, K. G. 1978 Interregional trade and the formation of gateway communities. *American Antiquity* 43, 35–45.

Hoare, R. Colt 1812 *The Ancient History of Wiltshire*. London: Miller.

Hodder, I. 1978 Social organisation and human interaction: the development of some tentative hypotheses in terms of material culture. In: I. Hodder (ed.) *The Spatial Organisation of Culture*, 199–269. London: Duckworth.

1979 Economic and social stress and material culture patterning. *American Antiquity* 44, 446–55.

1982a *Symbols in Action*. Cambridge: Cambridge University Press.

1982b Theoretical archaeology: a reactionary view. In: I. Hodder (ed.) *Symbolic and Structural Archaeology*, 1–16. Cambridge: Cambridge University Press.

1984 Burials, houses, women and men in the European Neolithic. In: D. Miller and C. Tilley (eds.) *Ideology, Power and Prehistory*, 51–68. Cambridge: Cambridge University Press.

1985 Post-processual archaeology. In: M. B. Schiffer (ed.) *Advances in Archaeological Method and Theory, Vol. 8*, 1–26. London: Academic Press.

1986 *Reading the Past*. Cambridge: Cambridge University Press.

1987 Contextual archaeology: an interpretation of Çatal Hüyük and a discussion of the origins of agriculture. *Bulletin of the Institute of Archaeology, London* 24, 43–56.

1988 Material culture texts and social change: a theoretical discussion and some archaeological examples. *Proceedings of the Prehistoric Society* 54, 67–76.

Hodder, I. and P. Lane 1982 A contextual examination of Neolithic axe distribution in Britain. In: J. Ericson and T. Earle (eds.) *Contexts for Prehistoric Exchange*, 213–35. London: Academic Press.

Hodder, I. and P. Shand 1988 The Haddenham long barrow: an interim statement. *Antiquity* 62, 349–53.

Hodges, R. 1982 *Dark Age Economics*. London: Duckworth.

Holgate, R. 1984 Neolithic settlement in the Upper Thames Valley. *Current Archaeology* 8, 374–5.

1988a *Neolithic Settlement of the Thames Basin*. Oxford: British Archaeological Reports 194.

1988b A review of Neolithic domestic activity in Southern Britain. In: J. Barrett and I. Kinnes (eds.) *The Archaeology of Context in the Neolithic and Bronze Age: Recent Trends*, 104–12. Sheffield: Department of Archaeology and Prehistory.

Houlder, C. 1968 The henge monuments at Llandegai. *Antiquity* 42, 216–31.

Howard, H. 1981 In the wake of distribution: towards an integrated approach to ceramic studies in prehistoric Britain. In: H. Howard and E. Morris (eds.) *Production and Distribution: A Ceramic Viewpoint*, 1–30. Oxford: British Archaeological Reports S120.

Howell, J. 1982 Neolithic settlement and economy in northern France. *Oxford Journal of Archaeology* 1, 115–18.

1983a *Settlement and Economy in Neolithic Northern France*. Oxford: British Archaeological Reports S157

1983b The late Neolithic in the Paris Basin. In: C. Scarre (ed.) *Ancient France*, 62–90. Edinburgh: Edinburgh University Press.

Hoy, D. C. 1986 Power, repression, progress: Foucault, Lukes and the Frankfurt School. In: D. C. Hoy (ed.) *Foucault: A Critical Reader*, 123–47. Oxford: Blackwell.

Hugh-Jones, C. 1978 Food for thought: patterns of production and consumption in Pira-Pirana society. In: J. S. La Fontaine (ed.) *Age and Sex as Principles of Social Differentiation*, 41–66. London: Academic Press

Huntingdon, R. and P. Metcalf 1979 *Celebrations of Death*. Cambridge: Cambridge University Press.

Ingold, T. 1981 The hunter and his spear: notes on the ecological mediation of social and ecological systems. In: A. Sheridan and G. Bailey (eds.) *Economic Archaeology*, 119–30. Oxford: British Archaeological Reports S96.

Jackson, J. W. 1956 Letter to H. Case. Buxton Museum.

Jameson, F. 1981 *The Political Unconscious: Narrative as a Socially Symbolic Act*. London: Methuen.

Jarman, M., G. Bailey and H. Jarman (eds.) 1982 *Early European Agriculture*. Cambridge: Cambridge University Press.

Jazdzewski, K. 1973 The relations between Kujavian barrows in Poland and megalithic tombs in N. Germany, Denmark and West European countries. In: G. Daniel and P. Kjaerum (eds.) *Megalithic Graves and Ritual*, 63–74. Copenhagen: Jutland Archaeological Society.

Jones, M. 1980 Carbonised cereals from Grooved Ware contexts. *Proceedings of the Prehistoric Society* 46, 61–3.

Jones, M. U. 1976 Neolithic pottery found at Lechlade, Glos. *Oxoniensia* 41, 1–5.

Keiller, A. and S. Piggott 1938 Excavations of an untouched chamber in the Lanhill long barrow. *Proceedings of the Prehistoric Society* 4, 122–50.

Kenward, R. 1982 A Neolithic burial enclosure at New Wintles Farm, Eynsham. In: H. J. Case and A. W. R. Whittle (eds.) *Settlement Patterns in the Oxford Region*, 51–4. London: Council for British Archaeology.

Kesby, J. D. 1979 The Rangi classification of animals and plants. In: R. Ellen and D. Reason (eds.) *Classifications in their Social Context*, 33–56. London: Academic Press.

Kinnes, I. 1975 Monumental function in British Neolithic burial practices. *World Archaeology* 7, 16–28.

1978 Neolithic pottery. In: J. Hedges and D. Buckley, Excavations at a Neolithic causewayed enclosure, Orsett, Essex, 1975. *Proceedings of the Prehistoric Society* 44, 219–308.

1979 *Round Barrows and Ring Ditches in the British Neolithic*. London: British Museum.

1981 Dialogues with death. In: R. Chapman, I. Kinnes and K. Randsborg (eds.) *The Archaeology of Death*, 83–91. Cambridge: Cambridge University Press.

1982 Les Fouaillages and megalithic origins. *Antiquity* 61, 24–30.

1985 Circumstance not context: the Neolithic of Scotland as seen from outside. *Proceedings of the Society of Antiquaries of Scotland* 115, 115–57.

Kinnes, I. A., A. Gibson and S. Needham 1983 A dating programme for British Beakers. *Antiquity* 57, 218–19.

Kinnes, I., T. Schadla-Hall, P. Chadwick and P. Dean 1983 Duggleby Howe reconsidered. *Archaeological Journal* 140, 83–108.

Kristiansen, K. 1984 Ideology and material culture: an archaeological perspective. In: M. Spriggs (ed.) *Marxist Perspectives in Archaeology*. Cambridge: Cambridge University Press.

Kruk, J. 1980 *The Earlier Neolithic Settlement of Southern Poland*. Oxford: British Archaeological Reports S93.

Kus, S. 1983 The social representation of space: dimensioning the cosmological and the quotidian. In: J. A. Moore and A. S. Keene (eds.) *Archaeological Hammers and Theories*, 277–98. London: Academic Press.

La Fontaine, J. 1978 Introduction. In: J. S. La Fontaine (ed.) *Sex and Age as Principles of Social Differentiation*, 1–20. London: Academic Press.

Laidler, D. and W. E. V. Young 1938 A surface flint assemblage from a site near Stonehenge. *Wiltshire Archaeological Magazine* 33, 150–60.

Lane, P. 1986 Past practices in the ritual present: examples from the Welsh Bronze Age. *Archaeological Review from Cambridge* 5, 181–92.

Lanting, J. N. and J. D. Van der Waals 1972 British Beakers as seen from the continent. *Helenium* 12, 20–46.

1976 Beaker Culture relations in the lower Rhine basin. In: J. N. Lanting and J. D. Van der Waals (eds.) *Glockenbecher Symposion Oberried 1974*, 1–80. Haarlem: Fibula-Van Dishoek.

Larrick, R. 1986 Age grading and ethnicity in Loikop (Samburu) spears. *Journal of Anthropological Archaeology* 4, 269–83.

Lawson, H. 1985 *Reflexivity: the Post-Modern Predicament*. London: Hutchinson.

Leach, E. 1976 *Culture and Communication: The Logic by which Symbols are Connected*. Cambridge: Cambridge University Press.

Leeds, E. T. 1923 A Saxon village near Sutton Courtenay, Berkshire. *Archaeologia* 73, 147–92.

1927 A Saxon village near Sutton Courtenay, Berkshire (second report). *Archaeologia* 76, 59–80.

1928 A Neolithic site at Abingdon, Berks. *Antiquaries Journal* 8, 461–77.

1934 Recent Bronze Age discoveries in Berkshire and Oxfordshire. *Antiquaries Journal* 14, 264–76.

1940 New discoveries of Neolithic pottery in Oxfordshire. *Oxoniensia* 5, 1–12.

Legge, A. 1981 Aspects of cattle husbandry. In: R. Mercer (ed.) *Farming Practice in British Prehistory*, 169–81. Edinburgh: Edinburgh University Press.

1989 Milking the evidence: a reply to Entwistle and Grant. In: A. Milles, D. Williams and N. Gardner (eds.) *The Beginnings of Agriculture*, 217–42. Oxford: British Archaeological Reports S496.

Lentricchia, F. 1980 *After the New Criticism*. London: Methuen.

Lévi-Strauss, C. 1966 *Structural Anthropology, Vol. 1*. Harmondsworth: Penguin.
1969 *Totemism*. Harmondsworth: Penguin.
1970 *The Raw and the Cooked*. Harmondsworth: Penguin.

Levitan, B., A. Audsley, C. J. Hawkes, A. Moody, P. Moody, P. L. Smart and J. S. Thomas 1988 Charterhouse Warren Farm Swallett, Mendip, Somerset: exploration, geomorphology, taphonomy and archaeology. *Proceedings of the University of Bristol Spealeological Society* 18, 171–339.

Lewis-Williams, J. D. and T. A. Dowson 1988 Signs of all times: entoptic phenomena in Upper Palaeolithic art. *Current Anthropology* 29, 201-45.

Llamazares, A. M. 1989 A semiotic approach in rock-art analysis. In: I. Hodder (ed.) *The Meanings of Things*, 242–8. London: Unwin Hyman.

Lloyd, C. 1986 *Explanation in Social History*. Oxford: Blackwell.

Longworth, I. 1959 Notes on excavations in the British Isles, 1958. *Proceedings of the Prehistoric Society* 25, 270–82.
1961 The origins and development of the primary series in the Collared Urn tradition in England and Wales. *Proceedings of the Prehistoric Society* 27, 263–306.

Lubbock, J. 1872 *Pre-Historic Times*. London: Williams and Norgate.

Lukis, W. 1867 Tumuli of north Wiltshire. *Proceedings of the Society of Antiquaries of London* 2nd series, 3, 213–16.

Lüning, J. 1982 Research into the Bandkeramik settlement of the Aldenhover Platte in the Rhineland. *Analecta Praehistorica Leidensia* 15, 1–30.

Lynch, K. 1972 *What Time Is This Place?* Massachusetts: Massachusetts Institute of Technology.

MacCormack, C. P. 1980 Nature, culture and gender: a critique. In: C. P. MacCormack and M. Strathern (eds.) *Nature, Culture and Gender*, 1–24. Cambridge: Cambridge University Press

Macdonnall, D. 1986 *Theories of Discourse*. Oxford: Blackwell.

Madsen, T. 1979 Earthen long barrows and timber structures: aspects of the early Neolithic mortuary practice in Denmark. *Proceedings of the Prehistoric Society* 45, 301–20.

Madsen, T. and H. J. Jensen 1982 Settlement and land use in early Neolithic Denmark. *Analecta Praehistorica Leidensia* 15, 63–86.

Maltby, J. M. 1979 *Faunal Studies on Urban Sites: the Animal Bones from Exeter 1971–1975*. Sheffield: Department of Prehistory and Archaeology.

Manby, T. G. 1970 Long barrows of northern England: structural and dating evidence. *Scottish Archaeological Forum* 2, 1–27.
1974 *Grooved Ware Sites in Yorkshire and the North of England*. Oxford: British Archaeological Reports 9.
1976 The excavation of Kilham long barrow, East Riding of Yorkshire. *Proceedings of the Prehistoric Society* 42, 111-60.

Marx, K. 1968 The eighteenth Brumaire of Louis Bonaparte. In: K. Marx and F. Engels, *Selected Works in One Volume*, 96–179. London: Laurence and Wishart.

Marx, K. and F. Engels 1970 *The German Ideology*. London: Laurence and Wishart.

Meadow, R. 1975 Mammal remains from Hajji Firuz: a study in methodology. In: A. T. Clason (ed.) *Archaeozoological Studies*, 265–83. Amsterdam: North Holland.

Megaw, J. V. S. and D. D. A. Simpson 1979 *An Introduction to British Prehistory*. Leicester: Leicester University Press.

Mercer, R. J. 1980 *Hambledon Hill: A Neolithic Landscape*. Edinburgh: Edinburgh University Press.

1981a Introduction. In: R. J. Mercer (ed.) *Farming Practice in British Prehistory*, ix–xxvi. Edinburgh: Edinburgh University Press.

1981b The excavation of a late Neolithic henge-type enclosure at Balfarg, Fife, Scotland. *Proceedings of the Society of Antiquaries of Scotland* 111, 63–171.

1982 Hambledon Hill, 1982: Interim report. Manuscript.

1988 Hambledon Hill, Dorset, England. In: C. Burgess, P. Topping, C. Mordant and M. Maddison (eds.) *Enclosures and Defences in the Neolithic of Western Europe*, 89–106. Oxford: British Archaeological Reports S403.

Metcalf, P. 1981 Meaning and materialism: the ritual economy of death. *Man* 16, 563–78.

Midgley, M. S. 1985 *The Origin and Function of the Earthen Long Barrows of Northern Europe*. Oxford: British Archaeological Reports S259.

Miket, R. 1981 Pit alignments in the Millfield Basin, and the excavation of Ewart 1. *Proceedings of the Prehistoric Society* 47, 137–46.

Miller, D. 1982 Structures and strategies: an aspect of the relationship between social hierarchy and cultural change. In: I. Hodder (ed.) *Symbolic and Structural Archaeology*, 89–98. Cambridge: Cambridge University Press.

1987 *Material Culture and Mass Consumption*. Oxford: Blackwell.

Minson, J. 1985 *Genealogies of Morals*. London: Macmillan.

Moffett, L., M. A. Robinson and V. Straker 1989 Cereals, fruit and nuts: charred plant remains from Neolithic sites in England and Wales and the Neolithic economy. In: A. Milles, D. Williams and N. Gardner (eds.) *The Beginnings of Agriculture*, 243–61. Oxford: British Archaeological Reports S496.

Moir, G. 1981 Some archaeological and astronomical objections to scientific astronomy in British prehistory. In: C. Ruggles and A. Whittle (eds.) *Astronomy and Society in Britain during the Period 4000–1000 B.C.*, 221–41. Oxford: British Archaeological Reports 88.

Moore, H. 1981 Bone refuse – possibilities for the future. In: A. Sheridan and G. Bailey (eds.) *Economic Archaeology*, 87–94. Oxford: British Archaeological Reports 96.

1982 The interpretation of spatial patterning in settlement residues. In: I. Hodder (ed.) *Symbolic and Structural Archaeology*, 74–9. Cambridge: Cambridge University Press.

1986 *Space, Text and Gender*. Cambridge: Cambridge University Press.

Moorey, P. R. S. 1982 A Neolithic ring ditch and Iron Age enclosure at Newnham Murren, near Wallingford. In: H. J. Case and A. W. R. Whittle (eds.) *Settlement Patterns in the Oxford Region*, 55–9. London: Council for British Archaeology.

Morgan, F. de M. 1959 The excavation of a long barrow at Nutbane, Hants. *Proceedings of the Prehistoric Society* 25, 15–51.

Morris, M. 1974 Megalithic exegesis: megalithic monuments as sources of socio-cultural meanings. *Irish Archaeological Research Forum* 1, 10–28.

Mortimer, J. R. 1905 *Forty Years' Researches in British and Saxon Burial Mounds of East Yorkshire*. London: A. Brown and Sons.

Needham, S. 1988 Selective deposition in the British Early Bronze Age. *World Archaeology* 20, 229–48.

Nielsen, P. O. 1986 The beginning of the Neolithic – assimilation or complex change? *Journal of Danish Archaeology* 5, 240–3.

Nietzsche, F. 1969 *On the Genealogy of Morals and Ecce Homo*. New York: Vintage.

Norris, C. 1982 *Deconstruction: Theory and Practice*. London: Methuen.

1987 *Derrida*. London: Fontana.

O'Kelly, C. 1969 Bryn Celli Ddu, Anglesey: a reinterpretation. *Archaeologia Cambrensis* 118, 17–48.

O'Kelly, M. and C. Shell 1979 Stone objects and a bronze axe from Newgrange, Co. Meath.

In: M. Ryan (ed.) *The Origins of Metallurgy in Atlantic Europe*, 127–44. Dublin: The Stationery Office.

O'Neil, H. E. 1966 Sale's Lot long barrow, Withington, Glos. *Transactions of the Bristol and Gloucester Archaeological Society* 85, 5–35.

Oswald, A. 1969 Excavations at Barford, Warwickshire. *Transactions of the Birmingham and Warwickshire Archaeological Society* 83, 3–54.

Pader, E. J. 1982 *Symbolism, Social Relations, and the Interpretation of Mortuary Remains*. Oxford: British Archaeological Reports S130.

Palmer, R. 1976 Interrupted ditch enclosures in Britain. *Proceedings of the Prehistoric Society* 42, 161–86.

Panoff, S. 1970 Food and faeces: a Melanesian rite. *Man* 5, 237–52.

Parker-Pearson, M. 1982 Mortuary practices, society and ideology: an ethnoarchaeological study. In: I. Hodder (ed.) *Symbolic and Structural Archaeology*, 99–113. Cambridge: Cambridge University Press.

Parrington, M. 1978 *The Excavation of an Iron Age Settlement, Bronze Age Ring-Ditches and Roman Features at Ashville Trading Estate, Abingdon*. London: Council for British Archaeology.

Passmore, A. D. 1923 Chambered long barrow in West Woods. *Wiltshire Archaeological Magazine* 42, 366–7.

   1938 Gatcombe Lodge. *Proceedings of the Prehistoric Society* 4, 124.

   n.d. *Field Diary and Scrapbook*. Devizes Museum.

Patrik, L. 1985 Is there an archaeological record? In: M. B. Schiffer (ed.) *Advances in Archaeological Method and Theory, Vol. 8*, 27–62. London: Academic Press.

Payne, S. 1975 Faunal changes at Franchthi Cave from 20,000 B.C. to 3,000 B.C. In: A. T. Clason (ed.) *Archaeozoological Studies*, 120–31. Amsterdam: North Holland.

Peacock, D. P. S. 1969 Neolithic pottery production in Cornwall. *Antiquity* 43, 145–9.

Penny, A. and J. Wood 1973 The Dorset Cursus complex – a Neolithic astronomical observatory? *Archaeological Journal* 130, 44–76.

Phillips, C. W. 1935 The excavation of Giant's Hill long barrow, Skendleby. *Archaeologia* 85, 37–106.

Pierpoint, S. J. 1979 Who's who in the northern British Bronze Age. In: B. C. Burnham and J. Kingsbury (eds.) *Space, Hierarchy and Society*, 31–46. Oxford: British Archaeological Reports S59.

Piggott, S. 1931 The Neolithic pottery of the British Isles. *Archaeological Journal* 88, 67–158.

   1936a Handley Hill, Dorset – a Neolithic bowl and the date of the entrenchment. *Proceedings of the Prehistoric Society* 2, 229–30.

   1936b A potsherd from the Stonehenge ditch. *Antiquity* 10, 221–2.

   1940 Timber circles: a re-examination. *Archaeological Journal* 96, 193–222.

   1952 The Neolithic camp on Whitesheet Hill, Kilmington Parish. *Wiltshire Archaeological Magazine* 54, 404–9.

   1954 *The Neolithic Cultures of the British Isles*. Cambridge: Cambridge University Press.

   1958 Native economies and the Roman occupation of North Britain. In: I. Richmond (ed.) *Roman and Native in North Britain*, 1–27. London: Nelson.

   1962 *The West Kennet Long Barrow*. London: HMSO.

Piggott, S. and C. M. Piggott 1944 The excavation of barrows on Crichel and Launceston Downs. *Archaeologia* 90, 47–80.

Piggott, S. and D. D. A. Simpson 1971 Excavation of a stone circle at Croft Moraig, Perthshire, Scotland. *Proceedings of the Prehistoric Society* 37, 1–15.

Pitt Rivers, A. L. F. 1898 *Excavations in Cranborne Chase near Rushmore, on the Borders of Dorset and Wilts., Vol. IV*. Privately printed.

Pitts, M. 1982 On the road to Stonehenge: report on the investigations beside the A344. *Proceedings of the Prehistoric Society* 48, 75–132.

Pitts, M. and R. Jacobi 1979 Some aspects of change in flaked stone industries of the Mesolithic and Neolithic in Southern Britain. *Journal of Archaeological Science* 6, 163–77.

Powell, T., J. W. X. P. Corcoran, F. Lynch and J. Scott 1969 *Megalithic Enquiries in the West of Britain*. Liverpool: Liverpool University Press.

Pred, A. 1977 The choreography of existence: comments on Hagerstrand's Time-Geography and its usefulness. *Economic Geography* 53, 207–21.

Proudfoot, E. 1965 Bishop's Cannings: Roughridge Hill. *Wiltshire Archaeological Magazine* 60, 132–3.

Pryor, F. 1988 Etton, near Maxey, Cambridgeshire: a causewayed enclosure on the fen-edge. In: C. Burgess, P. Topping, C. Mordant and M. Maddison (eds.) *Enclosures and Defences in the Neolithic of Western Europe*, 107–26. Oxford: British Archaeological Reports S403.

Pryor, F., C. French and M. Taylor 1985 An interim report on excavations at Etton, Maxey, Cambridgeshire. *Antiquaries Journal* 65, 275–311.

Radley, J. 1967 The York hoard of flint tools. *Yorkshire Archaeological Journal* 42, 131–2.

Randsborg, K. 1980 *The Viking Age in Denmark*. London: Duckworth.

Ray, K. W. 1987 Material metaphor, social interaction and historical interpretations: exploring patterns of association and symbolism in the Igbo-Ukwu corpus. In: I. Hodder (ed.) *The Archaeology of Contextual Meanings*, 66–77. Cambridge: Cambridge University Press.

1988 Context, meaning and metaphor in an historical archaeology: Igbo Ikwu, eastern Nigeria. Ph.D. thesis, University of Cambridge.

Redman, C. 1977 Man, domestication and culture in south-west Asia. In C. A. Reed (ed.) *Origins of Agriculture*, 523–41. The Hague: Mouton.

Rees, S. 1979 *Agricultural Implements in Prehistoric and Roman Britain*. Oxford: British Archaeological Reports 69.

Relph, E. 1976 *Place and Placelessness*. London: Pion.

Renfrew, A. C. 1972. *The Emergence of Civilisation: The Cyclades and the Aegean in the Third Millennium B.C.* London: Methuen.

1973 Monuments, mobilisation and social organisation in Neolithic Wessex. In: A. C. Renfrew (ed.) *The Explanation of Culture Change*, 539–58. London: Duckworth.

1976 Megaliths, territories and populations. In: S. de Laet (ed.) *Acculturation and Continuity in Atlantic Europe*, 98–120. Bruges: de Tempel.

1979 *Investigations in Orkney*. London: Society of Antiquaries.

Reugg, M. 1979 Metaphor and metonymy: the logic of structuralist rhetoric. *Glyph* 6, 141–57.

Reynolds, P. 1974 Experimental Iron Age pits: an interim report. *Proceedings of the Prehistoric Society* 40, 118–31.

1979 *Iron Age Farm*. London: British Museum.

1981 Deadstock and livestock. In: R. J. Mercer (ed.) *Farming Practice in British Prehistory*, 97–124. Edinburgh: Edinburgh University Press.

Richards, C. C. 1988 Altered images: a re-examination of Neolithic mortuary practices in Orkney. In: J. C. Barrett and I. A. Kinnes (eds.) *The Archaeology of Context in the Neolithic and Bronze Age: Recent Trends*, 42–56. Sheffield: Department of Archaeology and Prehistory.

Richards, C. C. and J. S. Thomas 1984 Ritual activity and structured deposition in later Neolithic Wessex. In: R. J. Bradley and J. Gardiner (eds.) *Neolithic Studies*, 189–218. Oxford: British Archaeological Reports 133.

Richards, J. 1982 The Stonehenge environs project: the story so far. *Scottish Archaeological Review* 1, 98–104.

1984 The development of the Neolithic landscape in the environs of Stonehenge. In: R. J. Bradley and J. Gardiner (eds.) *Neolithic Studies*, 177–88. Oxford: British Archaeological Reports 133.

1985 Scouring the surface: approaches to the ploughzone in the Stonehenge environs. *Archaeological Review From Cambridge* 4, 27–42.

Ricoeur, P. 1978 Metaphor. *Critical Enquiry* 5, 1–12.

1981 *Hermeneutics and the Human Sciences*. Cambridge: Cambridge University Press.

1984 *The Reality of the Historical Past*. Milwaukee: Marquette University.

Ritchie, A. 1983 Excavation of a Neolithic farmstead at Knap of Howar, Papa Westray, Orkney. *Proceedings of the Society of Antiquaries of Scotland* 113, 40–121.

Robertson-Mackay, M. E. 1980 A 'head and hoofs' burial beneath a round barrow. *Proceedings of the Prehistoric Society* 46, 123–76.

Robertson-Mackay, R. 1962 The excavation of the causewayed camp at Staines. *Middlesex Archaeological Newsletter* 7, 131–4.

1987 The Neolithic causewayed enclosure at Staines, Surrey: excavations 1961–63. *Proceedings of the Prehistoric Society* 53, 23–128.

Robinson, M. and R. Wilson 1987 A survey of environmental archaeology in the south Midlands. In: H. Keeley (ed.) *Environmental Archaeology: A Regional Review, Vol. 2*, 16–100. London: HBMC.

Rolleston, G. 1876 On the people of the long barrow period. *Journal of the Anthropological Institute* 5, 120–75.

Roth, P. 1988 Narrative explanations: the case of history. *History and Theory*, 27, 1–13.

Rowlands, M. J. 1976 *The Production and Distribution of Metalwork in the Middle Bronze Age in Southern Britain*. Oxford: British Archaeological Reports 32.

Rowley-Conwy, P. 1981 Slash and burn in the temperate European Neolithic. In R. J. Mercer (ed.) *Farming Practice in British Prehistory*, 85–96. Edinburgh: Edinburgh University Press.

1982 Forest grazing and clearance in temperate Europe with special reference to Denmark: an archaeological view. In: M. Bell and S. Limbrey (eds.) *Archaeological Aspects of Woodland Ecology*, 199–215. Oxford: British Archaeological Reports S146.

1983 Sedentary hunters: the Ertebølle example. In: G. Bailey (ed.) *Hunter-Gatherer Economy in Prehistory*, 111–26. Cambridge: Cambridge University Press.

Saville, A. 1981 Hazleton Excavation Project, Gloucestershire, 1981: interim report. Manuscript.

1982 Hazleton, Gloucestershire, excavations 1982: interim report. Manuscript.

1984 Preliminary report on the excavation of a Cotswold–Severn tomb at Hazleton, Gloucestershire. *Antiquaries Journal* 64, 10-24.

Saville, A., J. A. Gowlett and R. E. M. Hedges 1987 Radiocarbon dates for the tomb at Hazleton (Glos.): a chronology for Neolithic collective burial. *Antiquity* 64, 10–24.

Savory, H. N. 1956 The excavation of Pipton long cairn, Brecknockshire. *Archaeologia Cambrensis* 105, 7–48.

Saxe, A. A. 1971 Social dimensions of mortuary practices. Ph.D. thesis, University of Michigan.

Schiffer, M. B. 1972 Archaeological context and systemic context. *American Antiquity* 37, 156–65.

1976 *Behavioral Archaeology*. London: Academic Press.

Servet, J. M. 1982 Primitive order and archaic trade, part II. *Economy and Society* 11, 22–59.

Shanks, M. and C. Y. Tilley 1982 Ideology, symbolic power and ritual communication: a reinterpretation of Neolithic mortuary practices. In: I. Hodder (ed.) *Symbolic and Structural Archaeology*, 129–54. Cambridge: Cambridge University Press.

1987a *Social Theory and Archaeology*. London: Polity.

1987b *Re-Constructing Archaeology*. Cambridge: Cambridge University Press.

Shee Twohig, E. 1981 *The Megalithic Art of Western Europe*. Oxford: Clarendon.

Shennan, S. 1982 Ideology, change and the European Early Bronze Age. In: I. Hodder (ed.) *Symbolic and Structural Archaeology*, 155–61. Cambridge: Cambridge University Press.

1985 *Experiments in the Collection and Analysis of Archaeological Survey Data: The East Hampshire Survey*. Sheffield: Department of Archaeology and Prehistory.

1986 Interaction and change in third millennium BC western and central Europe. In: C. Renfrew and J. F. Cherry (eds.) *Peer Polity Interaction and Sociopolitical Change*, 127–48. Cambridge: Cambridge University Press.

Shepherd, I. A. G. 1986 *Powerful Pots: Beakers in North-East Prehistory*. Aberdeen: Anthropological Museum.

Sheridan, A. 1986 Megaliths and megalomania: an account, and interpretation, of the development of passage graves in Ireland. *Journal of Irish Archaeology*, 3, 17–30.

Sherratt, A. G. 1980 Water, soil and seasonality in early cereal cultivation. *World Archaeology* 11, 313–30.

1981 Plough and pastoralism: aspects of the secondary products revolution. In: I. Hodder, N. Hammond and G. Isaac (eds.) *Pattern of the Past*, 261–306. Cambridge: Cambridge University Press.

Shotton, F. W. 1978 Archaeological inferences from the study of alluvium in the lower Severn–Avon valleys. In: S. Limbrey and J. G. Evans (eds.) *The Effect of Man on the Landscape: The Lowland Zone*, 27–31. London: Council for British Archaeology.

Slichter van Bath, B. H. 1963 *The Agrarian History of Western Europe*. London: Edward Arnold.

Smart, B. 1986 The politics of truth and the problem of hegemony. In: D. C. Hoy (ed.) *Foucault: A Critical Reader*, 157–74. Oxford: Blackwell.

Smith, A. G., C. Grigson, G. Hillman and M. Tooley 1981 The Neolithic. In: I. Simmons and M. Tooley (eds.) *The Environment in British Prehistory*, 125–209. London: Duckworth.

Smith, I. F. 1956 The decorative art of Neolithic ceramics in S.E. England and its relations. Ph.D. thesis, University of London.

1965a *Windmill Hill and Avebury*. Oxford: Clarendon.

1965b Excavation of a bell barrow, Avebury G.55. *Wiltshire Archaeological Magazine* 60, 24–46.

1965c Neolithic pottery from Rybury Camp. *Wiltshire Archaeological Magazine* 60, 127.

1966 Windmill Hill and its implications. *Palaeohistoria* 12, 469–83.

1968 Report on late Neolithic pits at Cam, Glos. *Transactions of the Bristol and Gloucester Archaeological Society* 87, 14–28.

1971 Causewayed enclosures. In: D. D. A. Simpson (ed.) *Economy and Settlement in Neolithic and Early Bronze Age Britain and Europe*, 89–112. Leicester: Leicester University Press.

1974 The Neolithic. In: A. C. Renfrew (ed.) *British Prehistory: A New Outline*, 100–36. London: Duckworth.

Smith, I. F. and D. D. A. Simpson 1964 Excavation of three Roman tombs and a prehistoric pit on Overton Down. *Wiltshire Archaeological Magazine* 59, 68–85.

1966 Excavation of a round barrow on Overton Hill, north Wiltshire, England. *Proceedings of the Prehistoric Society* 32, 122–55.

Smith, R. 1924 Neolithic bowls from the Thames at Mongewell. *Antiquaries Journal* 4, 127.

Smith, R. W. 1984 The ecology of Neolithic farming systems as exemplified by the Avebury region of Wiltshire. *Proceedings of the Prehistoric Society* 50, 99–120.

Smith, W. G. 1915 Maiden Bower, Bedfordshire. *Proceedings of the Society of Antiquaries of London* 27, 143–61.

Starling, N. 1983 Neolithic settlement patterns in central Germany. *Oxford Journal of Archaeology* 2, 1–11.

1985a Colonisation and succession: the earlier Neolithic of central Europe. *Proceedings of the Prehistoric Society* 51, 41–58.

1985b Social change in the later Neolithic of central Europe. *Antiquity* 59, 30–8.

Stone, J. F. S. 1935 Some discoveries at Ratfyn, Amesbury and their bearing on the date of Woodhenge. *Wiltshire Archaeological Magazine* 47, 55–67.

1938 An Early Bronze Age grave in Fargo Plantation near Stonehenge. *Wiltshire Archaeological Magazine* 48, 357–70.

1949 Some Grooved Ware pottery from the Woodhenge area. *Proceedings of the Prehistoric Society* 15, 122–7.

Stone, J. F. S., S. Piggott and A. St J. Booth 1954 Durrington Walls, Wiltshire: recent excavations at a ceremonial site of the early second millennium BC. *Antiquaries Journal* 34, 155–77.

Stone, J. F. S. and W. E. V. Young 1948 Two pits of Grooved Ware date near Woodhenge. *Wiltshire Archaeological Magazine* 52, 287–304.

Strathern, A. 1982 Witchcraft, greed, cannibalism and death. In: M. Bloch and J. Parry (eds.) *Death and the Regeneration of Life*, 111–33. Cambridge: Cambridge University Press.

Stukeley, W. 1740 *Stonehenge: A Temple Restor'd to the British Druids*. London.

Tainter, J. 1978 Mortuary practices and the study of prehistoric social systems. In: M. B. Schiffer (ed.) *Advances in Archaeological Method and Theory, Vol. 1*, 105–41.

Tambiah, S. J. 1969 Animals are good to think with and good to prohibit. *Ethnology* 8, 423–59.

Ten Hove, H. A. 1968 The Ulmus fall and the transition Atlanticum/Sub-Boreal in pollen diagrams. *Palaeogeography, Palaeoclimatology, Palaeoecology* 5, 359–69.

Thomas, J. S. 1984 A tale of two polities. In: R. J. Bradley and J. C. Gardiner (eds.) *Neolithic Studies*, 161–76. Oxford: British Archaeological Reports 133.

1987 Relations of production and social change in the Neolithic of north-west Europe. *Man* 22, 405–30.

1988a Neolithic explanations revisited: the Mesolithic–Neolithic transition in Britain and south Scandinavia. *Proceedings of the Prehistoric Society* 54, 59–66.

1988b The social significance of Cotswold–Severn burial rites. *Man* 23, 540–59.

forthcoming. The hermeneutics of megalithic space. In: C. Tilley (ed.) *Interpretive Archaeology*. London: Routledge.

Thomas, J. S. and A. W. R. Whittle 1986 Anatomy of a tomb: West Kennet revisited. *Oxford Journal of Archaeology* 5, 129–56.

Thomas, K. 1982 Neolithic enclosures and woodland habitats on the South Downs in Sussex, England. In: M. Bell and S. Limbrey (eds.) *Archaeological Aspects of Woodland Ecology*, 147–70. Oxford: British Archaeological Reports S146.

Thomas, N. 1955 Excavations at Vicarage Field, Stanton Harcourt, 1951. *Oxoniensia* 20, 1–28.

1956 A Neolithic pit on Waden Hill. *Wiltshire Archaeological Magazine* 56, 167–71.

1964 The Neolithic causewayed camp at Robin Hood's Ball, Shrewton. *Wiltshire Archaeological Magazine* 59, 1–25.

Thomas, R. and J. Wallis 1982 Recent work on Neolithic and Early Bronze Age sites in the Abingdon area. *Council for British Archaeology Group 9 Newsletter* 12, 184–91.

Thompson, E. P. 1978 *The Poverty of Theory and Other Essays*. London: Merlin.

Thorpe, I. J. 1984 Ritual, power and ideology: a reconsideration of earlier Neolithic rituals in Wessex. In: R. J. Bradley and J. Gardiner (eds.) *Neolithic Studies*, 41–60. Oxford: British Archaeological Reports 133.

Thorpe, I. J. and C. C. Richards 1984 The decline of ritual authority and the introduction of

Beakers into Britain. In: R. J. Bradley and J. Gardiner (eds.) *Neolithic Studies*, 67–84. Oxford: British Archaeological Reports 133.

Thurnam, J. 1857 On a cromlech-tumulus called Lugbury, near Littleton Drew. *Wiltshire Archaeological Magazine* 6, 164–73.

1860 Barrows on the north Wiltshire downs. *Wiltshire Archaeological Magazine* 6, 317–36.

1869 On ancient British barrows, especially those of Wiltshire and the adjoining counties (part I, long barrows). *Archaeologia* 42, 161–244.

Tilley, C. Y. 1984 Ideology and the legitimation of power in the Middle Neolithic of southern Sweden. In: D. Miller and C. Tilley (eds.) *Ideology, Power and Prehistory*, 111–46. Cambridge: Cambridge University Press.

1989 Interpreting material culture. In: I. Hodder (ed.) *The Meanings of Things*, 185–94. London: Unwin Hyman.

Tinsley, H. and C. Grigson 1981 The Bronze Age. In: I. Simmons and M. Tooley (eds.) *The Environment in British Prehistory*, 210–49. London: Duckworth.

Tuan, Yi-Fu 1974 Space and place: humanistic perspective. *Progress in Geography* 6, 211–52.

1978 Space, time, place: a humanistic frame. In: T. Carlstein, D. Parkes and N. Thrift (eds.) *Making Sense of Time: Timing Space and Spacing Time, Vol. 1*, 7–16. London: Edward Arnold.

Turner, V. 1967 *The Forest of Symbols*. Ithaca: Cornell University Press.

1969 *The Ritual Process*. Harmondsworth: Penguin.

Van Gennep, A. 1960 *The Rites of Passage*. London: Routledge and Kegan Paul.

Vatcher, F. de M. 1961 The excavation of the long mortuary enclosure on Normanton Down, Wilts. *Proceedings of the Prehistoric Society* 27, 160–73.

1969 Two incised chalk plaques from Stonehenge bottom. *Antiquity* 43, 310–11.

Vatcher, F. de M. and L. Vatcher 1973 Excavation of three postholes in Stonehenge car park. *Wiltshire Archaeological Magazine* 68, 57–63.

Vulliamy, C. E. 1921 The excavation of a megalithic tomb in Breconshire. *Archaeologia Cambrensis* 76, 300–5.

Vyner, B. 1984 The excavation of a Neolithic cairn at Street House, Loftus, Cleveland. *Proceedings of the Prehistoric Society* 50, 151–96.

Wainwright, G. J. 1969 A review of henge monuments in the light of recent research. *Proceedings of the Prehistoric Society* 35, 112–33.

1971 The excavation of a late Neolithic enclosure at Marden, Wiltshire. *Antiquaries Journal* 51, 177–239.

1979a *Mount Pleasant, Dorset: Excavations 1970–71*. London: Society of Antiquaries.

1979b *Gussage All Saints – An Iron Age Settlement in Dorset*. London: HMSO.

Wainwright, G. J., P. Donaldson, I. Longworth and V. Swan 1971 The excavation of prehistoric and Romano-British settlements near Durrington Walls, Wiltshire, 1970. *Wiltshire Archaeological Magazine* 66, 76–128.

Wainwright, G. J. and I. Longworth 1971 *Durrington Walls: Excavations 1966–1968*. London: Society of Antiquaries.

Wallerstein, I. 1974 *The Modern World-System, Vol. 1*. London: Academic Press.

Ward, J. 1915 The St. Nicholas chambered tomb, Glamorgan. *Archaeologia Cambrensis* 6th series, 15, 253–320.

Warren, S. H., S. Piggott, J. G. D. Clark, M. C. Burkitt and H. and M. E. Godwin 1936 Archaeology of the submerged land-surface of the Essex coast. *Proceedings of the Prehistoric Society* 2, 178–210.

Waton, P. V. 1982 Man's impact on the chalklands: some new pollen evidence. In: M. Bell and S. Limbrey (eds.) *Archaeological Aspects of Woodland Ecology*, 75–91. Oxford: British Archaeological Reports S146.

Watson, P. J., S. Leblanc and C. Redman 1971 *Explanation in Archaeology: An Explicitly Scientific Approach.* New York: Columbia University Press.

Watson, S. L. 1982 Of flesh and bones: the management of death pollution in Cantonese society. In: M. Bloch and J. Parry (eds.) *Death and the Regeneration of Life*, 155–86. Cambridge: Cambridge University Press.

Welbourne, A. 1984 Endo ceramics and power strategies. In: D. Miller and C. Tilley (eds.) *Ideology, Power and Prehistory*, 17–24. Cambridge: Cambridge University Press.

Wheeler, R. E. M. 1943 *Maiden Castle, Dorset.* London: Society of Antiquaries.

Whimster, R. 1981 *Burial Practices in Iron Age Britain.* Oxford: British Archaeological Reports 90.

Whittle, A. W. R. 1977 *The Earlier Neolithic of Southern England and its Continental Background.* Oxford: British Archaeological Reports S35.

1978 Resources and population in the British Neolithic. *Antiquity* 52, 34–41.

1980a Two Neolithics? Part one. *Current Archaeology* 70, 329–34.

1980b Two Neolithics? Part two. *Current Archaeology* 71, 371–3.

1981 Later Neolithic society in Britain: a realignment. In: C. Ruggles and A. W. R. Whittle (eds.) *Astronomy and Society in Britain During the Period 4000–1500 BC*, 297–342. Oxford: British Archaeological Reports 88.

1985 *Neolithic Europe: A Survey.* Cambridge: Cambridge University Press.

1988a *Problems in Neolithic Archaeology.* Cambridge: Cambridge University Press.

1988b Windmill Hill 1988: preliminary report on excavations of the Neolithic causewayed enclosure. Manuscript.

1989 Millbarrow 1989: preliminary report on excavations of the Neolithic chambered tomb. Manuscript.

1990 A pre-enclosure burial at Windmill Hill, Wiltshire. *Oxford Journal of Archaeology* 9, 25–8.

Whittle, A. W. R. and R. Smith 1990 West Kennet. *Current Archaeology* 10, 363–5.

Williams, E. 1989 Dating the introduction of food production into Britain and Ireland. *Antiquity* 63, 510–21.

Wilson, D. 1975 'Causewayed camps' and 'interrupted ditch systems'. *Antiquity* 49, 178–86.

Woodburn, J. 1982 Social dimensions of death in four African hunting and gathering societies. In: M. Bloch and J. Parry (eds.) *Death and the Regeneration of Life*, 187–210. Cambridge: Cambridge University Press.

Young, W. E. V. 1930 Diary Vol. 1, April–July 1930. Unpublished.

1950 Beaker burial at Beckhampton Grange. *Wiltshire Archaeological Magazine* 53, 311.

Zvelebil, M. 1989 On the transition to farming in Europe, or what was spreading with the Neolithic: a reply to Ammerman (1989). *Antiquity* 63, 379–83.

Zvelebil, M. and P. Rowley-Conwy 1984 Transition to farming in northern Europe: a hunter-gatherer perspective. *Norwegian Archaeological Review* 17, 104–27.

1986 Foragers and farmers in Atlantic Europe. In: M. Zvelebil (ed.) *Hunters in Transition*, 67–93. Cambridge: Cambridge University Press.